To Ken Mercado,
Best of luck linking your
data!

Regards,

Linking Government Data

David Wood
Editor

Linking Government Data

 Springer

Editor
David Wood
3 Round Stones Inc.
Fredericksburg, VA
USA
david@3roundstones.com

ISBN 978-1-4614-1766-8   e-ISBN 978-1-4614-1767-5
DOI 10.1007/978-1-4614-1767-5
Springer New York Dordrecht Heidelberg London

Library of Congress Control Number: 2011941199

Printed on acid-free paper

Springer is part of Springer Science+Business Media (www.springer.com)

"Information on anything that's inspected, spent, enforced, or licensed. That's what I want, and that's what the public wants."

Jennifer LaFleur, Director of Computer-Assisted Reporting, ProPublica, defining desired data from the U.S. Government, March 18, 2011

Preface

The Linked Open Data Project started just four years ago in 2007. In that short time Linked Data has grown into an almost mainstream activity for many governments around the world. As of this writing, the US Government's open data site listed twenty one countries whose governments publish open data regarding the operations of their public sector, with roughly one third of them publishing Linked Data using the data standards of the World Wide Web Consortium[1]. Those numbers show every sign of increasing in the immediate future.

The World Wide Web of 2011 is a mature and trusted information system, allowing its broad adoption even by laggards. As an information system owned by no one and yet open to vendors, governments and private citizens, the Web has become a natural place to publish information for public dissemination. The wide availability of Web clients, be they on mobile phones, laptop or desktop computers, tablets or game consoles, and the provision of public access services (especially by libraries) has made publication on the Web a preferred way for governments to empower their citizenry, or at least pretend to do so.

The Web is mature, and yet ever changing. The use of the Web to facilitate clean and uncorrupt government is likewise both viable now and capable of so much more in the future. It is our privilege to be a part of that change. We hope the information presented in this book can assist readers to join us.

The uptake of open data publication in general and Linked Data approaches in specific has mirrored interest by the public in governmental transparency. Some activists, such as the non-profits Sunlight Foundation[2] and Transparency International[3], aim to foster governmental fairness and reduce opportunities for corruption, nepotism and other illegal activities. Although the thesis that governmental transparency initiatives will assist those goals has yet to be proven, Sunlight Foundation in particular has embraced the publication of governmental information on the Web.

---

[1] http://www.data.gov/opendatasites

[2] http://sunlightfoundation.com

[3] http://www.transparency.org

In their words, "redefining 'public' information as meaning 'online'."[4] The score of governments currently providing open data on the Web seem to agree.

This focus on the Web as both the default location of published information and the preferred location of information published by governments stands to only increase the depth of the ocean of data in which we swim. How can we hope to absorb the shear quantity of information being published? Clearly, we cannot, no more than we can read all the documents currently published on the Web. We need the equivalent of a Google, a Yahoo!, a Baidu, a Yandex for data, but one has not yet emerged. The full text indexing techniques commonly employed by document search engines don't work well for spreadsheets, database dumps and tables of statistics. There is, however, another way.

An alternative to search is discovery, implemented on the Web as the "follow your nose" architecture. One simply follows one hyperlink to the next. The term "surfing" was used on the early Web to denote not solely an act of accessing information, but the act of following hyperlinks from one to the other until one found oneself in unexpected territory. Surfing the Web of Data is indeed possible using Linked Data techniques. The ability of Linked Data to describe itself, to place itself in context, contributes to the usefulness of the underlying data and makes surfing less a mindless activity and more a valuable research technique.

Part I attempts to collect some emerging best practices for the creation, publication and maintenance of Linked Government Data. There is more than one way to make a mess of a Linked Data project: Not all Linked Data is useful. Linked Data can be useless merely by being lonely. If it is not linked, it is not Linked Data. If its identifiers are not reused or reusable, it is not useful. The chapters in Part I are intended to help implementors avoid some common pitfalls.

Bernadette Hyland and I first present a Linked Data "cookbook" for government data. During the review process we were accused of attempting to boil the ocean. I hope we succeeded in providing an overview of the entire process. So often we forget to describe the forest as we are busy planting trees. Boris Villazón-Terrazas, Luis. M. Vilches-Blázquez, Oscar Corcho and Asunción Gómez-Pérez follow with their own guidelines based on experiences in Spain.

Timothy Lebo, John Erickson, Li Ding and their colleagues from Rensselaer Polytechnic Institute describe the creation of a portal for linking Open Government data and describe the tools and techniques they developed for the process. Anchoring Part I, Tom Heath and John Goodwin report on their experience creating linked data from geographical information in the United Kingdom. Importantly, they show how generally reusable information can become the basis for applications aimed both internally to government and externally to the public.

The chapters in Part II address issues of Linked Data quality. Producing high quality Linked Data is more of a challenge for governments than it is for, say, Linked Data research centers. Governments do not generally handle embarrassment well and are often sensitive to criticism. The chapters in this section offer solutions to problems of particular importance to government projects.

---

[4] http://sunlightfoundation.com/about/

Matias Frosterus, Eero Hyvönen and Joonas Laitio suggest ways and means to create and publish metadata about open government data, whether that data is in RDF or not. They are not alone in realizing the importance of non-RDF data in the governmental mix (see the chapters by Hyland and Desrochers for other examples).

Richard Cyganiak, Michael Hausenblas and Eoin McCuirc of the Linked Data powerhouse DERI, Ireland's Digital Enterprise Research Institute, suggest ways to represent statistical data in RDF. Statistical data is bread and butter to many governmental agencies and this contribution is important to exposing that vast trove of information. Similarly, Percy Salas, José Viterbo, Karin Breitman and Marco Antonio Casanova address the mapping of relational database schemas into RDF. Along with geographical information, statistical data and information sourced from relational databases constitute the lion's share of governmental data.

Part III offers real world case studies consuming Linked Data. Like any published information, Linked Data is only useful if it is used. Pierre Desrochers of Library and Archives Canada presents his experience marrying Linked Data techniques with the deployed XML-based infrastructure of his government. Qing Liu, Quan Bai, Li Ding and their colleagues from Australia and the United States investigate the ability of Linked Data to support data discovery in support of sustainability science. Finally, Dominic DiFranzo, Alvaro Graves, John Erickson and yet more researchers from Rensselaer Polytechnic Institute report on their experience building mashups from governmental data.

Open government is not just a concern of the West, nor of English speaking nations. Although this book is written in English, its authors work in countries around the world and were often born in others. Open government, like the Web itself, is an international enterprise. We are pleased to include work originating in Australia, Brazil, Canada, Finland, Ireland, Spain, the United Kingdom and the United States. We trust that readers will take into account the international nature of this effort when noticing American and British spelling differences and phraseology uncommon among native speakers of English. We consider such diversity to be a feature, not a bug.

This book would not have been possible without the peer reviews provided by chapter authors and the following external reviewers, listed in alphabetical order: Irene Celino of CEFRIEL Politecnico di Milano, Bob DuCharme of TopQuadrant Inc., Paul Gearon of Revelytix Inc. and Mike Pendleton of the United States Environmental Protection Agency. Thank you to all.

Fredericksburg, Virginia, USA,   *David Wood*
                                                                                                   August 2011

Contents

Part II Improving Linked Data Quality

5   Creating and Publishing Semantic Metadata about Linked and Open Datasets   95
Matias Frosterus, Eero Hyvönen, and Joonas Laitio

6   StdTrip: Promoting the Reuse of Standard Vocabularies in Open Government Data   113
Percy Salas, José Viterbo, Karin Breitman, and Marco Antonio Casanova

List of Contributors

Quan Bai
Tasmanian ICT Centre, CSIRO, GPO BOX 1538, Hobart, TAS 7001, Australia,
e-mail: quan.bai@aut.ac.nz

Karin Breitman
Departamento de Informática, Pontifícia Universidade Católica do Rio de
Janeiro, R. Mq. de S. Vicente, 225, Rio de Janeiro/RJ, 22451-900, Brazil, e-mail:
karin@inf.puc-rio.br

Marco Antonio Casanova
Departamento de Informática, Pontifícia Universidade Católica do Rio de
Janeiro, R. Mq. de S. Vicente, 225, Rio de Janeiro/RJ, 22451-900, Brazil, e-mail:
casanova@inf.puc-rio.br

Yun Chen
CSIRO Land and Water, Black Mountain, GPO Box 1666, Canberra, ACT 2601,
Australia, e-mail: Yun.chen@csiro.au

Oscar Corcho
Ontology Engineering Group, Departamento de Inteligencia Artificial, Facultad
de Informática, Universidad Politécnica de Madrid, Madrid, España, e-mail:
ocorcho@fi.upm.es

Richard Cyganiak
DERI, NUI Galway, IDA Business Park, Lower Dangan, Galway, Ireland, e-mail:
richard.cyganiak@deri.org

Pierre Desrochers
Library and Archives Canada, 550 Boul. de la Cité, Gatineau, QC, K1A 0N4,
Canada, e-mail: pierre.desrochers@bac-lac.gc.ca

Dominic DiFranzo
Tetherless World Constellation, Rensselaer Polytechnic Institute, 110 8th St., Troy,
NY 12180, USA, e-mail: difrad@rpi.edu

John S. Erickson
Tetherless World Constellation, Rensselaer Polytechnic Institute, 110 8th St., Troy,
NY 12180, USA, e-mail: erickj4@rpi.edu

Peter Fitch
CSIRO Land and Water, Black Mountain, GPO Box 1666, Canberra, ACT 2601,
Australia, e-mail: peter.fitch@csiro.au

Johanna Flores
Tetherless World Constellation, Rensselaer Polytechnic Institute, 110 8th St., Troy,
NY 12180, USA, e-mail: florej6@rpi.edu

Peter Fox
Tetherless World Constellation, Rensselaer Polytechnic Institute, 110 8th St., Troy,
NY 12180, USA, e-mail: pfox@cs.rpi.edu

Matias Frosterus
Aalto University School of Science P.O. Box 11000 FI-00076 Aalto, Finland
University of Helsinki P.O. Box 68 00014 Helsingin Yliopisto, e-mail:
matias.frosterus@aalto.fi

Asunción Gómez-Pérez
Ontology Engineering Group, Departamento de Inteligencia Artificial, Facultad
de Informática, Universidad Politécnica de Madrid, Madrid, España, e-mail:
asun@fi.upm.es

John Goodwin
Ordnance Survey, Adanac Drive, Southampton, SO16 0AS, United Kingdom,
e-mail: john.goodwin@ordnancesurvey.co.uk

Alvaro Graves
Tetherless World Constellation, Rensselaer Polytechnic Institute, 110 8th St., Troy,
NY 12180, USA, e-mail: gravea3@rpi.edu

Michael Hausenblas
DERI, NUI Galway, IDA Business Park, Lower Dangan, Galway, Ireland, e-mail:
michael.hausenblas@deri.org

Tom Heath
Talis Systems Ltd, 43 Temple Row, Birmingham, B2 5LS, United Kingdom,
e-mail: tom.heath@talis.com

Jim Hendler
Tetherless World Constellation, Rensselaer Polytechnic Institute, 110 8th St., Troy,
NY 12180, USA, e-mail: hendler@cs.rpi.edu

Eero Hyvönen
Aalto University School of Science P.O. Box 11000 FI-00076 Aalto, Finland
University of Helsinki P.O. Box 68 00014 Helsingin Yliopisto, e-mail:
eero.hyvonen@tkk.fi

Bernadette Hyland
3 Round Stones Inc., Fredericksburg, VA 22408, USA, e-mail:
bernadette.hyland@3roundstones.com

Corné Kloppers
Tasmanian ICT Centre, CSIRO, GPO BOX 1538, Hobart, TAS 7001, Australia,
e-mail: Corne.kloppers@csiro.au

Joonas Laitio
Aalto University School of Science P.O. Box 11000 FI-00076 Aalto, Finland
University of Helsinki P.O. Box 68 00014 Helsingin Yliopisto, e-mail:
joonas.laitio@aalto.fi

Timothy Lebo
Tetherless World Constellation, Rensselaer Polytechnic Institute, 110 8th St., Troy,
NY 12180, USA, e-mail: lebot@rpi.edu

David Lemon
CSIRO Land and Water, Black Mountain, GPO Box 1666, Canberra, ACT 2601,
Australia, e-mail: David.lemon@csiro.au

Li Ding
Tetherless World Constellation, Rensselaer Polytechnic Institute, 110 8th St., Troy,
NY 12180, USA, e-mail: dingl@cs.rpi.edu

Xian Li
Tetherless World Constellation, Rensselaer Polytechnic Institute, 110 8th St., Troy,
NY 12180, USA, e-mail: lix15@rpi.edu

Qing Liu
Tasmanian ICT Centre, CSIRO, GPO BOX 1538, Hobart, TAS 7001, Australia,
e-mail: Q.Liu@csiro.au

Eoin McCuirc
Central Statistics Office, Skehard Road, Cork, Ireland,
e-mail: Eoin.McCuirc@cso.ie

Deborah L. McGuinness
Tetherless World Constellation, Rensselaer Polytechnic Institute, 110 8th St., Troy,
NY 12180, USA, e-mail: dlm@cs.rpi.edu

James Michaelis
Tetherless World Constellation, Rensselaer Polytechnic Institute, 110 8th St., Troy,
NY 12180, USA, e-mail: michaj6@rpi.edu

Evan Patton
Tetherless World Constellation, Rensselaer Polytechnic Institute, 110 8th St., Troy,
NY 12180, USA, e-mail: pattoe@rpi.edu

Huong Pho
Tasmanian ICT Centre, CSIRO, GPO BOX 1538, Hobart, TAS 7001, Australia,
e-mail: huong.pho@csiro.au

Percy Salas
Departamento de Informática, Pontifícia Universidade Católica do Rio de
Janeiro, R. Mq. de S. Vicente, 225, Rio de Janeiro/RJ, 22451-900, Brazil, e-mail:
psalas@inf.puc-rio.br

Zhenning Shangguan
Tetherless World Constellation, Rensselaer Polytechnic Institute, 110 8th St., Troy,
NY 12180, USA, e-mail: shangz@cs.rpi.edu

Paulo de Souza
Tasmanian ICT Centre, CSIRO, GPO BOX 1538, Hobart, TAS 7001, Australia,
e-mail: Paulo.deSouza@csiro.au

Luis. M. Vilches-Blázquez
Ontology Engineering Group, Departamento de Inteligencia Artificial, Facultad
de Informática, Universidad Politécnica de Madrid, Madrid, España, e-mail:
lmvilches@fi.upm.es

Boris Villazón-Terrazas
Ontology Engineering Group, Departamento de Inteligencia Artificial, Facultad
de Informática, Universidad Politécnica de Madrid, Madrid, España, e-mail:
bvillazon@fi.upm.es

José Viterbo
Instituto de Computação, Universidade Federal Fluminense, R. Passo
da Pátria, 156/Bloco E/3o andar, Niterói/RJ, 24210-240, Brazil, e-mail:
jviterbo@id.uff.br

Gregory Todd Williams
Tetherless World Constellation, Rensselaer Polytechnic Institute, 110 8th St., Troy,
NY 12180, USA, e-mail: greg@evilfunhouse.com

David Wood
3 Round Stones Inc., Fredericksburg, VA 22408, USA, e-mail:
david.wood@3roundstones.com

Jin Guang Zheng
Tetherless World Constellation, Rensselaer Polytechnic Institute, 110 8th St., Troy,
NY 12180, USA, e-mail: zhengj3@rpi.edu

Part I
Publishing Linked Government Data

Linked Data, RDF, OWL and other Semantic Web research has resulted in a tremendous number of academic publications, totaling over two hundred thousand results on Google Scholar[5] as of this writing. Introductory material, on the other hand, has been relatively scarce. It is appropriate that this book begins by attempting to rectify that oversight.

The first two chapters provide introductions to open government initiatives using Linked Data and present general methodological guidance concerning the flow of a Linked Data project. The similarities found in these chapters may give some solace to those worried about unknown complexities; they were written on both sides of the Atlantic Ocean. The experiences gathered from Linked Data projects seems to have been remarkably uniform to date.

The following two chapters offer a deeper look into some real world governmental Linked Data projects. Again these experiences span the Atlantic. The projects address two critical use cases for government agencies; the conversion of data from traditional sources and the reuse of governmental geographic information.

---

[5] http://scholar.google.com

Chapter 1
The Joy of Data - A Cookbook for Publishing Linked Government Data on the Web

Bernadette Hyland and David Wood

Abstract

Many governments have recently mandated the open publication of more information to the public, in attempts to facilitate the maintenance of open societies and in support of governmental accountability and transparency initiatives. Publication of structured data on the World Wide Web is in itself insufficient; in order to make use of such data, members of the public can best absorb data when it can be used with other published data. Linked Data approaches address key requirements of open government by providing a family of international standards and best practices for the publication, dissemination and reuse of structured data. Further, Linked Data, unlike previous data formatting and publication approaches, provides a simple mechanism for combining data from multiple sources across the Web. This chapter provides a six-step "cookbook" to model, create, publish and announce government Linked Data. We'll highlight the role of the World Wide Web Consortium, an international standards organization and its member organizations who are currently driving specifications and best practices for the publication of governmental data. The chapter concludes with guidance on the social contract government agencies implicitly adopt when they publish Linked Data on the Web.

1.1 Introduction

In an era of reduced federal, state and local budgets, there is strong economic motivation to reduce waste and duplication in data management and integration. Linked Open Data is a viable approach to publishing governmental data to the public, but only if it adheres to some basic principles. In this chapter we define the "ingredients" and steps necessary to publish Linked Data.

Correspondance author: Bernadette Hyland, 3 Round Stones Inc., Fredericksburg, VA 22408, USA, e-mail: bhyland@3roundstones.com. See the List of Contributors for full contact details.

To date, Linked Data has been largely a ground up effort by individuals, communities and organizations around the world. Linked Data publishers are commonly data curators or stewards who have data they believe is valuable to others. Some may be publishing Linked Data sets in response to requirements to make foundation or government funded research available to the greater research community; others may have a legislative or executive mandate to make content available to the public. Governments including Canada, the United States, United Kingdom, France, Spain, Sweden, Norway, Italy, Austria, Maldova, Greece, Hong Kong, Australia, New Zealand and Finland all have Open Data sites to make government data more easily accessible, and several of those are making their data available as Linked Data.[1]

Early publishers could not have anticipated the results of publishing their data using Linked Data principles. In 2009, Jay Myers, a manager from a large US electronics retailer, confirmed the positive impact of publishing data using standard vocabularies.[20] By 2011, Meyers detailed how product visibility and discovery had increased through publishing product information in HTML with additional RDFa markup.[21]

Leveraging the pioneering work of data publishers in the commercial sector (c.f. [33]), open government initiatives around the world are also beginning to see the benefits of publishing Linked Open Data. Sir Tim Berners-Lee met with with former Prime Minister Gordon Brown of the UK in 2009 where they discussed making government content available via the Web[6]. In the US, President Barak Obama issued his Memorandum on Transparency and Open Government on his first day in office in January 2009.[24] The next year the new UK Prime Minster David Cameron issued his "Letter to Government Departments to Open up Data" which propelled useful content to be published on data.gov.uk in January 2010.[9] Data.gov.uk was built using Open Source technology by ten people over approximately six months in 2009.[6]

Forums held in Washington DC and London in November 2010 discussed the fundamental goals:

1. Empowering citizens to make informed choices;
2. Holding public servants accountable; and
3. Sowing the seeds for economic growth.

Advocates of Open Government contended that taxpayers have paid for data governments produce and therefore should have access to this information. Public disclosure has proven to be a strong incentive for polluters to reduce their use of toxic chemicals according to the former New York District Attorney.[14] Anecdotal evidence shows that intra- and inter-government agencies, NGOs and policy makers are some of the first people to reuse publicly published government data, following the phenomenon of employees using their organization's Web site to source information they cannot find on their intranet, document management system or other enterprise systems.

---

[1] http://www.data.gov/community

Deputy Chief Technology Officer for Open Government, White House Office of Science and Technology Policy during 2008-2010, acknowledged that government agency decision makers are policy, not data, professionals and that third parties, with the right tools and enthusiasm, will take raw data and provide the technical, design and statistical acumen to transform data into meaningful information.[23]

the first US Chief Information Officer from 2009-2011, stated, "government will never be able to make the data perfect. We just have to push forward and publish it for review and use by others who are knowledgeable. Real data is dirty and we as knowledgable consumers will learn to separate out the cruft from nuggets of gold."[17] We will cover in greater detail in this chapter what useful information means and how data stewards can publish high quality information.

Publishing and consuming Linked Data allows for cooperation without coordination.[34] Data publishers may effectively cooperate to produce - individually - data sets that may be reused and recombined by unknown third parties. There is no need for Linked Data publishers to coordinate efforts. Use of the Linked Data guidelines (which include a mandate to reuse existing vocabularies and to publish details of new vocabularies used) is sufficient.

Future proofing one's technology choices in a rapidly changing IT landscape is prudent. No organization should be beholden to one vendor to store, access or analyze their organization's data. Indeed, through leveraging modern RDF data exchange formats and international Internet standards, organizations have every opportunity to avoid vendor lock-in permanently.

This chapter reviews and augments earlier Linked Data guidance and suggests particular guidance for governmental data publishers. We examined a number of published and Web-based cookbooks for publishing Linked Data on the Web, including those by Bizer, Cyganiak and Heath[7], and guidance by the W3C.[29][2]. Tom Heath has collected some frequently asked questions on the Linked Data community Web site[3].

A collection of patterns to be found in high-quality Linked Data has been created by Ian Davis and Leigh Dodds[4]. Rob Styles, a colleague of Davis and Dodds, has used his experience creating Linked Data to write about what people find difficult about the process[5]. Similarly, Mike Bergman has identified some common problems[6]. Tim Davies has written specifically in relation to publishing government Linked Data[7]. There are, of course, many others.

This chapter is simultaneously broader in scope and yet in many cases presented at a higher level. It combines and collects information from all of the above, but changes the focus. It is rarely necessary for those in government to understand the technical details of Linked Data formats, standards or protocols. It is necessary,

---

[2] W3C "Guidance on Linked Data", see http://www.w3.org/standards/semanticweb/data

[3] http://linkeddata.org/faq

[4] http://patterns.dataincubator.org/book/

[5] http://blogs.talis.com/platform-consulting/2010/11/15/what-people-find-hard-about-linked-data/

[6] http://www.mkbergman.com/917/practical-p-p-p-problems-with-linked-data/

[7] http://www.timdavies.org.uk/2010/11/25/defining-raw-data/

however, for them to understand *why* Linked Data provides value and by which policy decisions governmental interests may be better served. It is also necessary for governmental staff to be aware of industry trends that reflect emerging best practices for the management of governmental data. This chapter, then, attempts to fill an existing gap in the guidance for Linked Data publication.

1.2 State of the Linked Open Data Cloud

The Linked Open Data cloud is a globally distributed Web of data; in effect, it is a database that spans the entire Web. The Linked Open Data cloud has grown from about 40 million triples representing four data sets in 2007 to 203 data sets (qualified from the 215 submitted) consisting of over 25 billion RDF triples and 395 million RDF links, as of the end of 2010.[3] The rapid growth of the Linked Open Data project may be seen in the diagrams developed by Richard Cyganiak and Anja Jentzsch.[8]

The number of government catalogues and data sets continues to increase. As local, state, federal and multi-national organizations publish content there are understandable concerns about misinterpretation. Best practices are being formulated for and by the bourgeoning number of data publishers and consumers. Best practices for the Linked Data ecosystem are being defined and include guidance for departments and agencies on procurement, vocabulary selection, URI construction, versioning, stability, conversion from legacy data. A W3C Linked Data cookbook is being updated regularly as best practices evolve.[9]

The W3C Government Linked Data Working Group (launched June 2011) has a mission "to provide standards and other information which help governments around the world publish their data as effective and usable Linked Data."[31] This working group is part of the W3C eGovernment Activity[10] and is collecting and making available information about governmental Linked Data activities around the world. The members of W3C Government Linked Data working group are comprised of international researchers and developers, vendors of technology products and services, Linked Data domain experts, government employees and contractors. Together, they are formulating guidance best practices, procurement, vocabulary selection guidance, and a community directory based on Linked Open Data principles described in this chapter.

---

[8] http://richard.cyganiak.de/2007/10/lod/

[9] http://www.w3.org/2011/gld/wiki/LinkedDataCookbook

[10] http://www.w3.org/egov/

1.3 Open and Usable Data Formats

At the First International Open Government Conference[11], Sir Tim Berners-Lee recounted that British Prime Minister Gordon Brown said in 2007, "data does not belong to government but public." However, as Darlene Meskell aptly said, "more data does not always mean usable data. While it is important that the operations of government be open and that hearings and other meetings be broadcast, it is insufficient to share information for purely passive consumption instead of releasing data in open, structured and readable formats that make it possible for third parties to reuse, manipulate and visualize the data."[19],[13] In a more open information society, there will be more eyes watching.

According to Robert Schaefer, speaking on climate change and space weather critical needs at the November 2010 International Open Government Conference, "having Open Government data is good thing, but making sense of the data is difficult without the context of what the data implies. You need analysts and scientists to extract meaning from the knowledge. Then we have to get this information to policy makers."[26] It is precisely this context that Linked Data can record, by allowing an open and extensible schema with explanatory information that resolves on the Web and by interlinking with related data from many sources. The openness of Linked Data formats, and their definition in international standards, helps to facilitate the collection of contextual information.

Linked Open Data published by some governments is primarily found through catalog sites. Data formats available via open government data sites fall into the following general categories:

1. Raw data (i.e., CSV, JSON, PDF, XML, RSS, XLS, XLSX)
2. Geospatial data (i.e., SHP, KML)
3. RDF (Turtle, N3, RDF/XML)

Many of the recently published government data sets, including the ubiquitous comma-separated-value (CSV) format, are not immediately useful because column headings or schema are not defined. While someone looking at a CSV file may be able to derive some value from the column headings, there is no guarantee the meaning of the data has been communicated. That is why the modeling effort described below is so vital.

has its own common formats, but efforts are also being made to represent that data in Linked Data. See the chapter entitled "Linking Geographical Data for Government and Consumer Applications" by Tom Heath and John Goodwin.

Data in the RDF family of standards is well on its way to becoming Linked Data, but it is not there yet. The Linked Data principles still need to be applied.[5] It is our view that open government information should, whenever possible, be high quality, "5-star" Linked Data.

---

[11] Held November 15-17, 2010 in Washington, DC.

1.4 Ingredients

This chapter uses a recipe analogy as a guide for new "cooks." We describe the necessary ingredients and process for creating Linked Data, including how to model Linked Data, what to consider when defining URIs (Uniform Resource Identifiers), how to select vocabularies, and importantly how to publish and announce new Linked Data sets.

Season to taste and have fun!

Ingredients List: (serves millions)

- URIs
- Information resources
- Descriptions of non-information resources
- W3C family of RDF standards
- Your data

Publishing Linked Data is likely to cause you to undergo a new way of thinking. In the Linked Open Data world, we turn things upside down and think about data and how objects *are related to each other*. After your first experience of seeing a data set, preferably one with which you are familiar, combined with a new data set, you'll rapidly begin to see to possibilities. As Linked Data publishers, we'll need to come to peace with *not knowing* in advance *how* people will use the data we publish, nor *who* will use our data.

The saying, "think globally, act locally" (first expressed by Greddes in 1915 [15]) is germane to Linked Data. Publishers of Linked Data spend their valuable time preparing and contributing content on the Web so anyone can use it, no matter where they live or what language they speak.

1.4.1 Comparing Relational and Linked Data Models

There are several differences between how data is modeled for use in a relational system versus a Linked Data application. A relational model provides a declarative mechanism to specify data and how it may be queried. Most relational databases use a SQL data definition and query language. Relational modelers specify the tables and views and a database management system handles the underlying data structures for storage and retrieval via SQL queries. Entities and their attributes are often fragmented across several tables. In a relational model, the schema is described separately from the data. To understand a relational model, a developer *first* reviews the logical model to understand the data and then the application logic to determine how the data is used.

By contrast, Linked Data models are conceptual in nature. Linked Data schemas are described exactly the same way as the data itself is described. This is a simple and very powerful concept. *Linked Data schemas are part of the data.* Bizer and Heath describe *schema* in the Linked Data sense to be "the mixture of distinct terms from different RDF vocabularies that are used by a data source to publish data on the Web."[8]

As a practical convenience, Linked Data practitioners often publish their schema in a human-readable format (HTML), however, when data is loaded into a graph database, the schema and the data are loaded together. It is in this way that consumers of Linked Data can discover more (related) data and learn about the data schema itself as they "follow their nose" and follow links that are in the data itself. The Linked Data approach allows for greater heterogeneous data integration through the use of resolvable HTTP URIs.

The Web is scalable because it is loosely coupled, as is the Semantic Web and thus Linked Data. Practically, Linked Data systems often refer to schema information that may not resolve on the Web. As disturbing as this may be to traditional data professionals, missing information on the Linked Data Web is handled in the same manner as other missing information on the Web: Missing is not necessarily broken. The Web reminds us to be accepting of failures, dirty data and different ways of categorizing.

1.5 Peeling the Onion

Fresh ingredients with minimal processing are a hallmark of great French cuisine. The parallel distinguishing feature of Linked Data are de-referenceable HTTP URIs. URIs are to Linked Data what fleur de sel (sea salt) is to French cuisine. HTTP clients, such as a Web browser, can resolve a URI and get information from it. URIs are what make Linked Data so extensible. That simple yet powerful concept allows developers to remix and re-use data sets with unparalleled ease.

Let's review the basic ingredients: *information resources* and the *description of non-information resources* on the Web *expressed as URIs*. Nicholas Negroponte has said, "bits have always been the underlying particle of digital computing, but over the last twenty-five years we have greatly expanded our binary vocabulary to include much more than just numbers."[22] On the Web, information resources are a series of bits, such as Web pages, images and CSS files. Thus, information resources are things that computers understand. By contrast, non-information resources are broadly defined by Negroponte as "atoms" and include people, places, events, things and concepts.

Linked Data uses HTTP URIs to describe *both atoms and bits*. We as humans can easily distinguish between the two, but we need to give machines some hints. When URIs identify real-world objects (i.e., people, places, events, things and concepts) and abstract concepts, it is important to not confuse the real world object for example, the *person* Julia Child, with the Web page that describes her. To avoid ambiguity, we use a different URIs to identify the real-world person versus the document that describes the French chef. Data appears differently in human and machine readable formats:

1. a human-readable Web page;

2. a human-readable view of Linked Data;
3. machine-readable data for a Linked Data client to parse.[12]

The reader is encouraged to view the following URIs in a Web browser to quickly see the difference between:

1. The URI http://en.wikipedia.org/wiki/Julia_Child is a Web page that describes Julia Child in English for a human reader.
2. The URI http://dbpedia.org/page/Julia_Child is a human-readable representation of the data on Julia Child available from DBpedia. This page was automatically generated from the RDF.
3. http://dbpedia.org/data/Julia_Child is RDF and is intended for a browser or search engine to parse.

The first page demonstrates information available as a Web page for human consumption. On the second page, generated from an RDF description, we see links to other pages including Julia's television shows, awards, articles written about her, education affiliations, a photograph of the chef. This content is written for a global audience and contains abstract information using the DBpedia Ontology in multiple human-readable languages including Portuguese, German, Russian, Finish, and Chinese. The RDF data also follows the best practice of using existing vocabularies. We see RDF descriptions, OWL, DBpedia[13], Dublin Core, RDF Schema for alternate name, comments and labels, and FOAF for names. Finally, you will notice that file extensions were omitted from the URLs. It is best practice to omit an extension indicating the specific serialization and let HTTP content negotiation identify which serialization it wants rather than hard-coding the data as a particular serialization and creating a URL to reflect this choice. Content negotiation allows a Web client to propose what kind of content it prefers to see and in what order: Web browsers will prefer to see HTML, but Linked Data clients can request RDF from the same URL.

The Linking Open Data project started with the DBpedia Project, so data and vocabularies from it are often used in Linked Data applications. DBpedia is a community led effort to extract structured information from Wikipedia and publish it on the Web as Linked Data. DBpedia serves as a hub for the Linking Open Data project. DBpedia publishes this information under the terms of the Creative Commons Attribution-ShareAlike 3.0 License[14] and the GNU Free Documentation License[15], allowing its reuse elsewhere on the Web.

Good quality Linked Data has, as the name suggests, lots of links. This is known as the 4th Linked Data principle defined by Tim Berners-Lee when he described the original vision for Linked Data in 2006.[5] The power of Linked Data is in merging

---

[12] Some Linked Data clients are Callimachus (http://callimachusproject.org), Link Sailor (http://linksailor.com) and Drupal version 7 (http://drupal.org)

[13] http://wiki.dbpedia.org/Ontology

[14] http://en.wikipedia.org/wiki/Wikipedia:Text_of_Creative_Commons_Attribution-ShareAlike_3.0_Unported_License

[15] http://en.wikipedia.org/wiki/Wikipedia:Text_of_the_GNU_Free_Documentation_License

data with other data sets. Linked Data "success" is defined by others reusing your data in potentially unanticipated and meaningful ways.

Guidelines for merging Linked Data include recognizing that:

1. URIs name the resources we are describing;
2. Two people using the same URI are describing the same thing;
3. The same URI in two datasets means the same thing;
4. Graphs from several different sources can be merged;
5. There are no limitations on which graphs can be merged (other than that imposed by security restrictions).

1.6 Ready to Cook

1.6.1 Step #1 - Modeling the Data

Linked Data domain experts model data without context versus traditional modelers who typically organize data for specified Web services or applications. Modeling without context better enables data reuse and easier merging of data sets by third parties. Linked Data application logic does not drive the data schema. Below we summarize the process of modeling that can take anywhere from several hours for a simple data set to several weeks for experienced subject matter experts and Linked Data experts working iteratively together. That is a comparatively modest investment given that most organizations spend months or years carefully compiling and curating their data.

A criticism voiced by detractors of Linked Data suggest that Linked Data modeling is too hard or time consuming. We see the effort of modeling as Linked Data as the way forward to unlock data and make it more widely available within an organization or on the public Web. On the numerous projects where we have modeled content as Linked Data, the data owners or stewards were impressed with the speed and flexibility their information now expressed as RDF provided their organization. Here is an outline of the steps one should follow during a modeling process where the original data resides in a relational database:

1. Identify:

    1.1. Obtain a copy of the logical and physical model of the database(s).
    1.2. Obtain data extracts (e.g. CSV table extracts, data dictionaries) or create data in a way that can be replicated.
    1.3. Look for real world objects of interest such as people, places, things and locations.

2. Model:

    2.1. Sketch or draw the objects on a white board (or similar) and draw lines to express how they are related to each other.

2.2. Investigate how others are already describing similar or related data. Reuse common vocabularies to facilitate data merging and reuse.

2.3. If you're using existing data, look for duplication and (de)normalize the data as necessary.

2.4. Use common sense to decide whether or not to make link.

2.5. Put aside immediate needs of any application.

3. Name:

3.1. Use URIs as names for your objects.

3.2. Think about time and how the data will change over time.

4. Test the assumptions in the schema with subject matter experts familiar with the data.

Linked Data domain experts typically model two or three exemplar objects to begin the process. During this process, domain experts figure out the relationships and identify how each object relates to the real world, initially drawing on a large white board or collaborative wiki site. As you iterate, use a graphing tool to organize the objects and relationships and produce an electronic copy for others to review. It bears repeating, during the modeling process, one should not be contemplating how an application will use your data. Instead, focus on modeling real world things that are known about the data and how it is related to other objects. Take the time to understand the data and how the objects represented in the data are related to each other.

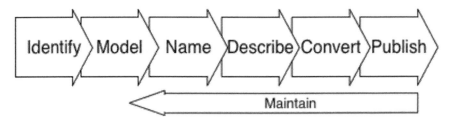

Fig. 1.1 A simplification of a typical Linked Data creation process.

1.6.2 Step #2 - Naming Things on the Web with URIs

You are now ready to name your objects that you modeled in Step #1. Give careful consideration to your URI naming strategy. This deserves careful consideration just like any form of public communication from your organization. Rob Styles has summarized this as, "choosing URIs is not a five minute task."[27]

The reader is encouraged to review both the guidance on Designing URIs Sets provided by the UK Cabinet Office.[28] This guide provides principles for choosing the right domain for URI sets, the path structure, coping with change, machine and human-readable formats. Additionally, the Linked Open Government Data (LOGD) team at Rensselaer Polytechnic Institute in New York documented URI Guidance for URI naming schemes.[16] The following is intended as a primer for designing public sector URIs:

Use HTTP URIs

URIs provide names for resources. You can say things about resources. Everyone knows what to do with HTTP URIs. They are a quick, easy and scalable lookup mechanism.

Use clean, stable URIs.

Try to abstract away from implementation details.

Use a Domain that You Control.

It is important to select a DNS domain that your department or agency controls. It is bad etiquette to use someone's domain that you do not own or control. In this way, you can also commit to its permanence and provide data at this address.

Use Natural Keys.

Use natural keys to make your URIs readable by people. This is not required, but is a very useful courtesy to those wishing to reuse your data. Take some care in defining these. Don't be cryptic. For example nobody can guess what http://.../984d6a means. Use containers in a URI path to help keep natural keys separate. Containers provide a logical place to put lists. For example, http://.../baked_goods/bread/rye-12, http://.../baked_goods/bread/rye-13

Use Neutral URIs.

A URI contains meaningful, natural or system-neutral keys. One can route these URIs to any implementation, meaning they can live forever. Therefore, don't include version numbers or technology names. Neutral URIs are also a wise choice as you're not advertising a specific technology choice that might change or where security vulnerabilities may exist.

---

[16] http://logd.tw.rpi.edu/instance-hub-uri-design

Use of hash URIs should be done cautiously.

The hash URI strategy builds on the characteristic that URIs may contain a special part that is separated from the base part of the URI by a hash symbol (#). This special part is called the fragment identifier.[8] Fragment identifiers are not sent to a server. This limits server side decision making, and limits granularity of the response. Fragment identifiers enable such URIs to be used to identify real-world objects and abstract concepts, without creating ambiguity.[25] Use fragment identifiers with caution.

Hash URIs are most useful for Linked Data schemas, where a URI for a schema term might resolve to a human-readable Web page (e.g. http://example.com/id/vocabulary#linked_data). Most Linked Data should use so-called Slash URIs that avoid fragment identifiers (e.g. http://example.com/id/vocabulary/linked_data/).

Use dates sparingly in URIs.

Dates provide a way to show data from a period in time. They are most useful for things like statistics, regulations, specifications, samples or readings from a given period.

The W3C is a well known exception this thumb rule. They use a convention for URIs related to the dates that working groups are established or documents are standardized. For example, the W3C RDF Recommendation was published 10 February 2004, so the convention they use is to path with the date as follows http://www.w3.org/TR/2004/REC-rdf-concepts-20040210/. This approach is acceptable however, it should be used with careful consideration on how things may change over time.

1.6.3 Step #3 - Reuse Vocabularies Whenever Possible

A relatively small number of vocabularies are routinely used to describe people, places, things and locations.[17] Any given Linked Data set may include terms from an existing and widely used vocabulary. This could include using terms from Dublin Core, which describes metadata about published works, or FOAF (Friend-of-a-Friend), used to describe people and their relationship to other people, or GeoNames a geographical database covers all countries and contains over ten million geographical names.

---

[17] Suggested by unpublished research at Talis conducted by Dr. Tom Heath.

It is a best practice to use existing authoritative vocabularies that are in widespread usage to describe common types of data.

In the traditional data modeling world, documentation is often not kept current after the system is launched, nor is it routinely published on the Web. However, in the Linked Data community, reuse is presumed. Reuse of authoritative vocabularies results in reduced costs because people can publish information more quickly. In many cases, the authoritative vocabulary is maintained by someone else, allowing many to benefit from the labor a few. Readers may be interested in following the Data Catalog Vocabulary Task Force within the W3C Interest Group on eGovernment[18]. Knowing how to use the commonly used vocabularies properly will help your organization find natural reuse potential and help identify areas for cross-linking with other Linked Data sets.

- To name things, use rdfs:label, foaf:name, skos:prefLabel
- To describe people, use FOAF, vCard
- To describe projects, use DOAP
- To describe Web pages and other publications, use dc:creator and dc:description
- To describe an RDF schema/vocabulary/ontology, use a VoID description
- To describe addresses, use vCard
- To model simple data, use RDF, RDFS, custom vocabularies
- To model existing taxonomies, use SKOS

The following summary of vocabularies is relevant for government agencies. It is not exhaustive. The typical practice is to combine a few terms from several different vocabularies, much like a smorgasbord. You may still need to define a few more customized terms depending upon the specific needs of your organization.

1. The (WGS84) vocabulary[19] defines terms for lat(itude), long(itude) and other information about spatially-located things, using WGS84 as a reference datum.
2. The (BIBO)[20] provides main concepts and properties for describing citations and bibliographic references (i.e. quotes, books, articles, etc).
3. The (CC) schema[21] defines terms for describing copyright licenses in RDF. Although data created by government agencies is generally under legislated ownership, the CC licenses are often used by government contractors to ensure that government agencies retain a right to use the material.
4. The **Description of a Project** (DOAP)[22] vocabulary (pronounced "*dope*") is a project to create a vocabulary to describe software projects, with particular emphasis on Open Source projects.

---

[18] http://www.w3.org/egov/wiki/Data_Catalog_Vocabulary

[19] http://www.w3.org/2003/01/geo/

[20] http://bibliontology.com/specification

[21] http://creativecommons.org/ns#

[22] http://trac.usefulinc.com/doap

5. The **Dublin Core Metadata Initiative (DCMI) Metadata Terms**[23] defines general metadata attributes for published works including *title, creator, date, subject* and *publisher.*
6. The **Friend-of-a-Friend** (FOAF)[24] vocabulary defines terms for describing people, their activities (collaboration) and their relations to other people and objects. There are extensions to FOAF for the Social Web. This helps describe how one relates to Facebook, Flikr, LinkedIn, etc.
7. The **GeoNames Ontology**[25] is a geographical database containing over 10 million geographical names.
8. The [26], an ontology for E-commerce that defines terms for describing products, price, and company data. The goal is to increase the visibility of products and services in search engines, recommender systems, and mobile or social applications.
9. The **Object Reuse and Exchange vocabulary**[27] defines standards for the description and exchange of aggregations of Web resources. These aggregations, called compound digital objects, may combine distributed resources with multiple media types including text, images, data, and video. Used by libraries and media publishers.
10. The **Semantically-Interlinked Online Communities vocabulary**[28] (SIOC, pronounced "shock") is designed for developers to describe information about an online community sites, such as users, posts and forums.
11. The **vocabulary**[29] is a file format for address books. It is an older but popular address book format that has since been ported to RDF and includes the basics of what is needed for representing addresses internationally.
12. The **Vocabulary of Interlinked Datasets**[30] (VoID) defines key metadata about RDF datasets. It is intended as a bridge between the publishers and users of RDF data, with applications ranging from data discovery to cataloging and archiving of datasets. Ideally, one will always publish a VoID description of your vocabulary so others can reuse it.

Those concerned with reusing existing vocabularies should see the chapter "StdTrip: Promoting the Reuse of Standard Vocabularies in Open Government Data" by Percy Salas and his colleagues. Those interested in describing their own data sets should also see the chapter "Creating and Publishing Semantic Metadata about Linked and Open Datasets" by Matias Frosterus and his colleagues.

---

[23] Dublin Core terms have also been published as IETF RFC 5013, ANSI/NISO Standard Z39.85-2007 and ISO Standard 15836:2009: http://dublincore.org/documents/dcmi-terms/

[24] http://xmlns.com/foaf/spec/

[25] http://www.geonames.org/ontology/ontology_v2.2.1.rdf

[26] http://www.heppnetz.de/projects/goodrelations/

[27] http://www.openarchives.org/ore/

[28] http://rdfs.org/sioc/spec/

[29] http://w3.org/TR/vcard-rdf/

[30] http://www.w3.org/2001/sw/interest/void/

If you determine that there is no existing or authoritative vocabulary for your subject domain, create one or more, following some basic conventions. We recommend *Semantic Web for the Working Ontologist: Effective Modeling in RDFS and OWL* as a resource.[16]

1.6.4 Step #4 - Publishing Human and Machine-Readable Descriptions

Consumers of Linked Data do not have the luxury of talking to a database administrator who could help them understand a schema. Therefore, a best practice for publishing a Linked Data set is to make it "self-describing." Self-describing data suggests that "information about the encodings used for each representation is provided explicitly within the representation.[29] Reusability is provided to others by modeling data outside of any one application's context. Validation of the data is specific to an application's context. Said another way, the application using a data set is responsible for validating the data. The ability for Linked Data to describe itself, to place itself in context, contributes to the usefulness of the underlying data.

> Be sure to include human-readable descriptions of your data as a Web page, in addition to your RDF data files.

By making available both human-readable and machine-readable formats that are self-contained, you will have moved your agency closer to achieving the goals of Open Government and making the data truly available for reuse.

Be sure to publish a VoID description of your RDF dataset. VoID is the de facto standard vocabulary for describing Linked Data sets because it helps users find the right data for their tasks.[31]

1.6.5 Step #5 - Converting Data to RDF

Once you have a schema that you are satisfied with, the next step is to convert the source data into a Linked Data representation or serialization. We are often asked, "what form of RDF should we publish?" There are several RDF serializations for example, RDF/XML[32], Notation-3 (N3)[33], Turtle[34], N-Triples, XHTML with em-

---

[31] A useful guide with examples for using VoID may be found on http://code.google.com/p/void-impl/wiki/ExampleVoidQueries.

[32] http://www.w3.org/TR/rdf-syntax-grammar/

[33] http://www.w3.org/DesignIssues/Notation3

[34] http://www.w3.org/TeamSubmission/turtle/

bedded RDFa[35], however, they are simply different ways of representing the same information. One is not necessarily better than the other, although some parse more quickly or are more readable by people, such as Turtle.

A best practice is to validate a representative sample set of your data format after converting it into one or more of the RDF serialization formats. One validation tool is provided by Joshua Tauberer.[36] Validation helps to avoid unnecessary errors when the data is loaded into an RDF database.

1.6.5.1 Conversion: Triplification vs. Modeling

Conversion approaches fall into three categories:

1. Automatic conversion sometimes called *triplification*
2. Partial scripted conversion
3. Modeling by human and subject matter experts, followed by scripted conversion

When converting content to RDF, it is *not* considered good practice to convert hierarchical data set into RDF/XML with few or no links. As Tim Berners-Lee says, "it is bad etiquette not to link to related external material. The value of your own information is very much a function of what it links to, as well as the inherent value of the information within the web page. So it is also in the Semantic Web."[2]

In specific cases, automatic conversion by script, sometimes called "triplification" is a valid strategy to help break the back of large conversions, for example large amounts of sensor data or geospatial information. However, automatic triplification does not produce high quality results. Skipping the important modeling step and converting solely by script may technically produce RDF content but without offering benefit in terms of re-use. If people don't use the Linked Data you publish, what was the point of simply converting it in the first place?

> Converting hierarchical data using one triple per record misses the key premise of Linked Data reusability.

The preferable approach is to include one or more SMEs and domain experts to review the data, logical and relational schemas. This is no different than what data modeling professionals have done for decades, with the exception that Linked Data experts name objects using URIs and openly publish human- and machine-readable schemas. The modeling process often occurs in two to four week sprints. Experts can model the subjects, predicates and objects for the data, identify existing vocabularies and define custom requirements to develop a reasonable object modeling guide. The modeling guide should be documented and reviewed with the subject matter experts and business stakeholders. It will form part of the human-readable

---

[35] http://www.w3.org/TR/rdfa-syntax/

[36] http://www.rdfabout.com/demo/validator/

documentation later produced and published online as part of the Linked Data. This collaboration need not be complex or particularly technical. Ideally, business owners will participate in the process and contribute to the discussion on cross linking content. The focus should be on the data and what it represents. Avoid the temptation to structure the data for a specific use or application. Collaboratively identify the objects and how they relate to other objects. There is plenty of time in the future to do complex ontology development; "walk before you run."

1.6.5.2 Choosing a Service Provider

To publish Linked Data, the data set must be physically copied onto a publicly accessible Web server. There are options ranging from in-house hosting to vendors offering hosting and support as a managed service. Search for "linked data hosting" to get a sense of some commercial providers. Government agencies may ask their procurement departments for commercial suppliers who offer "Linked Data services". The W3C Government Linked Data Working Group provides a community directory of vendors providing Linked Data hosting.[37]

At minimum, review vendor responses with respect to support for relevant standards. This includes, the RDF family of standards including the SPARQL Query Language, as well as, compliance with Linked Data principles that we've discussed above. Of particular importance is provision of a SPARQL endpoint and support for the SPARQL query language specification (currently SPARQL v1.1). If a vendor provides variations to the standard, there will be an elevated risk of vendor lock-in if non-standard features are adopted. RESTful APIs are very important, but are insufficient.

A goal should be to serve "5-star" Linked Data. A good vendor should be able to explain their ability to serve "5-star" Linked Data and knowledgeably discuss any variations of limitations.

The cost and ease of management of infrastructure will be a factor in deciding between local deployment versus software-as-a-service, as discussed above. In addition, a platform's ease of use is of critical importance. If it isn't easy to refresh Linked Data, it will become stale.

The following is an outline of questions a department/agency should consider reviewing as part of their decision to choose a service provider:

1. Is the infrastructure accessible and usable from developers' environment?
2. Is the documentation aimed at developers comprehensive and usable?
3. Is the software supported and under active development?
4. Is there an interface to load data and "follow your nose" through a Web interface?

---

[37] http://w3.org/2011/gld/wiki/Community_Directory

5. Can the data be queried programmatically via a SPARQL endpoint?
6. Does the vendor have reference sites? Are they similar to what you are considering in production?
7. What is the vendor's past performance with government departments/agencies?
8. Does the vendor provide training for the products or services?
9. What is the vendor's Service Level Agreement?
10. Is there a government approved contract vehicle to obtain this service or product?
11. Is the vendor or provider an active contributor to Open Source Software, Standards groups, activities associated with data.gov and Linked Open Data projects at the enterprise and/or government level.
12. Does the vendor or provider comply with the department/agency's published Open Source Policy?

When serving RDF data, it is very important to generate the correct MIME type. Many service providers do not properly configure their Web servers to correctly serve RDF data, so this becomes an important criterion when choosing a service provider. The Web's HTTP protocol uses Multipurpose Internet Mail Extensions (MIME) to identify content types, originally developed for multimedia attachments to electronic mail messages.[32] Linked Data uses MIME content types to identify whether a response is intended to be read by humans or machines. The server looks at the MIME type in order to provide the correct content type in its response.

1.6.6 Step #6 - Announcing a New Linked Data Set

Once you have created your data and converted it into reusable Linked Data format, it is time to serve it. Publication is your way to say, "Dinner is ready. Come and get it!"

1.6.6.1 Adding to the Organization's Communications Strategy

Publishing Linked Data is a form of public communication from your organization. It is advised that one check with their organization's communications and/or Web publishing team regarding data policies. Be sure data policies are spelled out for the new data set. Data policies should be in human-readable form and reference privacy, data quality and retention, treatment of data through secondary sources, citation and reference, public participation, and applicability of the data policy. For example, a data policy for government content might say something like, "All datasets accessed through this site are confined to public information and must not contain National Security information as defined by statute and/or Executive Order, or other information/data that is protected by other statute, practice, or legal precedent. The supplying Department/Agency is required to maintain currency with public disclosure requirements." This data policy happens to be for the US data.gov site.[38]

1.6.6.2 Sharing Your Data via SPARQL

It is helpful to provide a controlled access to the RDF datasets via a SPARQL endpoint. Note the word "controlled". Few sites allow unfettered access via a SPARQL endpoint because a poorly constructed SPARQL query could take down a server, much as poorly constructed SQL queries can crash a relational database. An endpoint may be either available only to authenticated users or if it is publicly available, limits may be put on the query syntax or the size of the result set. A SPARQL endpoint will allow Linked Data clients to issue queries against a published URL and get back a SPARQL results document in an XML format[1].

Some government agencies have one or more SPARQL endpoints, allowing people to perform searches across their data. For example, the UK Government allows access via http://data.gov.uk/sparql. They provide reference data that covers the central working of government, including organizational structures all available as RDF. Many sites host a Web-based text entry form that allows you to enter a query and immediately get results back. The US Government updated data.gov to include increased support for visualizations, in additional to allowing for downloads in various formats. The recently updated data.gov site does not appear to have a SPARQL endpoint as of this writing.

There are numerous Web-based guides to learn the SPARQL query language. We recommend Bob Ducharme's book Learning SPARQL: Querying and Updating with SPARQL 1.1.[10]

As with any form of database, there are performance considerations associated with running queries. Seek the advice of a Linked Data / SPARQL expert as you prepare your 'go live' data publishing strategy. Together, work through use cases and the audience for your data. There are decisions around utilization of servers, access, backup and failover that are important to consider as part of the organization's "social contract", as well as production support commitment.

1.6.6.3 Criteria for being added to the Linked Data Cloud

The best practice is to test your data and confirm that it complies with the Linked Data Principles. Next, confirm that your data meets the criteria to join the Linked Open Data cloud. Richard Cyganiak outlines those criteria in the following checklist:[39]

1. There must be resolvable http:// (or https://) URIs.

---

[38] US Government's Data Policy on data.gov, see http://www.data.gov/datapolicy

[39] "How can I get my data set into the LOD diagram?", see http://richard.cyganiak.de/2007/10/lod/

2. They must resolve, with or without content negotiation, to RDF data in one of the popular RDF formats (RDFa, RDF/XML, Turtle, N-Triples).
3. The dataset must contain at least 1000 triples.
4. The dataset must be connected via RDF links to a dataset in the LOD diagram.[40] This means, either your dataset must use URIs from the other dataset, or vice versa.
5. An arbitrarily recommendation is at least 50 links.
6. Access of the entire dataset must be possible via RDF crawling, via an RDF dump, or via a SPARQL endpoint.

1.6.6.4 Announcing a Data Set

With the hard work of modeling, vocabulary selection, minting URIs, converting the data and validating it now done, meet with the organization's communications and management who are supportive of Open Government initiatives. Consider the publication of a press release and blog posts announcing your new data set's public availability.

This is a rapidly evolving area and the reader is encouraged to review the latest recommendations from the W3C Government Linked Data Working Group[41] as one current source of information on applicable best practices for government Linked Data sets. The following is general advice:

1. Publish a human-readable description of the data;
2. Publish the schema as a VoID description;
3. List your data set on CKAN;[42] which is an open registry of data and content packages. See the "Guidelines for Collecting Metadata on Linked Data in CKAN"[43] for further details. It will be reviewed and added to the CKAN lodcloud group and will be updated on the next version of the diagram.
4. Submit your data set to semantic search engines such as Swoogle[44] and Sindice[45], which help people find published Linked Data;
5. Inform the Linked Data developer community of the existence of the dataset at http://linkeddata.org;
6. Announce your data set to search engines by opting in where required, adding RDFa hints for improved layout in search results; and
7. Include a SPARQL endpoint for all or some of your data, if possible.

---

[40] LOD Diagram published by Richard Cyganiak of DERI, NUI Galway and Anja Jentzsch of Freie Universitat Berlin. Retrieved 30 July 2011 from http://richard.cyganiak.de/2007/10/lod/

[41] http://www.w3.org/2011/gld/wiki/Main_Page

[42] CKAN, An Open Knowledge Foundation Project, http://ckan.net/

[43] Guidelines for Collecting Metadata on Linked Datasets in CKAN, `http://www.w3.org/wiki/TaskForces/CommunityProjects/LinkingOpenData/DataSets/CKANmetainformation`

[44] Swoogle, Semantic Web search engine, http://swoogle.umbc.edu/

[45] Sindice, Semantic Web search engine, http://sindice.com/

1.7 Social Responsibility as a Publisher

Publishers of Linked Data implicitly enter into an implicit *social contract* with users of their data. A problem on the Web is that it can be difficult to determine how much your information may matter to users. Publishers should feel a responsibility to maintain their data, to keep it fresh and up to date, to ensure its accuracy to the greatest degree possible and to repair reported problems. Publishers should assign a contact person or people to respond to enquires via some common mechanisms such as electronic mail or even telephone. If reuse is a priority, then following best practices such as modeling your data as high quality Linked Data, carefully considering your URI strategy and publishing VoID descriptions will form the foundation of your Open Government initiatives. Ensuring that your Linked Open Data set remains available where you say it will be is critical.

If you remove data that is published to the Web, you may break third party applications or mashups *without knowing*. This is considered rude for obvious reasons and is the basis for the social contract.

1.8 Licensing Linked Data Sets

It is a best practice to explicitly attach a license statement to each data set. Governments typically define ownership of works produced by government employees or contractors in legislation. For example, the US Government designates information produced by civil servants as a U.S. Government Work, whereas contractors may produce works under a variety of licenses and copyright assignments. U.S. Government Works are not subject to copyright restrictions in the United States. It is critical for US government officials to know their rights and responsibilities under the Federal Acquisition Regulations (especially FAR Subpart 27.4, the Contract Clauses in 52.227-14, -17 and -20 and any agency-specific FAR Supplements) and copyright assignments if data is produced by a government contractor. Similarly, the UK and many former Commonwealth countries maintain the concept of the Crown Copyright. It is important to know who owns your data and to say so. Additional work around the recording of legal implications and licensing may be undertaken by the W3C Government Linked Data Working Group[46] in coming years. It is recommended that governmental agencies publishing Linked Data review the Recommendations produced by the W3C.

---

[46] http://www.w3.org/2011/govdata/charter

1.9 Conclusions and Further Work

This chapter has attempted to collate a variety of guidance regarding the creation, publication and dissemination of Linked Data with a particular emphasis on the needs of governmental organizations. We highlighted new ways to think about publishing government data and proposed a step-by-step process for modeling, converting, publishing and announcing new data sets. A six-step "cookbook" was presented to ease the transition from traditional data management practices to Linked Data on the World Wide Web.

The first four years of the Linked Open Data project have taught some new lessons and reinforced some old ones. We already knew the importance of open standards, Open Source software and the collection of best practices. The combination of these approaches is also nothing new. However, the Linked Open Data project has shown how insufficient they can be; it required the immense effort of a small portion of the Web community to interlink structured data in order to start a revolution in data sharing and reuse. People matter.

Similarly, we are now accustomed to the Web. It has dominated our lives for most of the last generation. Yet, the Web way has not fully permeated governmental policy, our enterprise systems, nor our way of thinking about data. The Web, it seems, still has lessons to teach. We have attempted to collect some of those lessons in this chapter, such as modeling data for use by many, serving data in ways appropriate for many, thinking about openness, languages and even cultures. The Web reminds us to be accepting of failures, dirty data and different ways of categorizing.

This work is necessarily incomplete. Linked Data approaches and the Semantic Web techniques upon which they are based are still in a period of rapid innovation. Yet, the base standards are stable and we are years beyond the early success stories. Significant adoption by commercial companies and the maturation of tools, both commercial and Open Source, have allowed many governments to successfully expose data for view, reuse and further analysis. It is only through such open provision of governmental data that the public can fully participate in the business of democracy.

The real fun begins when others start using the data you've published and merge it with complementary data sets to derive new insights. We encourage all of you to explore the potential.

Acknowledgements The authors wish to thank our colleagues in the Linked Data community for producing the foundation from which we are all building. We wish to acknowledge and thank our clients including the US Environmental Protection Agency and US Government Printing Office for providing use cases.

References

1. Beckett, D. and Broekstra, J. (2008, January 15). SPARQL Query Results XML Format. W3C Recommendation. Retrieved June 7, 2011 from http://www.w3.org/TR/rdf-sparql-XMLres/
2. Beckett, D. and Berners-Lee, T. (2011, March 28). Turtle - Terse RDF Triple Language. W3C Team Submission. Retrieved June 7, 2011 from http://www.w3.org/TeamSubmission/turtle/
3. Bergman, M. (2010, October 4). "Dealing with the Four Ps to Broaden Actual Use". Message posted to http://www.mkbergman.com/917/practical-p-p-p-problems-with-linked-data/
4. Bergman, M. (2011, April 4). "Democratizing Information with Semantics". Retrieved 7 June, 2011 from http://www.mkbergman.com/953/democratizing-information-with-semantics/
5. Berners-Lee, T. (2009, June 18). Linked Data Design Issues. Retrieved June 18, 2009 from http://www.w3.org/DesignIssues/LinkedData.html
6. Berners-Lee, T. (2010, November 15). Keynote. First International Open Government Conference, US Department of Commerce, Washington DC.
7. Bizer, C., Cyganiak, R. and Heath, T. (2008, July 17). How to Publish Linked Data on the Web. Retrieved from http://www4.wiwiss.fu-berlin.de/bizer/pub/LinkedDataTutorial/
8. Heath, T. and Bizer, C. (2011). Linked Data: Evolving the Web into a Global Data Space (1st edition). Synthesis Lectures on the Semantic Web: Theory and Technology, 1:1, 1-136. Morgan & Claypool, New York. Retrieved 7 June 2011 from http://linkeddatabook.com/editions/1.0/#htoc11
9. Cameron, D. (2010, May 31). Letter to Government departments on opening up data. Retrieved June 7, 2011 from http://www.number10.gov.uk/news/statements-and-articles/2010/05/letter-to-government-departments-on-opening-up-data-51204
10. DuCharme, R. (2011). Learning SPARQL: Querying and Updating with SPARQL 1.1, O'Reilly Media, Sebastapol, California.
11. Duerst, M. and Suignard, M. (2005, January). Internationalized Resource Identifiers (IRIs). RFC 3987, Internet Engineering Task Force (IETF), Network Working Group. Retrieved June 7, 2011 from see http://www.ietf.org/rfc/rfc3987.txt
12. Forbus, K. and de Kleer, J. (1993). Building Problem Solvers. MIT Press.
13. Frantzich, S. and Sullivan, J. (1996). The C-Span Revolution. University of Oklahoma Press.
14. Geiselman, B. (2006). The States ask EPA to reconsider TRI changes. Waste & Recycling News.
15. Geddes, P. (1915). Cities in Evolution. Williams, pp. 397. Retrieved 7 June 2011 from http://www.archive.org/details/citiesinevolutio00gedduoft
16. Hendler, J. and Allemang, D. (2008). Semantic Web for the Working Ontologist: Effective Modeling in RDFS and OWL, Morgan Kaufmann, Waltham, Massachusetts.
17. Kundra, V. (2010, November 15). Keynote. International Open Government Conference, http://www.data.gov/conference
18. Masinter, L., Alvestrand, H., Zigmond, D. and Petke, R. (1999). Guidelines for new URL Schemes. Retrieved 7 June 2011 from http://www.ietf.org/rfc/rfc2718.txt
19. Meskell, D. (2007). New Opportunities for Involving Citizens in the Democratic Process. GSA no. 20 (Fall): 2-4.
20. Myers, J. (2009, June 5). Best Buy Local Store Sites Go Semantic With Good Relations Ontology. Message posted to http://jay.beweep.com/2009/06/05/best-buy-local-stores-goes-semantic-with-good-relations-ontology/
21. Myers, J. (2011, April 26). Released! Human Product Discovery via Machines, RDFa and "Shop URLs". Message posted to http://jay.beweep.com/2011/04/26/released-human-product-discovery-via-machines-rdfa-and-shop-urls/
22. Negroponte, N. (1995). Being Digital. Hodder & Stoughton, page 14.
23. Noveck, B. (2009). Wiki Government: How technology can make government better, democracy stronger, and citizens more powerful. Brookings Institution Press.

24. Obama, B. (2009, January 20). Transparency and Open Government. Memorandum for the Heads of Executive Departments and Agencies. Retrieved June 7, 2011 from http://www.whitehouse.gov/the_press_office/TransparencyandOpenGovernment/

25. Sauermann, L. and Cyganiak, R. (2008) Cool URIs for the Semantic Web. W3C Semantic Web Interest Group Note. Retrieved June 7, 2011 from http://www.w3.org/TR/cooluris/

26. Schaefer, R. (2010, November 15). "Climate Change & Space Weather - Critical Needs". First International Open Government Conference, US Department of Commerce, Washington DC.

27. Styles, R. (2011, April 21). "Choosing URIs is not a five minute task". Message posted to http://blogs.talis.com/platform-consulting/2011/04/21/choosing-uris-not-a-five-minute-task/

28. UK Cabinet Office (2010, May 10). "Designing URI Sets for the UK Public Sector". Retrieved 7 June 2011 from http://www.cabinetoffice.gov.uk/resource-library/designing-uri-sets-uk-public-sector

29. World Wide Web Consortium (2009, February 7). Guidance on The Self-Describing Web. Finding of the Technical Architecture Group. Retrieved 7 June 2011 from http://www.w3.org/2001/tag/doc/selfDescribingDocuments.html

30. World Wide Web Consortium (2011, May 10). "Open Web Platform Progress Drives Expanding Industry Interest". Press Release. Retrieved 7 June 2011 from http://www.w3.org/2011/05/membership-pr.html

31. World Wide Web Consortium (2011, June 6). "Government Linked Data Working Group Charter". Retrieved 7 June 2011 from http://www.w3.org/2011/gld/charter.html

32. Wood, D. (1999). Programming Internet Email. O'Reilly & Associates, Sebasapol, California.

33. Wood, D. (Ed.). (2011). Linking Enterprise Data. New York: Springer.

34. Wood, D. (2011, February 8). Semantic Web Elevator Pitch. Message posted to http://prototypo.blogspot.com/2011/02/semantic-web-elevator-pitch.html

Chapter 2
Methodological Guidelines for Publishing Government Linked Data

Boris Villazón-Terrazas, Luis. M. Vilches-Blázquez,
Oscar Corcho, and Asunción Gómez-Pérez

Abstract Publishing Government Linked Data (and Linked Data in general) is a process that involves a high number of steps, design decisions and technologies. Although some initial guidelines have been already provided by Linked Data publishers, these are still far from covering all the steps that are necessary (from data source selection to publication) or giving enough details about all these steps, technologies, intermediate products, etc. In this chapter we propose a set of methodological guidelines for the activities involved within this process. These guidelines are the result of our experience in the production of Linked Data in several Governmental contexts. We validate these guidelines with the GeoLinkedData and AEMETLinkedData use cases.

2.1 Introduction

Electronic Government (e-Gov) is an important application field [17] for the transformations that governments are undergoing and will continue to undergo in the following decades. Moreover, currently there is a trend to transform the e-Gov into the e-Governance[1], by means of opening government data to the public.

initiatives across the world are making large amounts of raw governmental data available to the public on the Web. Opening this data to citizens enables transparency, delivers more public services, and encourages greater public and commercial use and re-use of governmental information. Some governments have even

---

Correspondance author: Boris Villazón-Terrazas, Ontology Engineering Group, Departamento de Inteligencia Artificial, Facultad de Informática, Universidad Politécnica de Madrid, Madrid, España, e-mail: `bvillazon@fi.upm.es`. See the List of Contributors for full contact details.

[1] e-Governance is the application of Information and Communication Technology (ICT) for delivering government Services, exchange of information communication transactions, integration various stand-one systems and services between Government-to-citizens (G2C), Government-to-Business (G2B), Government-to-Government (G2G) as well as back office processes and interactions within the entire government framework [17].

created catalogs or portals, such as the United States[2] and the United Kingdom[3] governments, to make it easy for the public to find and use this data [23], which are available in a range of formats, e.g., spreadsheets, relational database dumps, RDF; and span through a wide range of domains, e.g., geospatial, statistics, transport.

The application of Linked Data principles to government datasets brings enormous potential [7]. However, this potential is currently untapped mostly because of the lack of resources required to transform raw data to high-quality Linked Data on a large scale [4].

Linked Data generation and publication does not follow a set of common and clear guidelines to scale out the generation and publication of Linked Data. Moreover, there is a lack of detailed guidelines and software catalogs to support the whole life cycle of publishing government Linked Data, and most of existing guidelines are intended for software developers, not for governments.

In this chapter we take the first step to formalize our experience gained in the development of government Linked Data, into a preliminary set of methodological guidelines for generating, publishing and exploiting Linked Government Data. This chapter is addressed to developers who pertain to public administrations, but governments may find the guidelines useful because these guidelines are based and have been applied in real case government scenarios. Therefore, the guidelines are very good starting point for local or national public administrations when they want to publish their data as Linked Data. The rest of the chapter is organized as follows: Section 2.2 presents a summary of the initiatives for helping governments to open and share their data. Section 2.3 explains the guidelines for the generation of government Linked Data. Then, Section 2.4 describes the application of these guidelines to particular use cases. Finally, Section 2.5 presents the conclusions and future work.

2.2 Open Government Initiatives

During the last years several initiatives emerged to improve the interface between citizens and government through effective use of Information and Communication Technology (ICT), and specifically through use standards-base of the Web. In this section, we present a summary of those efforts that help governments in the use of technology and the Web to implement the full promise of electronic government, by managing their data in a transparent and efficient way.

- Since 2008 The W3C eGovernment Activity[4] is promoting several charters for helping goverments to follow best practices and approaches to improve the use of the Web. Currently, this activity includes the eGovernment Interest Group[5]

---

[2] http://www.data.gov/

[3] http://data.gov.uk/

[4] http://www.w3.org/egov/Activity.html

[5] http://www.w3.org/2007/eGov/IG/

and the Government Linked Data Working Group[6]. Some of the results of this activity are described next.

- *Improving Access to Government through Better Use of the Web*[7], a W3C Interest Group Note that attempts to describe the challenges and issues faced by governments and their efforts to apply technologies of the 21st century. Moreover, the document introduces the definition of Open Government Data, describes its benefits and how to achieve Open Government Data. However, the document does not include a detailed set of guidelines.
- *Publishing Open Government Data*[8], a W3C Working draft that proposes a set of preliminary guidelines to help governments to open and share their data. This document enumerates the following straightforward steps to publish government data (1) publish well-structured data in its raw form, e.g., an XML file; (2) create an online catalog of the raw data; and (3) make the data machine and human readable. This document also introduces the four Linked Data principles, but does not provide detailed guidelines.

- Since 2004 the Open Knowledge Foundation[9], a not-for-profit organization is promoting open knowledge[10]. The Open Knowledge Foundation has released the Open Data Manual[11], which is a report that includes discussions about the legal, social and technical aspects of open data, and its target audience are those who are seeking to open up data. Although the report is focused on data from the public sector, the target audience of the report are not governments.
- Finally, it is worth mentioning the suggestion given by Tim Berners-Lee about the 5-star deployment scheme for Linked Open Data that are described with examples in `http://lab.linkeddata.deri.ie/2010/star-scheme-by-example/`.

After having reviewed the available efforts to help governments for managing their data in a transparent and efficient way, by means of Open Data initiatives, we can conclude that those efforts are not based in real case government scenarios, neither there is a report of having applied them into real case scenarios.

2.3 Methodological Guidelines

In this section we present our preliminary set of guidelines that are based on our experience in the production of Linked Data in several Governmental contexts. Moreover, the guidelines have been applied in real case government scenarios and include

---

[6] `http://www.w3.org/2011/gld/`

[7] `http://www.w3.org/TR/2009/NOTE-egov-improving-20090512/`

[8] `http://www.w3.org/TR/gov-data/`

[9] `http://okfn.org/`

[10] Any kind of data, which can be freely used, reused and redistributed.

[11] `http://opendatamanual.org/`

methods, techniques and tools for carrying out the activities and tasks involved in the Government Linked Data publishing process.

The process of publishing Government Linked Data must have a life cycle, in the same way of Software Engineering, in which every development project has a life cycle [20]. According to our experience this process has an iterative incremental life cycle model, which is based on the continuous improvement and extension of the Government Linked Data resulted from performing several iterations.

The guidelines, for the process of publication Government Linked Data, consist of the following main activities: (1) specification, (2) modelling, (3) generation, (4) publication, and (5) exploitation. Each activity is decomposed in one or more tasks, and some techniques and tools are provided for carrying out them. It is worth mentioning that the order of the activities and tasks might be changed base on particular needs of the government bodies. Moreover, we are continuously getting feedback about these guidelines, and therefore, we are improving them constantly. Figure 2.1 deptics the main activities that are described next.

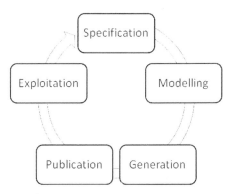

Fig. 2.1 Main Activities for Publishing Government Linked Data

2.3.1 Specification

As any other eGovernment project, aimed at the implementation and further development of e-administration and other IT solutions, the first activity is the drawing up of a detailed specification of requirements. It has been proved that detailed requirements provides several benefits [16], such as (a) the establishment of the basis for agreement between customers and suppliers on what the government application is supposed to do, (b) the reduction of the development effort, (c) the provision of a basis for estimating costs and schedules, and (d) the offer of a baseline for validation and verification.

When a government Linked Data application is being developed, government Linked Data requirements should be identified in addition to the application ones. Our experience in the publication of Linked Data in several Governmental contexts has showed that more critical than capturing software/application requirements was the efficient and precise identification of the government Linked Data requirements.

At this stage, the description of this activity is not intended to be exhaustive but it just introduces the most important points. The preliminary set of tasks identified for this activity are: (1) identification and analysis of the government data sources, (2) URI design, and (3) definition of license.

2.3.1.1 Identification and analysis of the government data sources

Within this task we identify and select the government data that we want to publish. In this task we have to distinguish between (i) open and publish data that government agencies have not yet opened up and published, and (ii) reuse and leverage on data already opened up and published by government agencies. Next, we describe briefly both alternatives.

- In the case of open and publish data that government agencies have not yet opened up and published, we will face, most of the time, a costly and tedious task that may require contacting to specific government data owners to get access to their legacy data.
- In the other case, when we want to reuse and leverage on data already opened up and published by government agencies, we should look for these data in public government catalogs, such as the Open Government Data[12], datacatalogs.org[13], and Open Government Data Catalog[14].

After we have identified and selected the government data sources, we have to (i) search and compile all the available data and documentation about those resources, including purpose, components, data model and implementation details; (ii) identify the schema of those resources including the conceptual components and their relationships; and (iii) identify the items in the domain, i.e., things whose properties and relations are described in the data sources, according to [7] the Web architecture term *resource* is used to refer to these *things of interest*.

2.3.1.2 URI design

The goal of the Linked Data initiative is to promote a vision of the Web as a global database, and interlink data the same way that Web documents. In this global database it is necessary to identify a resource on the Internet, and precisely URIs are thought for that. According to [15] URIs should be designed with simplicity, stability and manageability in mind, thinking about them as identifiers rather than as names for Web resources.

There are some existing guidelines for URI design, for example (1) *Cool URIs for the Semantic Web W3C Interest Group Note* [15], which introduces a useful guidance on how to use URIs to describe things that are not Web documents; (2)

---

[12] http://opengovernmentdata.org/data/catalogues/

[13] http://datacatalogs.org/

[14] http://datos.fundacionctic.org/sandbox/catalog/

Designing URI Sets for the UK Public Sector[15], a document from the UK Cabinet Office that defines the design considerations on how to URIs can be used to publish public sector reference data; and (3) *Sytle Guidelines for Naming and Labelling Ontologies in the Multilingual Web* [11], which proposes guidelines for designing URIs in a multilingual scenario.

Based on the aforementioned guidelines and on our experience we propose the following design decisions regarding the assignment of URIs to the elements of the dataset.

- Use meaningful URIs, instead of opaque URIs, when possible. Since one of the goals is to publish data to citizens, it is recommended to put into the URI as many information as possible.
- Use slash (303) URIs, instead of hash URIs, when possible. In spite of the fact that there is some criticism of the slash URIs because using them requires two HTTP requests to retrieve a single description of an object, they are appropriate for dealing with resource descriptions that are part of very large datasets [7].
- Separate the TBox (ontology model) from the ABox (instances) URIs. Therefore, we have to manage the following URI elements

  - Base URI structure. Here we need to choose the right domain for URIs, and this domain will expect to be maintained in perpetually, support a direct response to agency servers. Governments can follow the UK cabinet Office guides for choosing the right domain for URIs, for example for the Bolivian Government[16] `http://data.gov.bo`, and for a particular government sector, in this case health, `http://health.data.gov.bo`.
  - TBox URIs. We recommend to append the word *ontology* to the base URI structure, following our previous example we would have
    `http://data.gov.bo/ontology/`.
    Then, we would append all the ontology elements, classes and properties.
  - ABox URIs. We recommend to append the word *resource* to the base URI structure, again following our previous example we would have
    `http://data.gov.bo/resource/`.
    Additionally, we recommend to use *Patterned URIs*[17] by adding the class name to the ABox base URI. For example we want to identify a particular province, we would have
    `http://data.gov.bo/resource/province/Tiraque`.

- Use the main official language of the government, when possible. In some cases we will deal with some special characters depending on the language. Following our previous example, within the Bolivian Government we should use Spanish, therefore we would have for identifying the Tiraque Province `http://data.gov.bo/resource/Provincia/Tiraque`

---

[15] `http://www.cabinetoffice.gov.uk/resource-library/designing-uri-sets-uk-public-sector`

[16] The URI examples for the Bolivian Government are fictitious.

[17] `http://patterns.dataincubator.org/book/patterned-uris.html`

2.3.1.3 Definition of the license

Within the government context it is important to define the license of the data that governments are publishing. Currently, there are several licenses that can be used for government data. Next, we list a few of them.

- The UK Open Government License[18] was created to enable any public sector information holder to make their information available for use and reuse under its terms.
- The Open Database License[19] (ODbL) is an open license for databases and data that includes explicit attribution and share-alike requirements.
- Public Domain Dedication and License[20] (PDDL) is a document intended to allow you to freely share, modify, and use a particular data for any purpose and without any restrictions.
- Open Data Commons Attribution License[21] is a database specific license requiring attribution for databases.
- The Creative Commons Licenses[22] are several copyright licenses that allow the distribution of copyrighted works.

It is also possible to reuse and apply an existing license of the government data sources.

2.3.2 Modelling

After the specification activity, in which the government data sources were identified, selected and analysed, we need to determine the ontology to be used for modelling the domain of those data sources. The most important recommendation in this context is to reuse as much as possible available vocabularies[23] [2]. This reuse-based approach speeds up the ontology development, and therefore, governments will save time, effort and resources. This activity consists of the following tasks:

- Search for suitable vocabularies to reuse. Currently there are some useful repositories to find available vocabularies, such as, SchemaWeb[24], SchemaCache[25], Swoogle[26], and LOV[27]. For choosing the most suitable vocabularies we recom-

---

[18] http://www.nationalarchives.gov.uk/doc/open-government-licence/

[19] http://opendatacommons.org/licenses/odbl/

[20] http://opendatacommons.org/licenses/pddl/

[21] http://opendatacommons.org/licenses/by/

[22] http://creativecommons.org/

[23] Along this chapter we use vocabulary or ontology without distinction.

[24] http://schemaweb.info/

[25] http://schemacache.com/

[26] http://swoogle.umbc.edu/

[27] Linked Open Vocabularies http://labs.mondeca.com/dataset/lov/index.html

mend to follow the guidelines proposed in [19] that detail how to reuse vocabularies at different levels of granularity, i.e., reusing general ontologies, domain ontologies, and ontology statements.

- In case that we did not find any vocabulary that is suitable for our purposes, we should create them, trying to reuse as much as possible existing resources, e.g., government catalogues, vocabularies available at sites like http://semic.eu/, etc. Within this task, we recommend to follow the guidelines proposed in [22] that state how to (1) search government resources from highly reliable Web Sites, domain-related sites and government catalogs; (2) select the most appropriate government resources; and (3) transform them into ontologies.
- Finally, if we did not find available vocabularies nor resources for building the ontology, we have to create the ontology from scratch. To this end, we can follow the first scenario proposed in the NeOn Methodology [18].

There are several tools that provide technological support to this activity and some of them are Neologism[28], Protégé[29], NeOn Toolkit[30], TopBraid Composer[31], and Altova Semantic Works[32].

2.3.3 Generation

The Resource Description Framework, RDF[33], is the standard data model in which the government information has to be made available, according to the Linked Data principles. Therefore, in this activity we have to take the data sources selected in the specification activity (see Section 2.3.1), and transform them to RDF according to the vocabulary created in the modelling activity (see Section 7.3). The generation activity consists of the following tasks: (1) transformation, (2) data cleansing, and (3) linking.

2.3.3.1 Transformation

The preliminary guidelines proposed in this chapter consider only the transformation of the whole data source content into RDF, i.e., following an Extract, Transform, and Load ETL-like[34] process, by using a set of RDF-izers, i.e., RDF converters.

---

[28] http://neologism.deri.ie/

[29] http://protege.stanford.edu/

[30] http://www.neon-toolkit.org

[31] http://www.topquadrant.com/products/TB_Composer.html

[32] http://www.altova.com/semanticworks.html

[33] http://www.w3.org/RDF/

[34] Extract, transform, and load (ETL) of legacy data sources, is a process that involves: (1) extracting data from the outside resources, (2) transforming data to fit operational needs, and (3) loading data into the end target resources [9]

Guidelines for this task are based on the method proposed in [22] that provides guide for transforming the content of a given resource into RDF instances. The requirements of the transformation are (1) full conversion, which implies that all queries that are possible on the original source should also be possible on the RDF version; and (2) the RDF instances generated should reflect the target ontology structure as closely as possible, in other words, the RDF instances must conform to the already available ontology/vocabulary.

There are several tools that provide technological support to this task, and the format of the government data source is relevant for the selection of a particular tool. Next, we provide a list of some those tools[35] grouped by the common formats of government data.

- For CSV and spreadsheets: RDF Extension of Google Refine[36], XLWrap[37], RDF123[38], and NOR$_2$O[39].
- For relational databases: D2R Server[40], ODEMapster[41], Triplify[42], Virtuoso RDF View[43], and Ultrawrap[44]. It is worth mentioning that the RDB2RDF Working Group[45] is working on R2RML[46], a standard language to express mappings between relational databases and RDF.
- For XML: GRDDL[47] through XSLT, TopBraid Composer, and ReDeFer[48].
- For other formats any23[49], and Stats2RDF[50].

2.3.3.2 Data cleansing

The paradigm of generating, publishing and exploiting government linked data (and linked data in general) has inevitably led to several problems. There are a lot of noise which inhibits applications from effectively exploiting the structured information

---

[35] For a complete list see http://www.w3.org/wiki/ConverterToRdf

[36] http://lab.linkeddata.deri.ie/2010/grefine-rdf-extension/

[37] http://xlwrap.sourceforge.net/

[38] http://rdf123.umbc.edu/

[39] http://www.oeg-upm.net/index.php/en/downloads/57-nor2o

[40] http://sites.wiwiss.fu-berlin.de/suhl/bizer/d2r-server/

[41] http://www.oeg-upm.net/index.php/en/downloads/9-r2o-odemapster

[42] http://triplify.org/

[43] http://virtuoso.openlinksw.com/whitepapers/relational%20rdf%20views%20mapping.html

[44] http://www.cs.utexas.edu/~miranker/studentWeb/UltrawrapHomePage.html

[45] http://www.w3.org/2001/sw/rdb2rdf/

[46] http://www.w3.org/TR/r2rml/

[47] http://www.w3.org/TR/grddl/

[48] http://rhizomik.net/redefer/

[49] http://any23.org/

[50] http://aksw.org/Projects/Stats2RDF

that underlies linked data [8]. This activity focuses on cleaning this noise, e.g., the linked broken data. It consists of two steps

- To identify and find possible mistakes. To this end, Hogan et al. [8] identified a set of common errors

  - http-level issues such as accessibility and derefencability, e.g., HTTP URIs return 40x/50x errors.
  - reasoning issues such as namespace without vocabulary, e.g., `rss:item`; term invented in related namespace, e.g., `foaf:tagLine` invented by Live-Journal; term is misspelt version of term defined in namespace, e.g., `foaf:image` vs. `foaf:img`.
  - malformed/incompatible datatypes, e.g., "true" as `xsd:int`.

- To fix the identified errors. For this purpose Hogan et al. [8] also propose some solutions at the (1) application side, i.e., all the issues have a suitable antidote once we are aware of them; (2) publishing side, by means of all-in-one validation service such as the RDF Alerts[51].

One outstanding initiative within the context of data cleansing is driven by "The Pedantic Web Group"[52] that aims to engage with publishers and help them improve the quality of their data.

2.3.3.3 Linking

Following the fourth Linked Data Principle, *Include links to other URIs, so that they can discover more things*, the next task is to create links between the government dataset and external datasets. This task involves the discovery of relationships between data items. We can create these links manually, which is a time consuming task, or we can rely on automatic or supervised tools. The task consists of the following steps:

- To identify datasets that may be suitable as linking targets. For this purpose we can look for data sets of similar topics on the Linked Data repositories like CKAN[53]. Currently there is no tool support for this, so we have to perform the search in the repositories manually. However, there are approaches to peform this step, such as [13] and [10].
- To discover relationships between data items of government dataset and the items of the identified datasets in the previous step. There are several tools for creating links between data items of different datasets, for example the SILK framework [3], or LIMES [12].
- To validate the relationships that have been discovered in the previous step. This usually is performed by government domain experts. In this step we can use

---

[51] http://swse.deri.org/RDFAlerts/

[52] http://pedantic-web.org/

[53] http://ckan.net/group/lodcloud

tools like *sameAs Link Validator*[54] that aims to provide a user friendly interface for validating *sameAs* links.

2.3.4 Publication

In this section we review the publication of RDF data. In a nutshell, this activity consists in the following task (1) dataset publication, (2) metadata publication, and (3) enable effective discovery. These activities are described next.

2.3.4.1 Dataset publication

Once we have the legacy data transformed into RDF, we need to store and publish that data in a triplestore[55]. There are several tools for storing RDF datasets, for example Virtuoso Universal Server[56], Jena[57], Sesame[58], 4Store[59], YARS[60], and OWLIM[61]. Some of them already include a SPARQL endpoint and Linked Data frontend. However, there are some tools like Pubby[62], Joseki[63], and Talis Platform[64] that provide these functionalities. A good overview of the recipes for publishing RDF data can be found in [7].

2.3.4.2 Metadata Publication

Once our dataset is published we have to include metadata information about it. For this purpose there are vocabularies like (1) VoID[65] that allows to express metadata about RDF datasets, and it covers general metadata, access metadata, structural metadata, and description of links between datasets; and (2) Open Provenance Model[66] that is a domain independent provenance model result of the Provenance

---

[54] http://oegdev.dia.fi.upm.es:8080/sameAs/

[55] A triplestore is a purpose-built database for the storage and retrieval of RDF.

[56] http://virtuoso.openlinksw.com/

[57] http://jena.sourceforge.net/

[58] http://www.openrdf.org/

[59] http://4store.org/

[60] http://sw.deri.org/2004/06/yars/

[61] http://www.ontotext.com/owlim

[62] http://www4.wiwiss.fu-berlin.de/pubby/

[63] http://www.joseki.org/

[64] http://www.talis.com/platform/

[65] http://www.w3.org/TR/void/

[66] http://openprovenance.org/

Challenge Series[67]. The provenance of the government datasets plays an important role when browsing and exploring government resources.

2.3.4.3 Enable effective discovery

The last task of the publication activity is the one related to enable the effective discovery and synchronization of the government dataset. This task consists in the following steps

- In this step we deal with Sitemaps[68] that are the standard way to let crawlers know about the pages on a website. When sitemaps provide time indications using *lastmod*, *changefreq* and *priority* fields, they can be used to have (semantic) web search engines download only new data and changed pages. This step aims at allowing (semantic) web search engines to discover what is new or recently changed in the government dataset in an efficient and timely manner. In this step is necessary (1) to generate a set of sitemap.xml files from the government SPARQL endpoint, and (2) to submit the sitemap.xml files into (semantic) web search engines, such as Google[69] and Sindice[70]. In this step we can rely on automatic tools like sitemap4rdf[71].
- The second step aims to include the government dataset in the LOD cloud diagram[72]. To this end, we have to add an entry of dataset in the CKAN repository[73]. The Linking Open Data Task Force provides some guidelines for collecting metadata on linked datasets in CKAN at their site[74].
- The goal of the final step is to include the dataset in the available open data government catalogues, such as datacatalogs.org[75], and Open Government Data Catalog[76].

2.3.5 Exploitation

The final goal of opening government data (legacy data, streaming data, and services), is to enable transparency, deliver more public applications, and encourage

---

[67] http://twiki.ipaw.info/bin/view/Challenge/OPM

[68] http://www.sitemaps.org/

[69] https://www.google.com/webmasters/tools/

[70] http://sindice.com/main/submit

[71] http://lab.linkeddata.deri.ie/2010/sitemap4rdf/

[72] http://richard.cyganiak.de/2007/10/lod/

[73] http://ckan.net/group/lodcloud

[74]   http://www.w3.org/wiki/TaskForces/CommunityProjects/ LinkingOpenData/DataSets/CKANmetainformation

[75] http://datacatalogs.org/

[76] http://datos.fundacionctic.org/sandbox/catalog/

public and commercial use and re-use of the governmental information. Therefore, we have to develop applications on top of the Linked Open Government Data that exploit these data and provide rich graphical user interfaces to the citizens.

According to [7] we can categorize the Linked Data applications in generic applications and domain-specific applications. Regarding generic applications, we can have (i) Linked Data Browsers, e.g., Disco[77], Tabulator browser[78], LinkSailor[79], and LOD Browser Switch[80]; (ii) Linked Data Search Engines, e.g., Sig.ma[81], and VisiNav[82]. As for domain-specific applications, we have US Global Foreing Aid[83] that combines and visualizes data from different branches of the US Government, Talis Aspire[84] that helps educators to create and manage lists of learning resouces, and DBPedia Mobile[85] that helps tourists to explore a city.

It is worth mentioning that Linked Data applications have to integrate data from different provides (governmental and non-governmental) in a more comprehensive view. In section 2.4 we provide examples of specific applications that exploit the government linked data by providing rich graphical user interface to the final users.

2.4 Use Cases

In order to validate the understandability, applicability and usability of the guidelines proposed in this chapter, we conducted two experiments in real case scenarios within GeoLinkedData and AEMETLinkedData.

2.4.1 GeoLinkedData

GeoLinkedData[86] is an open initiative whose aim is to enrich the Web of Data with Spanish geospatial data into the context of INSPIRE themes[87]. This initiative has started off by publishing diverse information sources belonging to the National Geographic Institute of Spain, onwards IGN, and the National Statistic Institute in Spain, onwards INE. Such sources are made available as RDF knowledge bases ac-

---

[77] http://www4.wiwiss.fu-berlin.de/bizer/ng4j/disco/

[78] http://www.w3.org/2005/ajar/tab

[79] http://linksailor.com/

[80] http://browse.semanticweb.org/

[81] http://sig.ma/

[82] http://visinav.deri.org/

[83] http://data-gov.tw.rpi.edu/demo/USForeignAid/demo-1554.html

[84] http://www.talisaspire.com/

[85] http://wiki.dbpedia.org/DBpediaMobile

[86] http://geo.linkeddata.es/

[87] The INSPIRE Directive addresses 34 spatial data themes needed for environmental applications. http://inspire.jrc.ec.europa.eu/index.cfm/pageid/2/list/7

cording to the Linked Data principles, and following the guidelines proposed in this chapter.

2.4.1.1 Specification

This section presents the specification of GeoLinkedData according to our guidelines. This specification is not intended to be exahustive, but it just describes the most important points.

Identification and analysis of the government data sources

Regarding the government data sources we followed two paths

- We reused and leveraged on data already opened up and published by INE, at its open catalog[88].
- We opened and published data that IGN had not yet opened up and published.

Table 2.1 depicts the datasets that we have chosen for their publication, together with the format in which they are available. All the datasets correspond to Spain, so their content is available in Spanish or in any of the other official languages in Spain (Basque, Catalan and Galician).

Table 2.1 Government Datasets

Data	Provenance	Format
Population	INE	Spreadsheet
Dwelling	INE	Spreadsheet
Industry	INE	Spreadsheet
Building Trade	INE	Spreadsheet
Hydrography	IGN	Relational database (Oracle)
Beaches	IGN	Relational database (MySQL)
Administrative boundaries	IGN	Relational database (MySQL)

URI design

Following the guidelines introduced in section 2.3.1.2, within GeoLinkedData we are using meaningful URIs, and slash (303) URIs. Moreover, we manage the following URI elements

- Base URI structure. For the Spanish Linked Data initiatives we have bought the domain `http://linkeddata.es/`, and specifically, for the Spanish geospatial information we have created the subdomain `http://geo.linkeddata.es/`.

---

[88] `http://www.ine.es/inebmenu/indice.htm`

- TBox URIs. We appended the word *ontology* to the base URI structure for including concepts and properties available in our ontologies
  `http://geo.linkeddata.es/ontology/{conceptorproperty}.`
- ABox URIs. We appended the word *resource* to the base URI structure for including the available instances. In addition we include the type of resource in the URI, e.g.,
  `http://geo.linkeddata.es/resource/{resourcetype}/{resourcename}`

Definition of the license

In the case of GeoLinkedData, we are reusing the original license of the government data sources. IGN and INE data sources have their own license, similar to Attribution-ShareAlike 2.5 Generic License[89].

2.4.1.2 Modelling

In the case of GeoLinkedData our chosen datasets contain information such as time, administrative boundaries, unemployment, etc. For modelling of the information contained in the datasets we have created an ontology network [5]. The vocabulary that models the information contained in the datasets has been developed by reusing available vocabularies/ontologies. Next, we describe briefly each one the subvocabularies that compose the resultant vocabulary/ontology.

For describing statistics, we chose the **Statistical Core Vocabulary (SCOVO)** [6], which provides a modelling framework for statistical information. This vocabulary[90] is currently defined in RDF(S) and terms and labels are provided in English. However, we are going to change it for **RDF Data Cube Vocabulary**[91] that is an extension and improved vocabulary for modelling statistical information.

Regarding geospatial vocabulary we chose diverse ontologies.

- The **FAO Geopolitical Ontology**[92]. This OWL ontology includes information about continents, countries, and so on, in English. We have extended it to cover the main characteristics of the Spanish administrative division.
- Regarding the hydrographical phenomena (rivers, lakes, etc.) we chose **hydrOntology** [21], an OWL ontology that attempts to cover most of the concepts of the hydrographical domain. Its main goal is to harmonize heterogeneous information sources coming from several cartographic agencies and other international resources.

---

[89] `http://creativecommons.org/licenses/by-sa/2.5/`

[90] `http://purl.org/NET/scovo`

[91]   `http://publishing-statistical-data.googlecode.com/svn/trunk/specs/src/main/html/cube.html`

[92] `http://www.fao.org/countryprofiles/geoinfo.asp?lang=en`

- With respect to geometrical representation and positioning we reuse the **GML ontology**[93] (an OWL ontology for the representation of information structured according to the OGC Geography Markup Language - GML3.0-) and the **WSG84 Vocabulary**[94] (a basic RDF vocabulary, published by the W3C Semantic Web Interest Group, that provides a namespace for representing lat(itude), long(itude) and other information about spatially-located things, using WGS84 as a reference datum).
- Regarding the time information we chose the **Time Ontology**[95], an ontology for temporal concepts developed into the context of World Wide Web Consortium (W3C). This ontology provides a vocabulary for expressing facts about topological relations among instants and intervals, together with information about durations, and about date-time information.

2.4.1.3 Generation

As described in section 2.3.3, RDF is the standard data model in which the government information has to be made available. Therefore, the following tasks describe the transformation of the INE and IGN data sources to RDF following the model we have developed.

Transformation

Given the different formats in which the selected datasets were available, we used three different RDF-izers for the conversion of data into RDF. Next we describe some details of them.

The generation of RDF from spreadsheets was performed using the NOR_2O [22] software library. This library performs an (ETL) process of the legacy data sources, transforming these non-ontological resources (NORs) [22] into ontology instances.

The transformation of the relational database content into RDF was done using the integrated framework R_2O+ and ODEMapster+ [1], which is available as a NeOn Toolkit plugin[96]. This framework allows the formal specification, evaluation, verification and exploitation of semantic mappings between ontologies and relational databases.

For transforming the geospatial information we have used geometry2rdf[97] that converts geometrical data, which could be availabe in GML[98] or WKT[99], into RDF.

---

[93] http://loki.cae.drexel.edu/~wbs/ontology/2004/09/ogc-gml.owl

[94] http://www.w3.org/2003/01/geo/wgs84_pos

[95] http://www.w3.org/TR/owl-time/

[96] http://www.neon-toolkit.org

[97] http://www.oeg-upm.net/index.php/en/downloads/151-geometry2rdf

[98] http://www.opengeospatial.org/standards/gml

[99] http://iwkt.com/

Data cleansing

In the context of GeoLinkedData we have identified and fixed errors like unescaped characters and encoding problems. Those errors produced by the fact we were generating and publishing linked data in Spanish, therefore we had URIs that contain special characters such as *á,é, ñ*, and it was necessary to encoded those URIs, for example

For the province of *Málaga*

```
http://geo.linkeddata.es/resource/Provincia/M%C3%A1laga
```
For the *Miñor* river

```
http://geo.linkeddata.es/resource/R%C3%ADo/
Mi%C3%B1or%2C%20R%C3%ADo
```

Linking

In the context of GeoLinkedData, we have identified as initial data sets to link with DBpedia[100] and Geonames[101], because these data sets include similar topics of GeoLinkedData.

The task of discovering relationships between data items was based on the SILK framework. First, we have used SILK to discover relationships between RDF published of Spanish provinces, DBpedia[102] and GeoNames[103] data sources. This process allows setting (*owl:sameAs*) relationships between data of these sources. Next, we present an example of these relationships:

```
<http://geo.linkeddata.es/resource/Provincia/Granada>
<owl:sameAs>
<http://dbpedia.org/resource/Province_of_Granada>
```

The task of result validation was performed by domain experts. This task shows a value of accuracy equal to 86%.

2.4.1.4 Publication

In GeoLinkedData, for the publication of the RDF data we relied on Virtuoso Universal Server[104]. On top of it, Pubby[105] was used for the visualization and navigation of the raw RDF data.

---

[100] http://dbpedia.org/

[101] http://www.geonames.org/

[102] http://dbpedia.org/About

[103] http://www.geonames.org/

[104] http://virtuoso.openlinksw.com/

[105] http://www4.wiwiss.fu-berlin.de/pubby/

We used VoID for describing the government dataset, and we already created an entry in CKAN for this dataset[106]. Finally, we submitted the sitemap files, generated by sitemap4rdf, to Sindice.

2.4.1.5 Exploitation

As described in section 2.3.5 we need to develop applications that unlock the value of data to provide benefits to citizens. To this end, we have developed an application, map4rdf[107], to enhance the visualization of the aggregated information. This interface combines the faceted browsing paradigm [14] with map-based visualization using the Google Maps API[108]. Thus for instance, the application is able to render on the map distinct geometrical representations such as *LineStrings* that depict to hydrographical features (reservoirs, beaches, rivers, etc.), or *Points* that show province capitals.

2.4.2 AEMETLinkedData

AEMETLinkedData[109] is an open initiative whose aim is to enrich the Web of Data with Spanish metereological data. Within this initiative we are publishing information resources from the *Agencia Estatal de Meteorlogía* (Spanish Metereological Office), ownwards AEMET, as Linked Data.

2.4.2.1 Specification

Here we present the specification of AEMETLinkedData according to our guidelines. This specification just describes the most important points.

Identification and analysis of the government data sources

Regarding the government data sources we reused and leveraged on data already opened up and published by AEMET. Recently, AEMET made publicly available meteorological and climatic data registered by its weather stations, radars, lightning detectors and ozone soundings. AEMET has around 250 automatic weather stations registering pressure, temperature, humidity, precipitation and wind data every 10 minutes. These data from the different stations are provided in CSV files, updated every hour and kept for seven days in the AEMET FTP server, linked from its website.

---

[106] http://ckan.net/package/geolinkeddata

[107] http://oegdev.dia.fi.upm.es/projects/map4rdf/

[108] http://code.google.com/apis/maps/index.html

[109] http://aemet.linkeddata.es/

URI design

Following the guidelines introduced in section 2.3.1.2, within AEMETLinkedData we are using meaningful URIs, and slash (303) URIs, and managing the following URI elements

- Base URI structure. For the Spanish metereological information we have created the subdomain `http://aemet.linkeddata.es/`.
- TBox URIs. We appended the word *ontology* to the base URI structure for including concepts and properties available in our ontologies
  `http://aemet.linkeddata.es/ontology/{conceptorproperty}`.
- ABox URIs. We appended the word *resource* to the base URI structure for including the available instances we have. In addition we include the type of resource in the URI, e.g.,
  `http://aemet.linkeddata.es/resource/{resourcetype}/`
  `{resourcename}`

Definition of the license

In the case of AEMETLinkedData, we are reusing the original license of the government data sources. AEMET data sources have their own license, an Spanish copyright license. However, this government agency is changing the publication policy and therefore their data sources will adopt a new license in the near future.

2.4.2.2 Modelling

In the case of AEMETLinkedData our chosen datasets contain information related to the metereology domain. For modelling that domain we have developed a network of ontologies [5], by reusing available ontologies and non-ontological resources. Next, we present a high level overview each one of the vocabularies that compose the resultant ontology.

- **Observations ontology**. This vocabulary models the knowledge related to metereological observations. For its development the NOR_2O[110] tool was used to transform non-ontological resources provided by AEMET to ontological resources, i.e., ontology of measurements.
- **Location ontology**. The vocabulary models the knowledge about locations, such as administrative limits and coordinates. The WGS84 vocabulary has been reused with the aim of supporting the representation of geospatial positioning by means of the *Point* concept.

---

[110] `http://www.oeg-upm.net/index.php/en/downloads/57-nor2o`

- **Time ontology**. The ontology is for representing knowledge about time such as temporal entities, units, instants, intervals, etc. This ontology was mainly developed by reusing the OWL Time ontology[111].
- **Sensors ontology**. The vocabulary models sensors networks and weather stations. For this ontology we have been reused the Semantic Sensor Network Ontology (SSN)[112].

2.4.2.3 Generation

As described in section 2.3.3, RDF is the standard data model in which the government information has to be made available. Therefore, the following sections describe the transformation of the AEMET data sources to RDF following the model we have developed.

Transformation

The RDF was generated with ad-hoc Python scripts that were executed in two steps, integrating with ease the generation of RDF and the crawling of the FTP server where the CSV files are located. Next, we describe briefly the two steps.

- The first step generates the RDF data about the automatic stations. Since this information is static, only needs to be executed once.
- The second step generates the RDF data about the observations. The observations are obtained by crawling the AEMET FTP server. Whenever new files are added or old files are modified, the script downloads and processes the files.

Data cleansing

In AEMETLinkedData we are finishing the first iteration of the process, and so far we have not yet deeply analyzed the RDF generated. We are planning to do it in the next iteration of the process.

Linking

Within AEMETLinkedData we have identified as initial dataset to link with GeoLinkedData, since we are working with Spanish metereological data.

The task of discovering relationships between data items was based on the SILK framework. First, we have used SILK to discover relationships between AEMET weather stations and their locations in GeoLinkedData resources. This process allows setting (*geo:isLocatedIn*) relationships between data of these sources. Next, we present an example of these relationships:

---

[111] http://www.w3.org/TR/owl-time/

[112] http://www.w3.org/2005/Incubator/ssn/ssnx/ssn

```
<http://aemet.linkeddata.es/resource/Estacion/Estacion_08430>
<geo:isLocatedIn>
<http://geo.linkeddata.es/resource/Provincia/Murcia>
```

The task of result validation was performed by one person from AEMET. This task shows a value of accuracy equal to 80%.

2.4.2.4 Publication

In AEMETLinkedData, for the publication of the RDF data we relied on Virtuoso Universal Server[113]. On top of it, Pubby[114] was used for the visualization and navigation of the raw RDF data.

We used VoID for describing the government dataset, and we already created an entry in CKAN for this dataset[115]. Finally, we submitted the sitemap files, generated by sitemap4rdf, to Sindice.

2.4.2.5 Exploitation

As described in section 2.3.5 applications have to be developed to unlock the value of data to provide benefits to citizens. Within AEMETLinkedData we have enhanced the visualization capabilities of map4rdf, by including a chart that displays the evolution of a given variable, e.g., temperature. Figure 2.2 shows an example of this visualization.

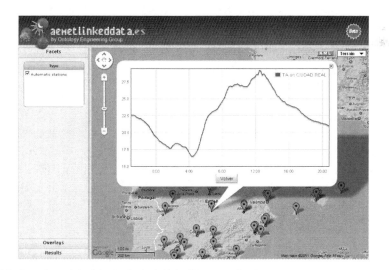

Fig. 2.2 Overview of the Metereological Linked Data Application

---

[113] http://virtuoso.openlinksw.com/

[114] http://www4.wiwiss.fu-berlin.de/pubby/

[115] http://ckan.net/package/aemet

2.5 Conclusions

In this chapter we have introduced a set of preliminary guidelines for generating, publishing and exploiting Linked Government Data. These guidelines are based on our experience in the production of Linked Data in several Governmental contexts.

According to our experience this process has an iterative incremental life cycle model, which is based on the continuous improvement and extension of the Government Linked Data resulted from performing several iterations. It is worth mentioning that the order of the activities and tasks, involved in this process, might be changed base on particular needs of the government bodies. Moreover, in order to validate the understandability, applicability and usability of the guidelines proposed in this chapter, we have presented two experiments in real case scenarios within GeoLinkedData and AEMET.

As future work, we will (1) continue formalizing the experiences we are gained in the different government contexts we are working; (2) develop more applications for the exploitation of the Government Linked Data; (3) include a validation activity, in which government agencies will validate the results according to the requirements identified in the specification activity; (4) perform more experiments to validate and refine our guidelines.

2.6 Acknowledgments

This work has been supported by the BabelData (TIN2010-17550) and myBigData (TIN2010-17060) Spanish projects. We would like to kindly thank the chapter reviewers for the very good comments. Finally, we would like to thank all OEG members involved in the Linked Data initiatives.

References

1. Barrasa, J., Corcho, O., and Gómez-Pérez, A. R2O, an Extensible and Semantically Based Database-to-Ontology Mapping Language. In *Second Workshop on Semantic Web and Databases (SWDB2004)*, 2004.
2. Bizer, C., Cyganiak, R. and Heath, T. How to publish Linked Data on the Web. Web page, 2007. Revised 2008. Accessed 01/01/2011.
3. Volz, J., Bizer, C., Gaedke, M., Kobilarov, G.: Discovering and Maintaining Links on the Web of Data. In: Bernstein, A., Karger, D. (eds.) The Semantic Web - ISWC 2009, pp. 731-746. Springer, Heidelberg (2009)
4. Cyganiak, R., Maali, F. and Peristeras, V. Self-service linked government data with dcat and gridworks. In *Proceedings of the 6th International Conference on Semantic Systems*, I-SEMANTICS '10, pages 37:1–37:3, New York, NY, USA, 2010. ACM.
5. Haase, P., Rudolph, S., Wang, Y., Brockmans, S., Palma, R., Euzenat, J. and d'Aquin, M. Networked Ontology Model. Technical report, NeOn project deliverable D1.1.1, 2006.
6. Hausenblas, M., Halb, W., Raimond, Y., Feigenbaum, L. and Ayers, D. SCOVO: Using Statistics on the Web of Data. In *ESWC*, volume 5554 of *LNCS*, pages 708–722. Springer, 2009.

7. Heath, T. and Bizer, C. *Linked Data: Evolving the Web into a Global Data Space*, volume 1. Morgan & Claypool, 2011.
8. Hogan, A., Harth, A., Passant, A., Decker, S. and Polleres, A. Weaving the Pedantic Web. In *Linked Data on the Web Workshop (LDOW2010) at WWW'2010*, 2010.
9. Kimball, R. and Caserta, J. *The Data Warehouse ETL Toolkit: Practical Techniques for Extracting, Cleanin*. John Wiley & Sons, 2004.
10. Maali, F. and Cyganiak, R. Re-using Cool URIs : Entity Reconciliation Against LOD Hubs. *Library*, 2011.
11. Montiel-Ponsoda, E., Vila-Suero, D., Villazón-Terrazas, B., Dunsire, G., Rodríguez, E.E. and Gómez-Pérezi, A. Style Guidelines for Naming and Labeling Ontologies in the Multilingual Web. In *Proceedings of the 2011 International Conference on Dublin Core and Metadata Applications*, DCMI '11. Dublin Core Metadata Initiative, 2011.
12. Ngonga Ngomo, A.-C. and Auer, S. Limes - a time-efficient approach for large-scale link discovery on the web of data, 2011.
13. Nikolov, A. and dAquin, M. Identifying Relevant Sources for Data Linking using a Semantic Web Index. *Search*, 2011.
14. Oren, E., Delbru, R. and Decker, S. Extending faceted navigation for RDF data. In *ISWC*, pages 559–572, 2006.
15. Sauermann, L., Cyganiak, R., Ayers, D. and Volkel, M. Cool URIs for the semantic web. Interest Group Note 20080331, W3C. Web page, 2008.
16. I. E. E. E. Computer Society, Sponsored B. The, and Software Engineering Standards Committee. IEEE Recommended Practice for Software Requirements Specifications IEEE Std 830-1998. Technical report, 1998.
17. Sommer, G.G. *The World of E-Government*. Haworth Press, January 2005.
18. Suárez-Figueroa, M.C. *NeOn Methodology for Building Ontology Networks: Specification, Scheduling and Reuse*. PhD thesis, Facultad de Informática, Universidad Politécnica de Madrid, Madrid, Spain, 2010.
19. Suarez-Figueroa, M.C, and Gómez-Pérez, A. NeOn Methodology for Building Ontology Networks: a Scenario-based Methodology. In *(S3T 2009)*, 2009.
20. Taylor, J. *Project Scheduling and Cost Control: Planning, Monitoring and Controlling the Baseline*, volume 1. J. Ross Publishing, 2008.
21. Vilches-Blázquez, L.M., Gargantilla, J.A.R., López-Pellicer, F.J., Corcho, O., and Nogueras-Iso, J. An Approach to Comparing Different Ontologies in the Context of Hydrographical Information. In *IF&GIS*, pages 193–207, 2009.
22. Villazón-Terrazas, B., Suárez-Figueroa, M.C. and Gómez-Pérez, A. A Pattern-Based Method for Re-Engineering Non-Ontological Resources into Ontologies. *International Journal on Semantic Web and Information Systems*, 6(4):27–63, 2010.
23. W3C. Publishing Open Government Data. W3C Working Draft. Web page, 2009.

Chapter 3
Producing and Using Linked Open Government Data in the TWC LOGD Portal

Timothy Lebo, John S. Erickson, Li Ding, Alvaro Graves, Gregory Todd Williams, Dominic DiFranzo, Xian Li, James Michaelis, Jin Guang Zheng, Johanna Flores, Zhenning Shangguan, Deborah L. McGuinness, and Jim Hendler

Abstract As open government initiatives around the world publish an increasing number of raw datasets, citizens and communities face daunting challenges when organizing, understanding, and associating disparate data related to their interests. Immediate and incremental solutions are needed to integrate, collaboratively manipulate, and transparently consume large-scale distributed data. The Tetherless World Constellation (TWC) at Rensselaer Polytechnic Institute (RPI) has developed the TWC LOGD Portal based on Semantic Web principles to support the deployment of Linked Open Government Data. The portal is not only an open source infrastructure supporting Linked Open Government Data production and consumption, but also serves to educate the developers, data curators, managers, and end users that form the growing international open government community. This chapter introduces the informatic challenges faced while developing the portal over the past two years, describes the current design solutions employed by the portal's LOGD production infrastructure, and concludes with lessons learned and future work.

3.1 Introduction

In recent years the release of Open Government Data (OGD) has become more common and has emerged as a vital communications channel between governments and their citizens. Since 2009, governments around the world[1] including the United States, United Kingdom, Australia, Norway, and Greece have built Web portals to provide datasets to their citizens and worldwide consumers alike. These datasets provide a wide range of information significant to the daily lives of citizens such as locations of toxic waste dumps, regional health-care costs, and local govern-

Correspondance author: Timothy Lebo, Tetherless World Constellation, Rensselaer Polytechnic Institute, 110 8th St., Troy, NY 12180, USA, e-mail: `lebot@rpi.edu`. See the List of Contributors for full contact details.

[1] http://www.data.gov/community/

51

ment spending. Citizens have become consumers of OGD: a study conducted by the Pew Internet and American Life Project reported that 40% of adults went online in 2009 to access some kind of government data[19]. One direct benefit of OGD is richer governmental transparency: citizens may now access the data sources behind previously-opaque government applications, enabling them to perform their own analyses and investigations not supported by existing tools. Moreover, instead of merely being *read-only* end users, citizens may now participate in collaborative government information access, including *mashing up* distributed government data from different agencies, discovering novel facts and rules, developing customized applications, and providing government agencies specific feedback about how to more effectively perform their governmental role.

Several technological challenges requiring significant time and effort must be overcome to fully realize this potential. Although many open government datasets are available for public access, most have been published using formats that do not permit distributed linking and do not help consumers understand their content. As stewards of a vast and diverse collection of official government data, the cost of individual agencies deploying Linked Open Government Data by themselves is prohibitive. Due to interoperability, scalability and usability constraints, "raw" OGD datasets are typically released *as is*; many datasets are encoded in formats not conducive to automated machine processing, and datasets from different sources are encoded using heterogeneous structures with ambiguous or differing meanings.

Since substantial human effort is needed to make raw datasets comprehensible, only a small proportion of the government data available has been published in an easily-reusable form using open principles. To accelerate the progress of opening more government data, new approaches are required to produce Linked Open Government Data as quickly as possible while allowing for incremental improvements developed by a broad community with diverse knowledge, skills, and objectives.

Instead of employing Linked Data principles, OGD release efforts such as Sunlight Foundation's National Data Catalog, Socrata, and Microsoft's OData use Web-friendly RESTful APIs to address these infrastructural challenges. However, data APIs provide only a partial solution. By their nature, APIs abstract away details and thus restrict access to the underlining data; there is typically no way for consumers to inspect, reuse, or extend the data model behind an API. This poses problems for application developers and end users because the data itself cannot be easily shared and reused, causing each API to act as an isolated silo of data that requires effort from each application developer to connect.

A global community of developers is applying Semantic Web technologies and Linked Data principles to overcome data integration challenges and take full advantage of OGD [1, 2]. The emerging Linked Open Data methodology[2] enables full data access using Web standards. Publishers can release raw data dumps instead of devoting time to design special-purpose data access APIs that make assumptions about consumer needs. Instead, consumers can integrate distributed government data in

---

[2] http://linkeddata.org/

Linked Data form without advance coordination with publishers, allowing others to benefit without waiting for each agency to adopt linked data design principles.

Since only a few government agencies have released their data in RDF formats, they need tools, infrastructure, and guidance to impart a wide variety of data with appropriate structure for human and machine consumption and to make data elements linkable. The TWC LOGD Portal has been designed and deployed to serve as a resource for the global LOGD community and has helped make the LOGD vision real. It stands as a reference model for the practical application of using Linked Data techniques to integrate disparate and heterogeneous government data.

This chapter describes our approach to fulfilling these needs and is organized as follows. Section 3.2 provides an overview of the TWC LOGD Portal, which provided motivation, context, and design constraints for the production workflow described in Section 3.3. Section 3.4 discusses the challenges faced when republishing third party data and the approaches taken to increase transparency of the production workflow. Section 3.5 discusses aspects of deploying LOGD on the portal and its use to create mashups. Section 3.6 reviews work related to producing and consuming government data with and without Linked Data principles. Section 3.7 concludes with a summary of our research, deployment contributions, and an outline of future directions.

3.2 The TWC LOGD Portal

The LOGD production workflow described in this chapter was developed to support the TWC LOGD Portal[3], described more fully in [8]. To serve the growing international open government community, the portal was created to meet three challenges:

- *LOGD Production*: Because many OGD datasets are released by different agencies using various formats and vocabulary, developers spend a lot of effort cleaning, restructuring, and linking related OGD datasets before they can develop applications. To reduce these initial costs, we created a persistent and incremental LOGD production infrastructure to incorporate and reuse individual efforts.
- *LOGD Consumption*: Using LOGD as a basis, developers can quickly develop and replicate government data mashup applications on the Web. To illustrate the benefits of LOGD in government applications, our team has developed more than fifty demonstrations using a wide range of readily-available Web technologies.
- *LOGD Community*: LOGD stakeholders need community support to collaborate and share best practices. To this end, the TWC LOGD Portal implements social semantic Web and provenance technologies to inter-link demos and tutorials that demonstrate best LOGD practices. Supporting open source principles is essential in developing the LOGD community, so the portal uses third-party

---

[3] http://logd.tw.rpi.edu

open source code including Virtuoso and Drupal6; hosts `csv2rdf4lod`[4] on GitHub; hosts all converted data, conversion configurations, and metadata on the Web; and hosts demo code and SPARQL queries on a Google Code project[5].

3.3 Producing Linked Open Government Data

The LOGD production workflow is the centerpiece of the TWC LOGD Portal. In this section, we introduce six stages of dataset integration. Five of these stages are designed to minimize human effort for incorporating a new dataset as Linked Data, while the remaining stage enables data modelers to add well-structured and well-connected descriptions to the initial representation. We describe enhancement types that a data modeler is most likely to use[6], along with a selection of more advanced enhancement types that elucidate the diversity of structural schemes employed by tabular government datasets. Throughout this section, we use portions of the White House Visitor Access Records[7] as a running example.

We describe an extension of the VoID[8] Dataset class to establish a three level dataset hierarchy that accounts for the RDF data resulting from incremental activities when accumulating new datasets, enhancing existing datasets, and handling new releases of those datasets already accumulated. Further, we highlight the correspondence between a dataset's URI and its role within the three-level VoID hierarchy. We then describe how this same correspondence is reused in our design to populate a SPARQL endpoint's named graphs.

After applying the five stages to create initial Linked Data from an OGD dataset and taking advantage of a sixth stage to enhance its representation, we describe how to handle an inevitable situation: a source organization releases a new version of a dataset we have already incorporated, published – and are using in applications. We use this situation to highlight several data organization challenges and how we solve them using a three-level namespace decomposition that simultaneously supports naming entities within and across datasets, establishing vocabularies that apply at different breadths, and performing bottom-up incremental integration of diverse datasets within and across source organizations – and among the Web of Data.

---

[4] http://purl.org/twc/id/software/csv2rdf4lod

[5] http://code.google.com/p/data-gov-wiki/

[6] Based on our experience with curating hundreds of datasets during the past two years.

[7] http://purl.org/twc/pages/whitehouse-visitor-access-records

[8] Vocabulary of Interlinked Datasets is described at http://www.w3.org/TR/void/

3.3.1 Producing Initial Conversions with Minimal Human Effort

As illustrated in Figure 3.1, data integration is achieved by iteratively following a few stages for each dataset of interest. These stages are designed to minimize initial human effort so that all data is available as Linked Data as quickly as possible, yet focused human efforts to understand, use, and enrich particular portions of the data are accumulated for sharing among the rest of the community. The six major stages are *Name*, *Retrieve*, *Adjust*, *Convert*, *Enhance*, and *Publish*. Two of these stages are optional and can be omitted or postponed in situations where the source data is already in an amenable format (*Adjust*) and/or consumers do not yet have a compelling use case to warrant enhancement (*Enhance*).

Name: To name a dataset, three identifiers are assigned; the first identifies the **source** organization providing the data, the second identifies the particular **dataset** that the organization is providing, and the third identifies the **version** (or release) of the dataset. For example, *whitehouse-gov*, *visitor-records*, and *0510* identify the data that was available from whitehouse.gov[9] on July 8th, 2010. These identifiers are used to construct the URI for the dataset itself[10], which in turn serves as a namespace for the entities that the dataset mentions. These three identifiers should be assigned thoughtfully and consistently, as they provide the basis for the entire naming convention and may be used by third party consumers to orient with and navigate among the resulting data. Decisions for these three identifiers should be guided by reusing the source organization's terminology. To identify the source organization, we recommend reusing a form of their Web domain name, such as *london-gov-uk* or *ncdc-noaa-gov*. To identify the dataset, we recommend reusing a title[11] that the source organization provides or would recognize and associate to their collection.

Retrieve: After naming a dataset, its associated data files and documentation are retrieved. Such a retrieval creates a snapshot of the dataset available, while subsequent retrievals of the same dataset will create potentially different snapshots (since the source may remove, replace, or augment previous offerings). The assigned version identifier distinguishes the data from each snapshot. When possible, we recommend reusing version identifiers provided by the source organization (such as *release-23* for USDA's nutrition dataset[12]), but we have found that these are rarely provided by data publishers[13]. In the absence of a more suitable identifier, we recommend assigning a version identifier according to the publish, last-modified, or retrieval dates[14] in the form *2011-Mar-17*[15]. A provenance-enabled URL fetch util-

---

[9] http://www.whitehouse.gov/files/disclosures/visitors/WhiteHouse-WAVES-Released-0510.csv

[10] http://logd.tw.rpi.edu/source/whitehouse-gov/dataset/visitor-records/version/0510

[11] If acronyms are expanded, titles are more informative to a broader audience.

[12] http://www.ars.usda.gov/services/docs.htm?docid=8964

[13] A version identifier is gleaned from the White House by inspecting part of its data file URLs.

[14] These three types of dates are listed in order of preference because, for example, the publish date more closely identifies the source organization's dataset than the date one happened to retrieve it.

[15] This date format was chosen to facilitate human readability and to follow the hierarchical nature of the URI; date information that one would want to query should be – and is – encoded in RDF.

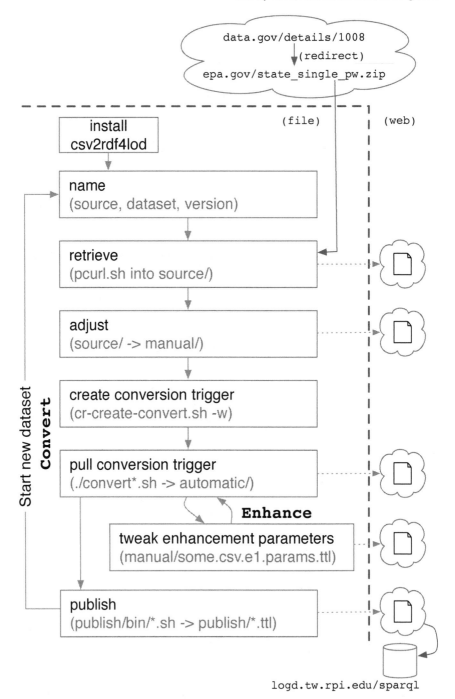

Fig. 3.1 The major stages of the LOGD production workflow are performed on the server, while the final and intermediate results are made available on the Web as dump files and through a SPARQL endpoint. Entities described in the SPARQL endpoint are available as resolvable Linked Data. Associations among the retrieved files and conversion results are encoded in RDF by provenance-aware utilities. Five of the six production stages require minimal human effort; the sixth enhancement stage can be perform as needed without disrupting applications built against earlier results.

ity is used to retrieve URLs, which stores a PML file[13] in the same directory as the retrieved file and records provenance including the user account initiating retrieval, the government URL requested, time requested, and checksum of the file received.

Adjust: Although manually modifying files retrieved from authoritative sources should be avoided, unrepeatable human intervention may be necessary to accommodate the format required by the conversion process. Manual adjustments are minimized by specifying appropriate conversion parameters (discussed in Section 3.3.2), but process transparency is maintained by storing results separately from their originals and recording the provenance associating the adjusted files to their predecessors, indicating the type of process applied, and citing the user account reporting the modifications.

Convert: `csv2rdf4lod`[16] converts tabular data files to RDF according to interpretation parameters encoded using a conversion vocabulary[17]. The use of parameters instead of custom code to perform conversions enables repeatable, easily inspectable, and queryable transformations; provides more consistent results; and is an excellent source of metadata. XML-based data files can be converted to RDF using parameter-driven utilities such as Krextor[10]. Output from `csv2rdf4lod` includes provenance for the RDF dump files it produces by citing its invocation time, the converter version and hash, the input file, the transformation parameters used, the parameter authors, and the user account invoking the conversion. Each conversion that uses different transformation parameters is named with a **layer identifier**[18] to distinguish it from other interpretations of the same input files retrieved. An initial *raw layer* is produced with minimal effort by providing only the three identifiers already assigned (source, dataset, and version). Although easy to create, the *raw layer* is the result of a *naive* interpretation; rows become subjects, column headers become predicates, and cells assert a single triple with an untyped string literal. Enhancing *raw* to make more meaningful RDF is highly encouraged.

Enhance: Because the enhancement stage is the only one of six that requires significant human effort, it is described more completely in Section 3.3.2. Enhancement can be performed after (or instead of) the initial conversion and it can be published well after (or instead of) publishing the initial conversion. In either case, the well-structured, well-connected addition will augment what has already been published and will not interfere with applications built against the initial conversion. Further, applications are able to discover the new enhancements of previous layers, may automatically adjust to use it, and can fall back if the enhancements are "too" different.

Publish: Publication begins with the conversion results and can include making dump files available for download, loading results into a triple store, and hosting resolvable URIs so they are available to Linked Data utilities. Different portions of the full RDF dataset are aggregated into separate dump files to allow consumers to retrieve specific portions that fulfill their needs. A complete dump file is hosted on

---

[16] `csv2rdf4lod`'s URI is http://purl.org/twc/id/software/csv2rdf4lod

[17] The conversion vocabulary namespace is http://purl.org/twc/vocab/conversion/

[18] Because their meanings are difficult to name concisely and uniformly, enhancement layers are distinguished using incrementing counting numbers to provide a simple temporal ordering.

the Web and includes the raw layer, any enhancement layers, *owl:sameAs* triples, retrieval provenance, conversion provenance, and metadata describing its VoID hierarchy. The SPARQL endpoint is loaded by retrieving the RDF dump files that the production workflow previously hosted on the Web. This transparency allows anyone else to reproduce the state of the triple store for their own purposes. Provenance of loading a named graph with an RDF file from the Web is stored in the named graph itself, enabling users to trace data from what they are querying, through the conversion process and retrieval, and to the original government data. The data files originally retrieved from the government along with any other intermediate files are also hosted on the Web and associated by RDF assertions, enabling consumers to inspect and repeat the integration processes responsible for the data offered.

3.3.2 Enhancing an Initial Conversion by Creating a Second Layer

Although the rapid production of large quantities of Linked Open Government Data may be useful, such data will be much more valuable if attention has been given to correctly model dataset content by reusing existing vocabularies, referencing entities commonly recognized from other data sources, and structuring in more natural (and less record-like) representations. The five stages described in the previous section quickly produce an initial conversion that permits exploration using standard Linked Data utilities. These stages provide a concrete basis for learning the content, discussing with experts, determining more "appropriate" RDF representations of the domain, and developing prototypes.

As described earlier, the initial conversion is *naive*; rows become subjects, columns become predicates, and cells assert a single triple with an untyped string literal. The initial interpretation of the tabular structure creates the first *layer* of descriptions for entities in a versioned dataset. For example, two triples in an initial layer (*:thing_2 raw:namefirst "CHRISTINE"; raw:access_type "VA"*) are illustrated in Figure 3.2. Enhancing the same versioned dataset creates a second *layer* that adds more descriptions for the same entities[19] (*:visitor_2 foaf:firstName "CHRISTINE"; e1:access_type a:Visitor_Access*). A *layer* can be defined as the set of triples whose predicates fall within a given namespace. For example, one could specify a FOAF layer of the Billion Triple Challenge datasets or a Dublin Core layer of the latest DBPedia dataset. Since each conversion provides a new interpretation of the original data, predicates from each conversion need to be in distinct layers. For example, the enhanced layer in Figure 3.2 changed *access_type*'s range from a Literal to a Resource; using the same predicate across layers would cause logical issues when applying OWL reasoning, or would break applications expecting literal values when the enhancement is added. To avoid these issues, predicates are named within a namespace specific to the layer.

---

[19] When renaming subjects, older names point to newer names using http://prefix.cc/con

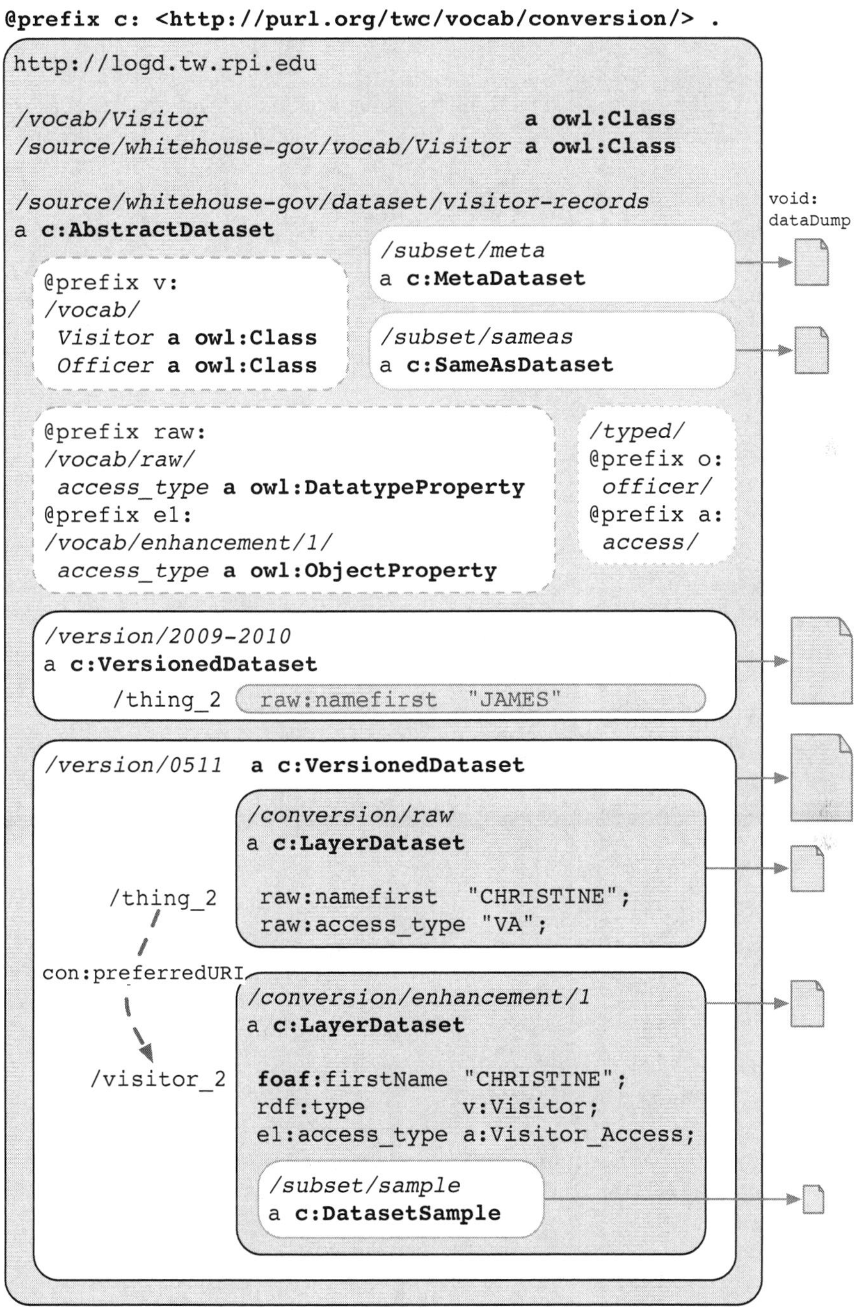

```
@prefix c: <http://purl.org/twc/vocab/conversion/> .
```

http://logd.tw.rpi.edu

/vocab/Visitor   **a owl:Class**
/source/whitehouse-gov/vocab/Visitor **a owl:Class**

/source/whitehouse-gov/dataset/visitor-records   void:
a **c:AbstractDataset**   dataDump

> @prefix v:
> /vocab/
>   Visitor **a owl:Class**
>   Officer **a owl:Class**

/subset/meta
a **c:MetaDataset**

/subset/sameas
a **c:SameAsDataset**

> @prefix raw:
> /vocab/raw/
>   access_type **a owl:DatatypeProperty**
> @prefix el:
> /vocab/enhancement/1/
>   access_type **a owl:ObjectProperty**

/typed/
@prefix o:
  officer/
@prefix a:
  access/

/version/2009-2010
a **c:VersionedDataset**
          /thing_2   raw:namefirst   "JAMES"

/version/0511   **a c:VersionedDataset**

/conversion/raw
a **c:LayerDataset**

          /thing_2   raw:namefirst   "CHRISTINE";
                      raw:access_type "VA";

con:preferredURI

/conversion/enhancement/1
a **c:LayerDataset**

          /visitor_2 **foaf:firstName** "CHRISTINE";
                      rdf:type   v:Visitor;
                      el:access_type a:Visitor_Access;

/subset/sample
a **c:DatasetSample**

Fig. 3.2 Namespaces decompose according to *source*, *dataset*, and *version* identifiers assigned when retrieving data from other organizations; and *layer* identifiers assigned when interpreting it in different ways. Each step in the namespace decomposition corresponds to a void:Dataset URI that is a VoID superset of the datasets named within its namespace. URIs for entities, properties, and classes created from a dataset are named in namespaces corresponding to their breadth of applicability. Data integration is achieved incrementally by reinterpreting source data to use entities, properties, and classes from broader namespaces within this namespace decomposition or from existing vocabulary that is already used in the Semantic Web. For grammar defining URIs, see [8].

csv2rdf4lod converts tabular data files to RDF according to interpretation parameters encoded using a conversion vocabulary. The following sections highlight the enhancements[20] most frequently used, where the prefix c: abbreviates the conversion vocabulary namespace[21]. Similarities between the enhancement names and the axioms in RDFS and OWL were a design goal, since the enhancements behave in analogous ways when considering the triple or property created from each cell situated within a particular column. The distinction between csv2rdf4lod and traditional RDFS/OWL reasoners is that the former produces RDF inferences from tabular literals while the latter produce RDF inferences from existing RDF triples. This allows an LOGD publisher to choose between materializing the inferences with csv2rdf4lod to avoid using an inferencing engine at query time, or delaying the inferences until query execution and installing an additional inference engine.

3.3.2.1 Most Popular Row-Based Enhancements

Enhancements can control the triple's subject[22]. **c:domain_template** is used to rename the subject of the triple. In the example shown in Figure 3.2, it was used to rename the subject from *:thing_2* to *:visitor_2*. Variables specified in the template are used to name the subject according to one or more values from the row. For example, one could name the visitor *:CHRISTINE_ADAMS* by using the template *"[#2]_[#1]"*. A string label provided by **c:domain_name** is used to type the subject[23]. A full class URI is created within the dataset's vocabulary namespace. For example, specifying *"Visitor"* will create the class *v:Visitor* in Figure 3.2 and type *:visitor_2* to *v:Visitor*. **c:subclass_of** is used to associate class URIs in the dataset's namespace to any class URI. This is done by associating the local class label to its superclass (e.g., *"Visitor"* to foaf:Person). Templates may also be used to specify the superclass (e.g., *"Visitor"* to *"[/]/vocab/Visitor"*).

Enhancements can control the triple's predicate. **c:label** is used to rename the property created from a column. For example, we could have renamed the *raw:access_type* property to *e1:has_access*. Renaming properties also enables one to merge properties from multiple columns[24]. **c:equivalent_property** is used to omit a local predicate in favor of an external one. For example, in Figure 3.2, we omit *e1:namefirst* and use *foaf:firstName* instead. **c:comment** will create an *rdfs:comment* on the predicate created. When we find the documentation[25] *"Type of access to the complex (VA = Visitor Access)"* for *access_type*, we can use this enhancement so that all conversions will further describe the predicate created.

---

[20] The full list of enhancements is at http://purl.org/twc/vocab/conversion/Enhancement.html

[21] The conversion vocabulary namespace is http://purl.org/twc/vocab/conversion/

[22] Due to space considerations, we are omitting an entire class of enhancements that specify structural characteristics of the input file. These are critical because they significantly reduce the need for manual edits to "prepare" an input file for conversion.

[23] Row subjects are left untyped until an enhancement can provide a meaningful one.

[24] The initial conversions never create the same predicate for two columns in the same table.

[25] http://www.whitehouse.gov/files/disclosures/visitors/WhiteHouse-WAVES-Key-1209.txt

Enhancements can describe how to interpret the value of a cell. **c:interpret** is used to replace entire cell values with alternative values. For example, we can specify that *"VA"* should be interpreted as *"Visitor Access"*. This can serve as a codebook for archaic abbreviations that the source organization uses. A special case of this can also specify that triples with empty object strings or values like *"!NULL!"* should be omitted. The **c:*pattern** enhancements specify how to interpret the cells as dates and date times. For example *"M/d/yy HH:mm"* will cast the value into an *xsd:dateTime*. **c:delimits_object** can indicate a regular expression to use to delimit a single cell's value into multiple tokens. For example, the cell value *"AAPL,T"* would become two triples; one for *nyse:AAPL* and one for *nyse:T*.

Enhancements can control the triple's object. **c:range_template** is used to rename the object in the same way that **c:domain_template** renames the subject. **c:range** can cast the cell value to a typed literal[26], an *rdfs:Resource*, or keep it as an *rdfs:Literal*. **c:range_name** will type the object in the same way that **c:domain_name** types the subject (**c:subclass_of** is used in the same way, too). **c:links_via** specifies an RDF data source from which to assert *owl:sameAs* triples. For example, if a cell value is *"POTUS"*, we can point to an RDF dataset containing the triple *http://dbpedia.org/resource/President_of_the_United_States dct:identifier "POTUS"*. When promoting the cell value to a local resource (with **c:range**), it will also reference DBPedia's URI for the President of the United States[27]. This enhancement behaves like a locally-scoped *owl:InverseFunctionalProperty*.

3.3.2.2 Advanced Row-Based Enhancements

More advanced enhancements are also available. Table entries describing multiple concepts are "normalized" using **c:bundled_by**, which changes the subject of a cell's triple from the row URI to a URI created from another cell or a URI minted for an implicit entity. For example, the *raw:namelast*, *raw:namefirst*, and *raw:namemid* predicates in the White House Visitor Access Records dataset could be bundled into an implicit *foaf:Person*. The same dataset would actually be best represented by bundling values to about a half dozen different entities involved in a visit (e.g., the appointment caller, officer making the appointment, the meeting location, and a few time intervals). **c:object_search** is used to match arbitrary regular expressions against the cell value to assert descriptions of the subject by populating predicate and object templates with the expression's captured groups. For example, a regular expression finding stock ticker symbols in tweet texts can result in annotating the tweet's URI with *sioc:subject* triples citing the stock's URI. This eliminates the need for applications to use the SPARQL *regex* filter. **c:predicate/c:object** pairs can also be used to add arbitrary descriptions to the subjects and objects created from a converted cell. **c:ExampleResource** annotates particular rows as exemplary, which

---

[26] xsd:integer, xsd:decimal, xsd:boolean, xsd:date, xsd:dateTime

[27] *:POTUS owl:sameAs http://dbpedia.org/resource/President_of_the_United_States .*

become void:exampleResources in the resulting conversion. **c:multiplier** will scale
values when casting to numeric datatypes.

3.3.2.3 Beyond Binary Relations: Enhancing with Cell-Based Subjects

The initial conversion interprets columns as *binary* relations; where rows become
subjects, columns become predicates, and cells assert a single triple with an untyped
string literal. However, many tabular data represent *n-ary* relations. For example,
life expectancy in Wales by region, age, and time[28]; estimated and actual budgets for
U.S. federal agencies by fiscal year and program type[29]; and states that have instated
anti-smoking laws in bars, restaurants, and workplaces over several years[30] are all
poorly represented with an interpretation that assumes a binary relation. Although
many tabular data that require n-ary interpretations are statistical, they need not be.

When a table expresses an n-ary relationship, the columns are not *relations*, but
entities involved in a relation. This situation is better represented by using the cell
as the subject of the triple and asserting many triples from the cell to other values
in the row, one or more entities in the column header(s), and the cell value[31]. The
following example illustrates the results of interpreting the U.S. budget statistics
as row-based binary relationships versus a cell-based n-ary relationship. The latter
permits the addition of new entities without requiring new predicates and modified
queries to account for them, which is an objective of the RDF Data Cube effort[32].

```
:thing_6
  raw:agency                                        "NIH 2";
  raw:fiscal_year                                   "FY 2010";
  raw:estimate_request                              "Estimate";
  raw:high_end_computing_infrastructure_and_application "468.3".

:thing_6_4
  base_vocab:agency           typed_agency:NIH;
  base_vocab:fiscal_year      :FY_2010;
  e1:estimate_request         :Estimate;
  e1:program_component_area   :HECIA;
  rdf:value                   468300000;
  muo:measuredIn              dbpedia:United_States_dollar .
```

---

[28] http://purl.org/twc/pages/qb-example

[29] http://purl.org/twc/tiny-url/nitrd-fy11

[30] http://purl.org/twc/tiny-url/nci-nih-smoking-law-coverage

[31] https://github.com/timrdf/csv2rdf4lod-automation/wiki/Converting-with-cell-based-subjects

[32] http://publishing-statistical-data.googlecode.com

3.3.3 Extending VoID to Organize Incremental Developments

In Sections 3.3.1 and 3.3.2, we noted that three identifiers (*source, dataset, version*) are assigned when creating an initial LOGD conversion and a fourth identifier (*layer*) is assigned when enhancing it. Now that we have introduced the six *stages* of the LOGD production workflow, we can revisit three of them to consider the *sets of data* resulting from their completion. Three specializations of void:Dataset are used to group triples resulting from different incremental stages that are performed. Figure 3.2 illustrates the void:subset hierarchy of one abstract dataset, two versioned datasets, and three[33] layer datasets. Merely **naming** a dataset with *source* and *dataset* identifiers does not result in any data triples. However, this abstract dataset is often the first level at which a data consumer will discover it[34] or the only level at which a data publisher will maintain its offerings[35]. For example, Figure 3.2 illustrates the abstract dataset *visitor-records* that is named with a URI created by appending its source and dataset identifiers to a base URI[36]. Merely **retrieving** data files also does not result in any data triples, but will lead to RDF when they are converted. Figure 3.2 shows the URIs for two versioned datasets (ending in *2009-2010* and *0511*), which are VoID subsets of the abstract dataset *visitor-records*. Versioned datasets are named with URIs formed by appending their version identifier to the abstract dataset's URI. Finally, **converting** the data files[37] from *0511* creates a layer dataset named *raw* that is a VoID subset of the versioned dataset. A second layer dataset (*enhancement/1*) of *0511* is created when a second interpretation is applied to the same input data. Although other specializations of void:Dataset are shown in Figure 3.2, they do not delineate sets of triples resulting from one of the six LOGD production stages.

3.3.4 Reusing Dataset URIs for Named Graph Names

Organizing RDF datasets (*abstract, versioned,* and *layer*) according to results of three incremental integration stages (*name, retrieve,* and *enhance*) that reflect three levels of granularity and are consistently named according three provenance-based identifiers (*source, dataset,* and *version*) allows a data consumers to navigate, evaluate, and adopt the portions of LOGD appropriate for their use. To complete this consistency from retrieval to publishing, datasets are loaded into a triple store's named graphs whose names correspond to the URIs of the datasets being loaded. This allows a data consumer to anticipate a dataset's location within a triple store

---

[33] To abbreviate, the *raw* layer of versioned dataset *2009-2010* is neither named nor typed.

[34] For example, we mentioned the abstract dataset "White House Visitor Records" when introducing our running example in the beginning of Section 3.3.

[35] For example, data.gov does not distinguish among dataset versions, just abstract datasets.

[36] For a grammar that defines most of the URI design, see [8].

[37] http://www.whitehouse.gov/files/disclosures/visitors/WhiteHouse-WAVES-Released-0511.zip

when knowing only the URI of the dataset, which is consistently constructing knowing only the source, dataset, and version of interest. Practically, loading the RDF
of a particular dataset is achieved by resolving its URI, selecting the URL of its
void:dataDump, and loading the dump file into the triple store's named graph. To
facilitate data cataloging and exploration, all c:MetaDataset void:subsets are found
and loaded into a single named graph.

3.3.5 Handling Updated Datasets by Creating a Second Version

After naming, retrieving, adjusting, converting, enhancing, and publishing a dataset
from another organization, data curators are likely to face the situation where the
source organization updated the dataset's original data files. Although the change
could happen for a variety of reasons (it could contain corrections, augment the
previous, or simply replace it), they all present challenges that can be addressed
using a three-level (*source, dataset, version*) URI naming scheme.

As mentioned earlier, the source, dataset, and version identifiers *whitehouse-gov*,
visitor-records, and *0510* identify the data that was available from the White House
on July 8th, 2010. Although the requirement to assign a version identifier for a
dataset before retrieving any data may seem superfluous, its importance becomes
evident when we revisit the same dataset page on August 30th, 2010 to find that the
previous file has been replaced with a new one[38]. While the structure of the table
– and its intended interpretation – did not change, the content completely changed.
Assigning a new version identifier (*whitehouse-gov*, *visitor-records*, *0810*) distinguishes the RDF produced from this newly retrieved data file. The same is true for
0910 (last modified September 24, 2010 when it was retrieved on October 1, 2010),
0511 (last modified May 27, 2011 when it was retrieved on June 15, 2011), and
2009-2011 (last modified December 29, 2010 when retrieved on June 15, 2011).

As mentioned in Section 3.3.2, csv2rdf4lod uses enhancement parameters
encoded in RDF to create an enhancement layer. Since these were already defined
for the first version retrieved, they are reapplied to the data files of new versioned
datasets without requiring additional human effort to re-specify the parameters.

3.3.6 Using Dataset URIs as Namespaces for Entities and Vocabularies

Dataset URIs are used as namespaces for the entities that they describe and the
vocabularies they use to describe them. In general, we cannot assume that the entities described by rows in different versions of a table are identical. For example, comparing the first data row of versions *2009-1011* and *0511* in Figure 3.2,

---

[38] http://www.whitehouse.gov/files/disclosures/visitors/WhiteHouse-WAVES-Released-0827.csv

we see drastically different first names *"JAMES"* and *"CHRISTINE"*. So, different URIs are created for subjects (*:thing_2* in **2009-1011** versus *:thing_2* in **0511**). The URIs for predicates and objects, however, are shared across versions. For example, *raw:namefirst* and *a:Visitor_Access* are used in both versions. Although these characteristics are a fundamental aspect of being a data*set*, the enhancements **c:domain_template**, **c:equivalent_property**, and **c:range_template** are available to change this default behavior to suit different kinds of updates performed by a source organization.

Although decomposing the namespace according to provenance-based identifiers (*source*, *dataset*, and *version*) provides an effective way to distinguish among *who* "said" *what* (*when*), enhancements must be specified to integrate what is being said. Fortunately, the same namespace decomposition provides a natural scheme to incrementally integrate datasets of interest using a bottom-up technique. The URIs for entities, predicates, and classes are controlled by providing URI templates that are evaluated during conversion, giving curators control to create vocabularies and entity names at any level within the namespace or use external vocabularies directly – all within a single enhancement configuration. For example, in Figure 3.2, *v:Visitor* is scoped by the abstract dataset, but *Visitor* classes that apply across all White House datasets (*/source/whitehouse-gov/vocab/Visitor*) or across all source organizations (*/vocab/Visitor*) are also defined. The inverse operation becomes very powerful; we can now query for all datasets within our entire collection that mention visitors.

3.4 Transparent LOGD Production Using Provenance Metadata

Although Linked Data provides many benefits, the retrieval, conversion, enhancement, and republication of another organization's data raises important questions about the integrity of the resulting data products and any applications that rely upon them. An inherent consequence of integrating data from disparate sources is that *distinctions diminish*. Once integrated, important distinctions such as *who*, *where*, and *when* information came from are at risk. The preservation of these distinctions becomes increasingly important when the sources of integration vary significantly in degrees of authority, reputability, policies, and documentation. Ironically, an integrated content view obscures important answers about *how* it came to be.

Although the *results* from the LOGD production workflow are important and useful for the open government and linked data communities, we do not consider the workflow a success unless it also accounts for *how* those results came to be. To achieve this transparency, the workflow captures a wealth of context when performing each of the six stages of integration. When **naming** the dataset, identifiers for the *source*, *dataset*, and *version* are used to frame the integration process around *who* is providing *what* data, and *when* they provided it. By using these identifiers to construct the URI for the dataset, and by using the dataset URI as a namespace for the entities it mentions and the vocabulary it uses to describe them, we implicitly encode three aspects of provenance for datasets, their entities, and their vocabulary. When **retrieving**, the user account initiating retrieval, the government URL requested, time requested, a variety of HTTP interactions, and the received file's checksum are captured and encoded in RDF. This information is critical because it establishes the connection between the original source and all subsequent results. When **adjusting**, results are stored separately from their originals and are associated to their predecessors by indicating the type of process applied and citing the user account that reported the modifications. When **converting** and **enhancing**, the invocation time, converter version and hash, input file, enhancement parameters, enhancement authors, and the user account invoking the conversion are captured. When **publishing**, the intermediate and final results are hosted on the Web and associated with the provenance descriptions captured throughout the production process. Finally, provenance of loading a named graph with an RDF file from the Web is stored in the named graph itself, enabling users to trace data from what they are querying, through the conversion process and retrieval, and to the original source.

metadata describes the context of critical steps throughout the LOGD production workflow. Consumers that are merely looking for additional ways to understand the data or may even question the validity of the final product may use this additional information to determine for themselves whether the concerns they have are caused by the aggregation process or rest with the original data source. The ability to accurately and comprehensively acknowledge organizations and individuals contributing to a result is an additional benefit of having provenance information, which not only facilitates conformance with data usage policies, but also provides the basis of incentive structures to reward previous contributions while motivating additional contributions [17].

The application of provenance within the TWC LOGD Portal is an ongoing research area, but we have already established processes for data consumers to debug mashups collaboratively [15], access explanations for the workflows that lead to mashups [14], and have greater trust in mashup results [12]. The provenance at the triple level[39] that csv2rdf4lod provides allows inquiry and inspection at the assertion level, such as *How do you know that the UK gave Ethiopia $107,958,576 USD for Education in 2007/8?*, which is answered by clicking an *Oh yeah?*[40] link that provides URL of the original government spreadsheet, the cell that caused the triple, the interpretation parameters applied, and the author of the transformation parameters. This information is obtained by invoking a SPARQL DESCRIBE query on the triple's subject and predicate, causing provenance fragments of the original CSV's rows and columns to be combined by a custom Jena DESCRIBE handler.

The provenance of the LOGD workflow has been encoded primarily using the Proof Markup Language [13], but other popular provenance vocabularies such as Provenir [18], Hartig's Provenance Vocabulary [9], and OPM [16] have been incorporated to describe certain aspects when it is more natural to do so. Other more

---

[39] The triple-level provenance that csv2rdf4lod provides is reification-based, so the size of the provenance encoding is a function of the sum, *not* the product, of the table's rows and columns.

[40] The "Oh yeah?" button is described at http://www.w3.org/DesignIssues/UI.html

traditional vocabularies (e.g., FOAF, SIOC, DC Terms, NFO[41]) have also been used where appropriate.

3.5 LOGD Deployment and Usage

3.5.1 Cost-effective Deployment of Linked Open Government Data

Our work on LOGD production suggests architectural guidelines and design patterns for the development of LOGD ecosystems. The TWC LOGD Portal implementation demonstrates how LOGD can be generated quickly, at fairly low cost and can be incrementally improved through systematic enhancement. We have also found opportunities to further reduce human intervention in LOGD production through automation. For example, rather than relying on users to contribute links across LOGD datasets, several semi-automated methods have been developed [4, 10], including the automatic detection of special entities such as U.S. state identifiers that have been instantiated across different LOGD datasets, and using OWL inference to connect semantically-related properties.

Linked Open Government Data, together with relevant Semantic Web technologies, was officially deployed by the U.S. government as part of its open government data initiative in May 2010. As of May 2011 the TWC LOGD Portal hosts more than 9.9 billion RDF triples from 1,838 OGD datasets published by 82 different data sources from over twenty countries, including special political regions and international organizations; most of these datasets are from Data.gov. The Portal infrastructure has enhanced 1,505 datasets and has accumulated 8,335 *owl:sameAs* statements for 37 datasets (including 25 Data.gov datasets) linking to LOD datasets such as DBpedia, GeoNames and GovTrack.

TWC has made its `csv2rdf4lod` conversion tool, demo source code, SPARQL queries and configurations for dataset conversions available as open source. We are also currently working with several community-based organizations to mentor them in the creation and exploitation of LOGD directly from local-government data sources in their localities. We have also recently extended the TWC LOGD Portal with two key additions: an *Instance Hub* that will serve as a catalog of canonical URIs to be used when producing Linked Data based on U.S. government datasets, and a *International LOGD Dataset Catalog*[7][42] that provides a comprehensive, searchable, RDF-based inventory of over 300K OGD datasets by aggregating over 50 OGD dataset catalogs released by over 20 countries . We believe both the Instance Hub and International LOGD Dataset Catalog will be valuable resources that can be used and maintained by the LOGD community.

---

[41] http://www.semanticdesktop.org/ontologies/nfo/

[42] http://purl.org/twc/application/international-logd-dataset-catalog

3.5.2 Scalability and Quality in LOGD Production

It is computationally prohibitive to turn all OGD datasets into high quality enhanced data. Therefore, our LOGD production offers both *basic* LOGD production (using "raw" conversion configuration) requiring little if any human intervention, and *advanced* LOGD production (using "enhancement" conversion configuration) that enables users to use their domain knowledge to generate higher-quality LOGD data. The former approach is highly scalable since most of it is automated, while the latter approach supports the need for high quality LOGD production. Additional scalability is achieved through the social aspects of LOGD production. By decomposing the OGD data processing workflow into smaller stages it is possible to assign tasks to contributors with appropriate skill sets and domain knowledge.

3.5.3 Rapid LOGD Mashup Development using LOGD datasets

LOGD consumption complements its production. Producing well-structured and well-connected data facilitates the conception and creation of mashups to combine multiple government datasets or leverage datasets outside government domain. While we briefly discuss how LOGD datasets can be used to construct mashups here, a more detailed description of LOGD mashups, see *The Web is My Back-end* also in this issue.

LOGD datasets have been made available on the TWC LOGD Portal as downloadable RDF dump files. Application developers can load the LOGD datasets (typically LOGD produced from the latest version of a dataset) into a SPARQL endpoint to enable Web-based SPARQL queries. Applications then submit SPARQL queries to the endpoints to integrate multiple datasets and retrieve data integration results. LOGD datasets can be further linked by common entity URIs generated during the enhancement process.

Application developers may also query multiple SPARQL endpoints to achieve larger-scale data integration. A typical example might be to query the TWC LOGD Portal's SPARQL endpoint to retrieve government data (containing entities that map to DBpedia using owl:sameAs), and then query DBpedia for additional descriptions about the entities in government data. For example, the "Linking Wildland Fire and Government Budget" mashup[43] mashes up U.S. government budget information (released by OMB), statistics of wildland fire (released by Department of the Interior) with famous fires reported on Wikipedia.

The declarative, open source nature of LOGD datasets and the provenance metadata associated with LOGD data makes LOGD consumption more transparent. Developers can locate LOGD datasets used in demonstrations and learn to integrate multiple datasets by reading the corresponding SPARQL queries. For example, in recent Web Science courses at RPI senior undergraduate students in the Information

---

[43] http://logd.tw.rpi.edu/demo/linking_wildland_fire_and_government_budget

Technology program successfully completed course projects that required them to learn from the published LOGD datasets and corresponding demos on the TWC LOGD Portal.

3.6 Related Work

Dataset Catalog Services: Open government data initiatives typically begin with the publication of online catalogs of raw datasets; these catalogs usually feature keyword search and faceted browsing interfaces to help users find relevant datasets and retrieve corresponding metadata including dataset descriptions and download URLs. For example, Data.gov maintains three dataset catalogs including the *Raw Data Catalog*, *Tool Catalog* and *Geodata Catalog*: the first two share one faceted search interface, while the *Geodata Catalog* has a separate interface. Data.gov also uses a Microsoft BING-based search. The OpenPSI Project (http://www.openpsi.org) collects RDF-based catalog information about the UK's government datasets to support government-based information publishers, research communities, and Web developers. CKAN (Comprehensive Knowledge Archive Network) (http://ckan.net/) is an online registry for finding, sharing and reusing datasets. As of January 2011 about 1600 datasets had been registered with CKAN, and CKAN has been used to generate the LOD cloud diagram and to support dataset listings in Data.gov.uk. CKAN publishes its native dataset metadata in JSON format but is also experimenting with RDF encoding (http://semantic.ckan.net/). The TWC LOGD Portal publishes LOGD dataset metadata in RDF and provides a combined search over the three catalogs of Data.gov. As noted earlier, TWC is currently extending its metadata-based search technique to include federated government data from around world.

API-based OGD Data Access: As an alternative to making raw data directly available for download, several projects offer Web-based data APIs that enable developers to access government data within their applications. For example, the Sunlight Foundation (http://sunlightfoundation.com/) has created the National Data Catalog (http://nationaldatacatalog.com/) which makes federal, state and local government datasets available and provides data APIs via a RESTful Web service. Socrata (http://opendata.socrata.com) is a Web platform for publishing datasets that provides a full catalog of all their open government datasets, along with tools to browse and visualize data, and a RESTful Web API for developers. Microsoft has also entered this space with their OData (http://www.odata.org) data access protocol and their Open Government Data Initiative (OGDI) (http://ogdi.codeplex.com); recently a small number of OGD datasets have been published on Microsoft's Azure Marketplace DataMarket (https://datamarket.azure.com/). Currently, none of these platforms enable data to be linked specifically at the data level, and none of the APIs provide a way for developers to see or reuse the underlying data model, making it hard to extend the model or use it for further mashups.

Linked Open Government Data: There is an increasing number of Linked Data projects involving government data in the U.S. and around the world. Gov-Track (http://www.govtrack.us) is a civic project that collects data about the U.S. Congress and republishes the data in XML and as Linked Data. Goodwin et al. [8] used Linked Geographical Data to enhance spatial queries on the administrative geographic entities in Great Britain. Data.gov.uk has released LOGD datasets together with OGD raw datasets since its launch in January 2010. The LOD2 project [20] proposes a definition for *knowledge extraction* that can provide guidance in "better" or "worse" information modeling choices. According to their definition, knowledge extraction requires "the extraction result to go beyond the creation of structured information" by "reusing existing formal knowledge (identifiers or ontologies)" and "facilitating inferencing". The group surveyed tools and techniques for knowledge extraction, described them using an OWL Tool Survey Schema, and provide the results as linked data[44]. The diversity of tools in their survey and others like it[45] suggest a variety of requirements from different shareholders within the Linked Data community, and by extension the Linked Open Government Data community.

3.7 Conclusion and Future Work

The TWC LOGD Portal has been recognized as playing an important role in U.S. open government data activities including helping with the deployment of Semantic Web technologies within the Data.gov website, the official access point for open government data from U.S. federal government agencies. This success is due in part to the large volume of LOGD data (billions of RDF triples) produced by the TWC LOGD portal and the agile development of demonstrations of LOGD data published through the Portal. In particular, the LOGD production infrastructure demonstrates a scalable solution for converting raw OGD datasets into RDF, and an extensible solution for the incremental enhancement of LOGD to improve its quality.

TWC's LOGD production infrastructure makes both research and development contributions, especially: we designed a data organization model for LOGD datasets to support persistent and extensible LOGD production; we have developed a collection of open source tools, especially csv2rdf4lod, to provide infrastructural support to LOGD production automation; we have designed and captured provenance metadata, covering data structural relations and data processing workflow, to support deeper understanding of LOGD data and accountability evaluation over LOGD datasets from multiple sources.

Future work will always involve integrating additional OGD datasets, which is motivated by our recent international dataset catalog that aggregates metadata and download URLs for over three hundred thousand OGD datasets worldwide. While we have presented an infrastructure to systematically and repeatedly improve the

---

[44] http://data.lod2.eu/2011/tools/ket/

[45] http://www.mkbergman.com/sweet-tools/

quality of LOGD by linking entities and reusing existing ontologies, further work is needed to expose this functionality in a form approachable by users and their collaborators. One approach is our recent "instance hub" that will allow government agencies to define canonical URIs for entities frequently used in OGD datasets but not defined in Linked Data sources. Finally, as datasets become integrated and connect, it will be very interesting to begin to analyze this connectivity in general as well as for particular user interests.

3.8 Acknowledgements

The work in this paper was supported by grants from the National Science Foundation, DARPA, National Institutes of Health, Microsoft Research Laboratories, Lockheed Martin Advanced Technology Laboratories, Fujitsu Laboratories of America and LGS Bell Labs Innovations. Support was also provided by the Air Force Research Laboratory. Sponsorship details may be found on the TWC LOGD Portal.

References

1. Alani, H., Dupplaw, D., Sheridan, J., O'Hara, K., Darlington, J., Shadbolt, N. and Tullo, C. Unlocking the potential of public sector information with semantic web technology. In *ISWC/ASWC*, pages 708–721, 2007.
2. Berners-Lee, T. Putting government data online. http://www.w3.org/DesignIssues/GovData.html, accessed Sep 25, 2010, 2009.
3. DiFranzo, D., Graves, A., Erickson, J.S., Li, Ding, Michaelis, J., Lebo, T., Patton, E., Williams, G.T., Li, Xian, Zheng, Jin Guang, Flores, J., McGuinness, D.L. and Hendler, J. The web is my back-end: Creating mashups with linked open government data. In *Linked Open Government Data*, 2011.
4. Li, Ding, Difranzo, D., Graves, A., Michaelis, J., Li, Xian, McGuinness, D.L. and Hendler, J. Data-gov wiki: Towards linking government data. In *Proceedings of the AAAI 2010 Spring Symposium on Linked Data Meets Artificial Intelligence*, 2010.
5. Li, Ding, Difranzo, D., Graves, A., Michaelis, J., Li, Xian, McGuinness, D.L. and Hendler, J. Twc data-gov corpus: Incrementally generating linked government data from data.gov. In *Proceedings of the 19th International World Wide Web conference (WWW2010) (developer track)*, 2010.
6. Li, Ding, Lebo, T., Erickson, J.S., DiFranzo, D., Williams, G.T., Li, Xian, Michaelis, J., Graves, A., Zheng, Jin Guang, Shangguan, Z., Flores, J., McGuinness, D.L. and Hendler, J. Twc logd: A portal for linked open government data ecosystems. *Web Semantics: Science, Services and Agents on the World Wide Web*, In Press, Accepted Manuscript:–, 2011.
7. Erickson, J., Shi, Yongmei, Li, Ding, Rozell, E., Zheng, Jin and Hendler, J. Twc international open government dataset catalog (triplification challenge submission). In *Proceedings the 7th International Conference on Semantic Systems, I-SEMANTICS 2011, Graz, Austria.*, ACM International Conference Proceeding Series. ACM, 2011.
8. Goodwin, J., Dolbear, C. and Hart G. Geographical linked data: The administrative geography of great britain on the semantic web. *Transactions in GIS*, 12(s1):19–30, 2009.
9. Hartig, O. Provenance information in the web of data. In *Proceedings of the Linked Data on the Web (LDOW) Workshop at WWW*, Madrid, Spain, 2009.

10. Lange, C. Krextor – an extensible XML→RDF extraction framework. In Chris Bizer, Sören Auer, and Gunnar AAstrand Grimnes, editors, *Scripting and Development for the Semantic Web (SFSW)*, number 449 in CEUR Workshop Proceedings, Aachen, May 2009.
11. Lebo, T. and Williams, G.T. Converting governmental datasets into linked data. In *Proceedings of the 6th International Conference on Semantic Systems*, I-SEMANTICS '10, pages 38:1–38:3, 2010.
12. Li, Xian, Lebo, T. and McGuinness, D.L. Provenance-based strategies to develop trust in semantic web applications. In *The Third International Provenance and Annotation Workshop (IPAW 2010)*, pages 182–197, 2010.
13. McGuinness, D.L., Li, Ding, da Silva, P.P. and Chang, C. Pml 2: A modular explanation interlingua. In *Proceedings of the AAAI 2007 Workshop on Explanation-Aware Computing*, July 2007.
14. McGuinness, D.L., Furtado, V., da Silva, P.P., Li, Ding, Glass, A. and Chang, C. Explaining semantic web applications. In *Semantic Web Engineering in the Knowledge Society*, pages 1–24. Information Science Reference, 2008. (chapter 1).
15. Michaelis, J. and McGuinness, D.L. Towards provenance aware comment tracking for web applications. In *The Third International Provenance and Annotation Workshop (IPAW 2010)*, pages 265–273, 2010.
16. Moreau, L., Clifford, B., Freire, J., Futrelle, J., Gil, Y., Groth, P., Kwasnikowska, N., Miles, S., Missier, P., Myers, J., Plale, B., Simmhan, Y., Stephan, E. and Van den Bussche, J. The open provenance model core specification (v1.1). *Future Generation Computer Systems*, 27(6):743 – 756, 2011.
17. Parsons, M.A., Duerr, R., and Minster, J.B.. Data Citation and Peer Review. *EOS Transactions*, 91:297–298, August 2010.
18. Sahoo, S.S., Thomas, C. and Sheth, A. Knowledge modeling and its application in life sciences: A tale of two ontologies. In *Proceedings of WWW*, 2006.
19. Smith, A. Government online. URL: http://www.pewinternet.org/Reports/2010/Government-Online.aspx, accessed on Jan 25, 2011.
20. Hellmann, S, Unbehauen, J., Zaveri, A., Lehmann, J., Auer, S., Tramp, S., Williams, H., Erling, O., Thibodeau, T. Jr., Idehen, K., Blumauer, A. and Nagy, H. LOD2 - Creating Knowledge out of Interlinked Data. Deliverable 3.1.1. Report on Knowledge Extraction from Structured Sources. URL: http://static.lod2.eu/Deliverables/deliverable-3.1.1.pdf, accessed on August 15, 2011.

Chapter 4
Linking Geographical Data for Government and Consumer Applications

Tom Heath and John Goodwin

Abstract Given the influence of geography on our lives, it is of little surprise that this dimension runs through many of the data sets available on the Web as Linked Data, and plays a crucial ongoing role in many attempts to visualise and build applications upon these. The importance of opening access to governmental data resources is increasingly recognised, and those with a geographic flavour are no exception. In this chapter we describe how the national mapping agency of Great Britain approached the publication of various key data sets as Linked Data, detailing many of the data modelling decisions taken. We then explore a small sample of the applications that have been built on these and related data sets, demonstrating how governmental data sets can underpin government and consumer applications alike. The chapter concludes with presentation of a deployed approach for linking vast volumes of geographic data, thereby significantly increasing the density of links between geographic data sets in the Web of Data.

4.1 Introduction

Space and time are constructs that connect the most diverse aspects of our existence, frequently serving as lenses through which we view the world around us. The power and influence of geography as an organisational dimension for data provides the thematic backdrop to this chapter, in which we will explore some examples of how the concept of Linked Data [3] has been applied to geographical data, for use in governmental and consumer applications.

In their survey of the topology of the Web of Data, Heath and Bizer [7] report that data sets in the geographic domain contribute more than one fifth of the RDF

Correspondance author: Tom Heath, Talis Systems Ltd, 43 Temple Row, Birmingham, B2 5LS, United Kingdom, e-mail: tom.heath@talis.com. See the List of Contributors for full contact details.

triples in the Web of Data. Noteworthy landmarks in this area include *Geonames*[1] as well as Linked Data conversions of reference data sets such as *EuroStat*, the *CIA World Factbook*, the *US Census*, and *LinkedGeoData* [1], a Linked Data set of more than 350 million spatial features based on data from *OpenStreetMap*. In these latter cases, one party has been responsible for initial publication of the data under an open license, while a second party has undertaken its conversion to Linked Data and subsequent publication on the Web. A similar model has been adopted in various national initiatives to bring geographical information to the Web of Data[2][3].

In this chapter we will report on how one organisation has begun to publish Linked Data, at source, describing the complex administrative geography of Great Britain. We will then explore how this and related data sets are already supporting a range of government-related and consumer applications, before presenting mechanisms for increasing the degree of interconnectivity between sets of geographically-oriented Linked Data.

4.2 Publishing Administrative and Postal Geography as Linked Data

Ordnance Survey has recently begun to model the administrative and postal geography of Great Britain in RDF and publish this on the Web as Linked Data. In this section we will explore the data modelling decisions underpinning this initiative.

4.2.1 What is Ordnance Survey?

Ordnance Survey is the national mapping agency of Great Britain, with a responsibility for the collection, maintenance and distribution of a wide range of geographic information used regularly by government, business and individuals [9]. In this context, Ordnance Survey maintains a number of data sets that capture the administrative and postal geography of Great Britain – data sets that collectively underpin many aspects of the administrative and governmental functions of the nation.

---

[1] http://www.geonames.org/

[2] http://geo.linkeddata.es/

[3] http://data-gov.tw.rpi.edu/

4.2.2 What is the Administrative Geography?

The term *administrative geography* refers to the "hierarchy of areas relating to na-tional and local government in the UK"[4]. The administrative geography of Great Britain, which together with Northern Ireland makes up the United Kingdom, is based around a well defined, though sometimes confusing, structure. At the top level are the European regions, these include Scotland and Wales and the nine *Government Office Regions* (GORs) of England – the primary statistical subdivisions of England.

Each GOR covers a number of *local authority regions*. Local authority regions include *counties, unitary authorities, metropolitan districts* and the *Greater London Authority*, and *London boroughs*. Counties are further sub-divided into *districts*. Districts, metropolitan districts, unitary authorities and London boroughs are further broken down into *wards*. Electoral wards/divisions are the base unit of UK admin-istrative geography such that all higher units are built up from them. Wards are the regions used to elect local government councillors. At the lowest level are *parishes* and *communities*.

Running parallel to the administrative geography is the *civil voting geography*. This consists of *Westminster constituencies*, which form the basis by which Mem-bers of Parliament are elected to the House of Commons. Scotland is also made up of *Scottish Parliament electoral regions*, which in turn are made up of the *Scottish Parliament constituencies* used to elect members of the Scottish Government. Sim-ilarly, Wales is is made up of *Welsh Assembly electoral regions*, which in turn are made up of the *Welsh Assembly constituencies* used to elect members of the Welsh Assembly. The Greater London Authority is made up of *Greater London Authority Assembly constituencies* used to elect members of the London Assembly.

4.2.3 Publishing the Administrative Geography as Linked Data

The topological relationships between regions in the administrative geography are based on the eight qualitative spatial predicates defined in the *Region Connection Calculus* (RCC8) [6]:

- disconnected (DC)
- externally connected (EC)
- equal (EQ)
- partially overlapping (PO)
- tangential proper part (TPP)
- tangential proper part inverse (TPPi)
- non-tangential proper part (NTPP)
- non-tangential proper part inverse (NTPPi)

---

[4] http://www.statistics.gov.uk/geography/admin_geog.asp

Fig. 4.1 The eight qualitative spatial relations defined in the Region Connection Calculus (RCC8)

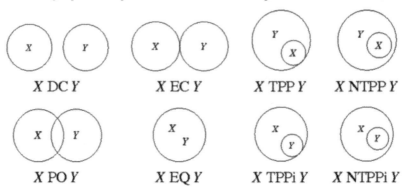

These relationships can be combined to form others. For example, a proper part relation can be constructed that is the *superproperty* of both *tangential proper part* and *non-tangential proper part*. The semantics of the RCC8 predicates are further defined in a composition table, and this can be used to perform qualitative spatial reasoning. For example, if *Region A* is *externally connected* to *Region B*, and *Region B* is a *non-tangential proper part* of *Region C* then we can infer that *Region A* either *partially overlaps Region C* or is a *proper part* of *Region C*.

4.2.3.1 The Spatial Relations Ontology

In order to represent the administrative geography in RDF a *Spatial Relations* ontology was created based on the RCC8 predicates. Some predicates were renamed in order to be more usable by those not expert in the Region Connection Calculus. Furthermore, the distinction between tangential and non-tangential proper parts was not always found to be useful. Consequently these terms were merged into a new `contains` relation, while their inverses were merged into a new `within` relation. The mapping between terms used in RCC8 and the Spatial Relations ontology[5] is as follows:

RCC8	Spatial Relations Ontology	Property Characteristics
disconnected	disjoint	symmetric
externally connected	touches	symmetric
partially overlapping	partiallyOverlaps	symmetric
equal	equals	symmetric, reflexive, transitive
proper part	within	transitive
proper part inverse	contains	transitive

---

[5] http://data.ordnancesurvey.co.uk/ontology/spatialrelations/

The *Web Ontology Language* (OWL)[6] can be used to capture many characteristics of these properties. For example, the contains relationship is *transitive*. This means that if *Region A* contains *Region B*, and *Region B* contains *Region C* then we can infer that *Region A* contains *Region C*. Relationships such as touches are *symmetric*, meaning that if *Region A* touches *Region B* then *Region B* touches *Region A*.

As described above, the administrative geography of Great Britain is formed from a number of well defined sub-geographies, such as local authority geography. These sub-geographies contain a number of well-defined containment hierarchies which are captured explicitly using the contains and within terms from the Spatial Relations ontology and expressed in RDF. The transitive closure of this hierarchy is also stated explicitly in the RDF data, meaning that not only are the county – district and district – parish containments listed, but so are the county – parish containments. However, containment is only stated explicitly for well defined nested geographies. For example, there are no explicit containment relationships between unitary authorities and Westminster constituencies so these are not reflected in the RDF. Explicit touches relationships are given between regions of the same type, and in some cases these are also stated between different regions where this makes sense (for example, where a county touches a unitary authority).

A number of extra predicates have been added to the data to enable query shortcuts, including sub-properties of contains and within which enable links between specific region types. For example, the predicate parish connects a region to all of the parishes contained in the region. These relations are listed in the table below.

Spatial Relation	Contextual Spatial Relation
contains	constituency, county, district, parish, ward, westminster-Constituency
within	inCounty, inDistrict, inEuropeanRegion, inRegion

4.2.3.2 Publication as Linked Data

Having been modelled according to the Spatial Relations ontology and described in RDF, the administrative geography was published as Linked Data at [7]. The first release of this data comprised of a gazetteer of the administrative regions of Great Britain, in which each administrative and voting region is identified by a URI of the form:

- http://data.ordnancesurvey.co.uk/id/*[16 digit identifier]*

For example, the URI for The City of Southampton is:

- http://data.ordnancesurvey.co.uk/id/7000000000037256

---

[6] http://www.w3.org/TR/owl2-overview

[7] http://data.ordnancesurvey.co.uk/

Dereferencing these URIs leads the client to a document describing the region identified by the URI, including properties such as its name and the coordinates of a representative point, guaranteed to lie within the region, and expressed in terms of both WGS84 lat/long and *British National Grid* eastings/northings.

4.2.3.3 Representing Boundary Geometry

As Ordnance Survey is responsible for surveying the boundaries of administrative areas, these RDF descriptions of regions can also include detailed boundary information. This might be used by spatial databases or GIS applications to perform quantitative spatial queries, such as finding all of the wards in *The County of Hampshire*. At present, however, the technology required to perform qualitative spatial queries based on coordinate and geometry information within RDF is rather immature and not widely deployed. For this reason, the topological relations between administrative regions was made explicit in the Linked Data, in the form of RDF triples connecting these regions, as described above.

Nevertheless, for completeness, the boundary geometry is also included in the Linked Data descriptions of the administrative geography. This can be achieved in a number of ways, with ongoing discussions on best practices[8] and no de facto standard at present. One option is to encode the geometry in the graph so that the polygon information can be interrogated using a SPARQL query. Another option favours the notion of geometrical primitives that can be manipulated through extensions to SPARQL. This would put geometrical objects like points, lines and polygons on the same footing as other datatypes, e.g. dates.

The initial release of the Ordnance Survey Linked Data adopted the latter approach, although this may be subject to change as best practices crystalise. This approach treats a geometry as a separate entity to the geographic region. The URI identifying the geometry is linked to the region URI via an `extent` predicate. The boundary information of the geometry is then encoded in an XML literal using the *Geographic Markup Language (GML)*. The geometry URI is linked to this XML literal through an `asGML` predicate, as shown below:

```
<http://data.ordnancesurvey.co.uk/id/geometry/96957>
  rdf:type geometry:AbstractGeometry ;
geometry:asGML
  '<gml:Polygon
    xmlns:gml="http://www.opengis.net/gml"
    srsName="os:BNG">
      <gml:exterior>
        <gml:LinearRing>
          <gml:posList srsDimension="2">
            443348.1
            108678.3
            443371.2
            108657.8
```

---

[8] http://vocamp.org/wiki/Geometry-vocab

```
          443483.2
          108558.5
          ...
          443348.1
          108678.3
        </gml:posList>
      </gml:LinearRing>
    </gml:exterior>
  </gml:Polygon>'^^rdf:XMLLiteral ;
```

4.2.4 Publishing the Postal Geography as Linked Data

The release of the administrative geography gazetteer was followed shortly by publication of Linked Data for every *postcode* in Great Britain. Postcodes, such as *SO17 1DP*, are unique references and identify an average of fifteen addresses. In some cases, where an address receives a substantial amount of mail, a postcode will apply to just one address. The maximum number of postal addresses a single postcode can serve is one hundred. A *postcode unit* is a region covered by a unique postcode. A *postcode sector* is a region comprising one or more *postcode units* and is distinguished by the number third from the end of a full postcode; for example, the postcode unit identified by the postcode *SO17 1DP* is located within the postcode sector *SO17 1*. There are approximately 9000 postcode sectors in Great Britain. Similarly, *postcode districts* (e.g. *SO17*) are built up from *postcode sectors*, and *postcode areas* (e.g. *SO*) are built up from *postcode districts*.

Postcode units, sectors, districts and areas are all described in the Ordnance Survey Linked Data describing the postal geography, also published at [9]. Each postcode unit within this data set is identified by a URI of the form:

- http://data.ordnancesurvey.co.uk/id/postcodeunit/*[postcode]*

British National Grid and WGS84 lat/long coordinates are also allocated to each postcode unit, with the exception of a small number of cases where this information is not available. These coordinates correspond to a representative point within that postcode unit. There are explicit topological `within` relationships between postcode units and their corresponding postcode sectors, districts and areas. Postcode units are also explicitly linked to their containing ward, district, country and, where applicable, county. It is worth noting that in some cases a postcode may fall within more than one region, in which case it will be associated with the region within which its given British National Grid coordinate falls.

The following code shows the typical RDF output for a postcode unit in the Ordnance Survey Linked Data:

```
<http://data.ordnancesurvey.co.uk/id/postcodeunit/SO171DP>
    rdf:type
```

---

[9] http://data.ordnancesurvey.co.uk/

```
   postcode:PostcodeUnit ;
rdfs:label
   "SO17 1DP" ;
spatialrelations:easting
   "442356"^^xsd:decimal ;
spatialrelations:northing
   "114001"^^xsd:decimal ;
geo:lat
   "50.923909"^^xsd:decimal ;
geo:long
   "-1.398739"^^xsd:decimal ;
spatialrelations:within
   <http://data.ordnancesurvey.co.uk/id/postcodearea/SO> ,
   <http://data.ordnancesurvey.co.uk/id/postcodedistrict/
      SO17> ,
   <http://data.ordnancesurvey.co.uk/id/postcodesector/
      SO171> ;
postcode:country
   ns1:england ;
postcode:district
   <http://data.ordnancesurvey.co.uk/id/7000000000037256> ;
postcode:ward
   <http://data.ordnancesurvey.co.uk/id/7000000000017707> .
```

4.3 Applications of Linked Geographical Data

In this section we will explore some Linked Data applications that have a geographical flavour, ranging from simple mashups that serve a specific purpose by combining
a handful of data sets, to more generic tools that provide a geographical view over
ad-hoc data sets.

4.3.1 Map-Based Mashups with Geographical Linked Data

Maps have long been used to demonstrate the outcomes of data integration efforts,
and those based on geographical Linked Data are no exception. Here we will discuss
several map-based mashups of geographical Linked Data, each of which draws on
one or more of the benefits of Linked Data, namely: (a) the use of common identifiers for items of interest; (b) the ability to easily look up those identifiers; and
(c) the use of a common data model that allows easy merging of data from disparate
sources.

4.3.1.1 CSAKTiveSpace

One of the earliest practical examples of a *Semantic Web* application, predating the emergence of the Linked Data principles and best practices, was CSAKTiveSpace[10][11]. This application enabled the exploration of the Computer Science research field in the UK along the dimensions of topics, people and geographic regions, with a map-based visualisation as its centre-piece.

4.3.1.2 BIS Research Funding Explorer

More recently, the BIS Research Funding Explorer[11] uses Linked Data from the *data.gov.uk* initiative[12] to enable users to browse UK research projects by subject and organisation. This view can be further refined to show which projects are being funded in each *government office region*. For example, the projects being funded at the West Midlands region are shown at [13].

Arguably it would also be advantageous to be able to view the geographic distribution of projects at a more fine grained level. This has been made possible by linking the research funding data to the geographical data from Ordnance Survey described above, in particular using the postcode information present in each data set (e.g. the postcode of the funded institution, in the case of the funding data) to make the connection. By exploiting the topographical relations present in the Linked Data from Ordnance Survey, the original research funding data can be enriched with knowledge about the ward, district and county (where applicable) of each institution. This means a user can now analyse research funding by local authority area as well as European region. This capability is illustrated in the screenshot at [14]. Using the spatial relationships in the Ordnance Survey Linked Data also enables more complex analyses. For example, a user could compare funding in one region with funding in its neighbouring region.

4.3.1.3 Driving Test Centres near Postcodes

This application is another example of a simple Linked Data mashup originating in the *data.gov.uk* initiative. The original data set contained no coordinates for the driving test centres, only an address and postcode. By aggregating data about driving test centres with postcode Linked Data from Ordnance Survey, the mashup provides a tool for finding the nearest driving test centres to a particular location, specified in terms of postcode or lat/long coordinate. The creation of these links, from driving

---

[10] http://www.aktors.org/technologies/csaktivespace/

[11] http://bis.clients.talis.com/

[12] http://data.gov.uk

[13] http://bis.clients.talis.com/region?uri=http%3A%2F%2Fstatistics.data.gov.uk%2Fid%2Fgovernment-office-region%2FF

[14] http://www.flickr.com/photos/tommyh/5986814401/

test centres to postcodes, also lowers the barrier for data consumers who wish to exploit this data in future geographical applications, as this integration process does not need to be repeated each time the data is reused. This mashup is shown in the screenshot at [15] and can also be explored at [16] and [17], which demonstrate the use of the Linked Data API [12] to map complex SPARQL queries to more familiar API requests.

4.3.1.4 English Heritage Site Browser

The *English Heritage Site Browser*[18] is a simple application that provides users with a map-oriented view of historically-significant sites in each borough of England. This is achieved through the merging of two existing data sets, the Ordnance Survey Administrative Geography data set, available as Linked Data and described above, and the English Heritage data set of historic sites, converted to Linked Data for this purpose. The availability of boundary data for England enables each historic site to be geolocated in one or more boroughs, while the availability of boundary data for each historic site enables their extent to be depicted on a map. This is illustrated in the screenshot at [19], which shows English Heritage sites on and around Liverpool's historic waterfront.

With Linked Data now available that connects historic sites and boroughs, third parties can combine these data sets with others and pose additional questions that may not be of interest to the original data publisher. For example:

- Which borough has the most historical sites?
- Which borough (or other administrative region) has the highest concentration of historic sites?
- Which historical sites are near to a particular school?
- Does concentration of historical sites correlate other social, cultural or economic measures?

4.3.2 Generic Applications for Linked Geographical Data

Geographically-oriented applications of Linked Data are not limited to task-specific mashups. The *LinkedGeoData Browser*[20], for example, provides a generic map-

---

[15] http://www.flickr.com/photos/tommyh/5987373536/
[16] http://labs.data.gov.uk/lod/os/postcode/SO171DP/driving-test-centre
[17] http://labs.data.gov.uk/lod/location/50.902093,-1.398722/driving-test-centre
[18] http://iandavis.com/2011/english-heritage/
[19] http://www.flickr.com/photos/tommyh/5986814599/
[20] http://browser.linkedgeodata.org/

based interface to the LinkedGeoData data set[1]. The SemaPlorer application[21] takes this concept one step further and presents a map-oriented view of data from the *Geonames, DBpedia* [5] and *Flickr* data sets, as well as individual *FOAF*[22] files published on the Web.

Each of these applications operates over a largely predetermined collection of data sets. In actuality, however, Linked Data enables ad-hoc discovery and integration of new data published on the Web, through traversal of RDF links. One application that exploits this feature is *DBpedia Mobile*[23] [2], which attempts to look up, from other sources on the Web, additional information about the resources represented in its map view.

4.3.3 Enabling a New Generation of Geographical Applications

While each of the applications described above reflect rather traditional notions of how data may be presented, other novel options have been demonstrated. For example, the *Postcode Paper*[24] [25] took data published via the *data.gov.uk* initiative and produced a local newspaper tailored to a specific postcode, including extensive local information such as neighbourhood statistics and transport information. In producing the paper, the creators had to manually integrate all the necessary information for the single postcode used to demonstrate the concept. As more and more Linked Data becomes available, the potential to automatically produce such a publication for every postcode becomes increasingly feasible.

4.4 Linking Geographical Data

Links that connect items in distinct data sets are critical to the efficacy and value of the Web of Data, as they streamline the discovery and integration of data from multiple sources. However, despite the critical importance of such links, they represent a relatively small proportion of the triples in the Web of Data. As of October 2010, fewer than one percent of the RDF triples in geographic data sets are links to related items in other data sets [4]. This sparsity of links poses significant challenges for application developers wishing to discover and consume data in this domain.

---

[21] http://www.uni-koblenz-landau.de/koblenz/fb4/institute/IFI/AGStaab/Research/systeme/semap

[22] http://xmlns.com/foaf/spec/

[23] http://beckr.org/DBpediaMobile/

[24] http://www.guardian.co.uk/technology/2009/nov/11/official-data-postcode-newspaper

[25] http://blog.newspaperclub.com/2009/10/16/data-gov-uk-newspaper/

Of those links that do exist, most are used to state equivalence between resources using the `owl:sameAs` predicate. For example, the official link set[26] connecting *DBpedia* to *Geonames* contains more than 86,000 links, all of which use the `owl:sameAs` property. Other sets of links represent aspects of adminstrative geography, as described above, however these are relatively small in number. In order to increase the volume and the utility of links in the Web of Data, a broader range of link types are required, including those that enable different forms of navigation between data sets.

For example, user needs will be best served in many consumer- and citizen-oriented application scenarios by links that connect things *near* to a particular location, enabling users to find nearby amenities of a particular type. This use case is not addressed by equivalence links, while precise definitions of administrative regions and their spatial relations are likely to be of less relevance in consumer applications (e.g. finding nearby restaurants) than in those related to government and administrative functions (e.g. finding all wards within a county).

Data sets such as LinkedGeoData [1] do enable users to find *points of interest (POIs)* near to a particular geographical location, but have the following limitations:

- This capability only extends to items within the same data set, i.e. proximity links are not made between items in different data sets.
- Proximity relations are only exposed through custom APIs, limiting the ability to *follow your nose* to related items.

Various frameworks, such as *Silk* [13] and *LIMES* [8], have been developed that enable links to be generated across different data sets, often producing `owl:sameAs` triples as output. LIMES computes estimates of the similarity between instances using text similarity metrics, and uses these estimates to reduce the number of comparisons needed between items in determining potential linkages. In addition to various string similarity metrics, Silk is able to exploit data from the surrounding graph for similarity assessment, and has support for a geographical distance metric, thereby offering some geographical linking capability.

A major limitation of these frameworks is their use of local or remote SPARQL endpoints for data access. Consequently, their performance will always be constrained by the performance of the underlying RDF storage and query implementations, while their ability to fully exploit data locality is limited. In the remainder of this section we will present a technique for generating large numbers of *proximity* links between items in geographically-oriented Linked Data sets. This technique is designed to operate at massive scale, generating a data set of immediate value for consumer applications that can be readily exploited without specialised geo-spatial reasoning infrastructure.

---

[26] `http://downloads.dbpedia.org/3.6/links/geonames_links.nt.bz2`

4.4.1 Snap-to-Grid Proximity Linking

The approach is based on the latitude/longitude grid of the WGS84 coordinate system[27]. The first stage in computing proximity links is to *snap* each geolocated item/POI in the input data to its nearest grid intersection point, as illustrated in Figure 4.2 (a).

This *snap-to-grid* process is achieved by computing a hash of the item's latitude/longitude. By exploiting collisions inherent in the design of the hash function, nearby items are frequently snapped to the same grid intersection point. In the simplest case, proximity links are then generated between each of these items. However, due to the design of the hash function, some nearby items will always snap to different grid points, as illustrated in Figure 4.2 (b), where the middle point is nearer to the left-most point, but snaps to a different grid point.

To overcome this issue, each item is snapped to its nearest grid point and also to the eight that surround it, as shown in Figure 4.2 (c). Proximity links are then created between all items snapped to a particular grid point, as before.

Proximity links are created in the form of RDF triples that use the `near` predicate defined in the OpenVocab namespace[28]. For example, the triple shown below states that *Birkby Junior School* is *near* the *Kirklees Incinerator*:

```
<http://education.data.gov.uk/id/school/107626>
   <http://open.vocab.org/terms/near>
      <http://dbpedia.org/resource/Kirklees_Incinerator> .
```

4.4.1.1 The Meaning of Near

At any specific position on the Earth's surface the notion of *near*, as it relates to this technique and data set, can be quantified in terms of the spacing in the latitude/longitude grid and the level of granularity applied in the *snap-to-grid* hashing function. A default granularity is used that broadly equates *near* to a moderate human walking distance. However, no attempt is made to further or more precisely quantify this notion, due to its highly subjective and context-dependent nature. The following factors may all influence the perception of proximity in a particular context:

- The geographic range of available **modes of transport**.
- Ease of travel as determined by features in the **surrounding terrain**, e.g. mountains, rivers or other natural barriers.
- The population density of the locale, and therefore the overall **density** of points of interest in the region; fewer points of interest in the surrounding area will likely result in a broader notion of proximity than in densely populated areas.
- The **type** and relative **scarcity** of points of interest; those points of interest that are by nature relatively scarce (e.g. airports) may be more readily considered

---

[27] http://earth-info.nga.mil/GandG/wgs84/
[28] http://open.vocab.org/terms/near

Fig. 4.2 (a) Each item is snapped to its nearest grid intersection point. (b) In the simple case, nearby items can snap to different grid intersection points. (c) Items are snapped to the nearest grid intersection point, and the eight that surround it.

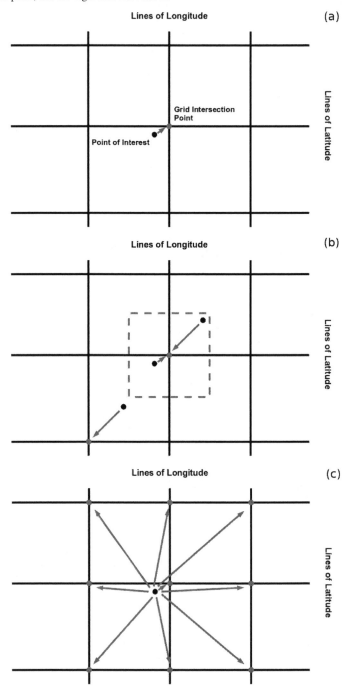

near than less scarce items (e.g. pharmacies), however the notion of *near* should be distinguished from *nearest*.

Given the diversity of these factors and the infeasibility of anticipating all subjective proximity judgements *a priori*, no attempt has been made to provide definitions of *near* that varies between different points on the globe. The one exception to this policy is the natural variation in our definition of proximity that stems from the nature of the latitude/longitude grid. The convergence of lines of longitude at the poles means that the definition of proximity becomes more narrow the further one travels from the equator. In contrast, the depth of the area within which points are snapped to the same grid intersection point remains constant across the globe as lines of latitude are parallel.

The limitation of a fixed yet globally inconsistent definition of *near* is addressed in the following way: each grid point represented in the data set is connected to the eight that surround it by further RDF triples that correspond to directional bearings between grid points, specifically *north, north-east, east, south-east, south, south-west, west, north-west*, e.g.:

```
<http://rdfize.com/geo/point/51.52/-0.13/>
  <http://open.vocab.org/terms/toSouthEast>
    <http://rdfize.com/geo/point/51.51/-0.12/> .
```

This additional degree of connectivity between points enables consumers of the data to traverse the graph, and consequently entire geographical areas, using the principle of *follow your nose*, whereby each link followed yields related data, including onward links that yield more, and so on. This feature of the data also enables consumers to define arbitrarily large areas within which they would like to locate items of interest, by following all bearing links from a specific point, outwards to a predetermined degree. This approach may be used to systematically scan the data set for things of a specific type (e.g. working outwards until an airport is found), or to increase the size of an initial bounding before computing true distances between the items it contains.

4.4.1.2 Computational Properties of the Approach

The ability to process very large volumes of input data was an essential design requirement of the approach. The $O(n)$ complexity of the hash function discussed above has enabled this scale requirement to be partially satisfied, with the $O(n^2)$ complexity of generating all pairwise proximity links limited to relatively small values of n.

To exploit these properties and take advantage of parallelisation, the entire data generation process is implemented as a series of jobs executed on the *Hadoop MapReduce* framework[29]. The last of these jobs is responsible for removing duplicate *near* statements that are an artefact of the approach: items that snap to the

---

[29] http://hadoop.apache.org/

same initial grid point will also snap to the same eight surrounding grid points, resulting in the generation of eight redundant proximity links that are removed in a final deduplication stage.

4.4.2 Results of the Approach

To give an indication of the results of applying the *snap-to-grid* approach described above, this section briefly reports on the output data generated when using the Geonames, DBpedia, and *Schools in Great Britain* data sets as input.

Table 4.4.2 illustrates the size of these input data sets, in terms of number of points of interest and number of RDF triples (the count of RDF triples refers to just those specifying latitude and longitude, and is therefore simply twice the number of points of interest):

Data Set	Size (POIs)	Size (RDF Triples)
Geonames	6,903,843	13,807,686
DBpedia	386,205	772,410
Schools in GB	64,180	128,360

Returning to the previous example of *Birkby Junior School*, the triples shown below state that the school is *near* a number of intersection points in the latitude/longitude grid (represented by the URIs in the `http://rdfize.com/geo/point/` namespace), as well as various other points of interest from the Geonames and DBpedia data sets:

```
<http://education.data.gov.uk/id/school/107626>
  <http://open.vocab.org/terms/near>
    <http://rdfize.com/geo/point/53.66/-1.78/> ,
    <http://rdfize.com/geo/point/53.65/-1.79/> ,
    <http://rdfize.com/geo/point/53.66/-1.79/> ,
    <http://rdfize.com/geo/point/53.67/-1.79/> ,
    <http://rdfize.com/geo/point/53.67/-1.77/> ,
    ...
    <http://dbpedia.org/resource/Kirklees_Incinerator> ,
    <http://dbpedia.org/resource/
      Rugby_League_Heritage_Centre> ,
    <http://dbpedia.org/resource/
      Huddersfield_Media_Centre_project> ,
    <http://dbpedia.org/resource/George_Hotel,_Huddersfield> ,
    <http://dbpedia.org/resource/Lawrence_Batley_Theatre> ,
    ...
    <http://sws.geonames.org/6466669/> ,
    <http://sws.geonames.org/6495178/> ,
    <http://sws.geonames.org/6511337/> .
```

The total size of the data set resulting from these inputs is 716,143,704 RDF triples. This includes all links within and between the input data sets, in addition to those triples that link points of interest in the input data with URIs minted to represent intersection points in the latitude/longitude grid, and the bearing links that connect those to each other. Table 4.4.2 shows the frequencies of new links created *within* and *between* the input data sets.

	Geonames	DBpedia	Schools in GB
Geonames	28,121,584	5,246,258	225,254
DBpedia		1,729,968	721,656
Schools in GB			59,938

At present the data set does not include any additional triples giving types to the resources in the input data set, or annotating them with labels or additional properties; the data set is purely new links. This decision was taken to avoid the redundancy that would arise from replicating, in this derived data set, data that can be retrieved by dereferencing the original resource URIs. A future iteration of the data set will likely add basic annotations to the grid intersection points, subject to assessment of the impact on the overall size of the data set.

4.4.3 Future Work

The approach described in this section produces a novel data set of immediate potential utility to those building consumer applications with a geographical component. In addition, by generating millions of new links between items in related data sets this approach significantly increases the density of the Web of Data in the geographical domain. According to [4] the number of *out-links* between geographic data sets in the *Linking Open Data Cloud*[30] stood, as of late 2010, at 16,539,378. Therefore, by generating 6,193,168 additional cross-data set links this approach has increased link density in the geographical domain by more than 37%.

Nevertheless, a number of challenges remain in developing the approach to improve the overall quality and utility of the data set. Figure 4.2 (b) highlighted how nearby points of interest that snap to different grid points could be overlooked when generating proximity links. This issue was addressed by also snapping each point to the eight surrounding grid points. This has the effect of increasing the size of the bounding box in which any particular point of interest is located, thereby effectively reducing the degree of skew in the positioning of the bounding box relative to the point of interest. While this modification significantly reduces the error inherent in the approach, some anomalies remain around the edges of the expanded bounding box. Future work should investigate additional strategies for mitigating this issue.

Related to this issue is the use of square bounding boxes to determine proximity relations. This has the effect of preferentially treating points of interest that occur close to the diagonal extremes of bounding boxes, at the expense of those that are closer but located elsewhere relative to the bounding box. This can be addressed in future work by using the *snap-to-grid* approach to define an initial working set of

---

[30] http://richard.cyganiak.de/2007/10/lod/

points of interest that is then analysed further to compute true distances between these. Use of this enhancement to the approach, in tandem with a bounding box that varies in size according to its position on the globe, could also address the issue of the narrowing definition of proximity the further one travels from the equator.

The introduction of a definition of proximity that varies according to the type of the items in question, while desirable, is considered infeasible at present for the following reason: not enough is known about how humans reason about the relative proximity of different types of objects. For example, what are the respective distances underlying a human judgement that a local grocery shop is near to one's home, versus a pharmacy or a supermarket? Without this essential background knowledge a meaningful data set can not be generated that takes type-specificity into account. However, one way in which this approach could benefit from some *type-awareness* is in the exclusion of points in the input data sets that are in fact centroids of wider areas, e.g. a city or country. If such cases could be reliably identified, they would be candidates for a hybrid approach that combines this proximity linking with some form of region-based reasoning, as described above.

One area that may be more promising is the introduction of a definition of proximity that varies according to the density of points of interest in the underlying region. As discussed above, densely populated areas will typically have more points of interest, and therefore possibly a more constrained notion of proximity. This may be accommodated in this approach by increasing the size of the bounding box in low density areas, until a minimal threshold for the number of items in the bounding box is reached.

Lastly, this data set can be used as input to post-processes that generate data with more rigid precision requirements. In addition to the more precise definitions of near described above, items from different data sets that are found to be *near* to each other could be examined to determined if they are in fact the same item. If this post-processing suggests, with a sufficient degree of confidence, that these two points of interest are in fact the same, their corresponding URIs may be linked by an additional triple using the owl:sameAs predicate, further increasing the density of the Web of data. This has the benefit of limiting the more expensive post-processing methods required for this form of instance linking to operating over data sets of significantly smaller sizes.

4.5 Conclusions

The role of geography is pervasive – in our daily lives, in the computing applications we use, and in the data sets that underpin them. As increasing volumes of governmental and public sector data are made openly available according to the Linked Data principles, there will be ever growing opportunities for development of novel applications with both a government and consumer flavour.

In this chapter we have described how Ordnance Survey, the national mapping agency of Great Britain, approached the publication of two pivotal geographic data sets as Linked Data. This exercise has a number of notable features, not least of which the degree of specificity in the data modelling, which enables the extensive topological relationships inherent in the data to be made explicit. This contrasts to and complements the significant number of resources already described on the Web using Linked Data, but modelled primarily in terms of points and coordinates. Furthermore, it demonstrates how Linked Data can be used to unify two data sets, namely the administrative and postal geographies, that have traditionally been perceived as rather disparate, thereby revealing the rich and extensive connections between them. Availability of these data sets has already spawned the creation of a number of simple end-user applications, detailed here, that would not otherwise have been feasible.

If the value of these data sets is to be fully realised, data consumers must be able to discover and integrate those portions relevant to their needs and applications. These discovery and integration processes are dependent on increasing the degree of interconnectivity between sets of Linked Data that have a geographic component. The linking approach presented in this chapter exploits the latitude/longitude grid to generate such links at very large scale, enabling the discovery of related data from disparate data sets and providing input to post-processes able to further increase the link density between geographic data sets.

References

1. Auer, S., Lehmann, J., Hellmann, S.: LinkedGeoData: Adding a Spatial Dimension to the Web of Data. In: Bernstein, A., Karger, D. (eds.) The Semantic Web - ISWC 2009, pp. 731-746. Springer, Heidelberg (2009)
2. Becker, C., Bizer, C.: Exploring the Geospatial Semantic Web with DBpedia Mobile. Web Semantics: Science, Services and Agents on the World Wide Web 7, 278–286 (2009)
3. Bizer, C., Heath, T., Berners-Lee, T.: Linked Data - The Story So Far. Int. J. Semantic Web Inf. Syst. 5, 1–22 (2009)
4. Bizer, C., Jentzsch, A., Cyganiak, R.: State of the LOD Cloud. Freie Universitaet Berlin (2011).
   http://www4.wiwiss.fu-berlin.de/lodcloud/state/. Cited 21 Apr 2011
5. Bizer, C., Lehmann, J., Kobilarov, G., Auer, S., Becker, C., Cyganiak, R., Hellmann, S.: DBpedia - A crystallization point for the Web of Data. Web Semantics: Science, Services and Agents on the World Wide Web 7, 154–165 (2009)
6. Cohn, A.G., Bennett, B., Gooday, J.M., and Gotts, N.: RCC: A calculus for region-based qualitative spatial reasoning. GeoInformatica 1, 275–316 (1997)
7. Heath, T., Bizer, C.: Linked Data – Evolving the Web into a Global Data Space. Morgan and Claypool (2011)
8. Ngonga Ngomo, A.C., Auer, S.: LIMES - A Time-Efficient Approach for Large-Scale Link Discovery on the Web of Data. University of Leipzig (2010).
   http://svn.aksw.org/papers/2011/WWW_LIMES/public.pdf. Cited 21 Apr 2011
9. Ordnance Survey: Annual Report 2009/10. Ordnance Survey (2010).
   http://www.ordnancesurvey.co.uk/. Cited 21 Apr 2011

10. Schenk, S., Saathoff, C., Staab, S., Scherp, A.: SemaPlorer–Interactive semantic exploration of data and media based on a federated cloud infrastructure. Web Semantics: Science, Services and Agents on the World Wide Web **7**, 298–304 (2009)
11. Shadbolt, N. R., Gibbins, N., Glaser, H., Harris, S. and schraefel, m. c.: CS AKTive Space or how we stopped worrying and learned to love the Semantic Web. IEEE Intelligent Systems **19**, 41–47 (2004)
12. Tennison, J.: A Developers' Guide to the Linked Data APIs. HM Government (2010). http://data.gov.uk/blog/guest-post-developers-guide-linked-data-apis-jeni-tennison. Cited 21 Apr 2011
13. Volz, J., Bizer, C., Gaedke, M., Kobilarov, G.: Discovering and Maintaining Links on the Web of Data. In: Bernstein, A., Karger, D. (eds.) The Semantic Web - ISWC 2009, pp. 731-746. Springer, Heidelberg (2009)
14. Wallis, R.: Linked Data Visualisation Launched at Prime Minister's Conference. Talis (2010). http://blogs.talis.com/nodalities/2010/02/linked-data-visualisation-launched-at-prime-ministers-conference.php. Cited 21 Apr 2011

Part II
Improving Linked Data Quality

Governments face several challenges in any data collection and publication effort, regardless of the techniques employed. Data must be accessible to new users, common practices should be applied across governmental agencies to facilitate consistency and the data should be generally useful. In this part, we look at the ways to address these key questions.

Making data sets accessible is a tall order. One approach is to ensure that data sets are adequately described and that the descriptions may be improved over time. Frosterus et al report on their successes improving descriptions of Linked Data sets in Finland. Next, Salas et al demonstrate the efforts the Brazilian government is taking to promote the reuse of standard Linked Data vocabularies. Finally, Richard Cyganiak and his colleagues present a mechanism for recording official statistics in Linked Data. Statistics naturally constitute one of the more generally reusable types of content that governments collect.

Together, these chapters describe methods to increase the quality of Linked Government Data.

Chapter 5
Creating and Publishing Semantic Metadata about Linked and Open Datasets

Matias Frosterus, Eero Hyvönen, and Joonas Laitio

Abstract The number of open datasets available on the web is increasing rapidly with the rise of the Linked Open Data (LOD) cloud and various governmental efforts for releasing public data in various formats, not only in RDF. However, the metadata available for these datasets is often minimal, heterogeneous, and distributed, which makes finding a suitable dataset for a given need problematic. Governmental open datasets are often the basis of innovative applications but the datasets need to be found by the developers first. To address the problem, we present a distributed content creation model and tools for annotating and publishing metadata about linked data and non-RDF datasets on the web. The system DATAFINLAND is based on a modified version of the VoiD vocabulary for describing linked RDF datasets, and uses an online metadata editor SAHA3 connected to ONKI ontology services for annotating contents semantically. The resulting metadata can be published instantly on an integrated faceted search and browsing engine HAKO for human users, as a SPARQL end-point for machine use, and as a source file. As a proof of concept, the system has been applied to LOD and Finnish governmental datasets.

5.1 Semantic Metadata Service for Datasets

Linked Data [15] refers to data published on the web in accordance with four rules [4] and guidelines [5] that allow retrieving metadata related to data entities, and linking data within and between different datasets. The datasets and their relations are represented using RDF (Resource Description Framework) and entities are identified by Uniform Resource Identifiers (URIs)[1], which allows using the HyperText

Correspondance author: Matias Frosterus, Aalto University School of Science P.O. Box 11000 FI-00076 Aalto, Finland University of Helsinki P.O. Box 68 00014 Helsingin Yliopisto, e-mail: matias.frosterus@aalto.fi. See the List of Contributors for full contact details.

[1] http://www.w3.org/TR/uri-clarification/

Transfer Protocol (HTTP) to retrieve either the resources themselves, useful descriptions of them, or links to related entities [6].

The Linked Open Data community project[2] has collected a large number of datasets and mappings between them. However, little metadata about the datasets is provided aside from short, non-uniform descriptions. As the number of linked datasets [13] grows, this approach does not allow for easy understanding of what kind of dataset are offered, who provides them, what is their subject, how they interlink with each other, possible licensing conditions, and so on. Such information should be available both to human users as well as to the applications of the Semantic Web.

Aside from linked datasets in RDF format, various organizations have also began publishing open data in whatever format they had it in. From a semantic web viewpoint, using the linked data would be an optimal dataformat, but opening data in any form is in general better than not publishing data at all [4]. For example, The governments of the United States and the United Kingdom have been releasing their governmental data in an open format[3] in different data formats (CSV, data dumps, XML etc.) and other governments are following suit. Such datasets are released with varying amounts of heterogenous associated metadata, which creates new challenges for finding and interlinking them to each other and with linked data datasets. The work presented in this chapter aims at

1. setting up a uniform metadata schema and vocabularies for annotating all kinds of datasets on the semantic web, as well as
2. a tool for collaborative distributed production of metadata and
3. an effective search tool that helps developers to find the datasets in order to use them for new applications.

There are search engines for finding RDF and other datasets, such as ordinary search engines, SWSE[4] [17], Swoogle[5] [11], Watson[6] [10], and others. However, using such systems—based on the Google-like search paradigm—it is difficult to get the general picture of the contents of the *whole* cloud of the offered datasets. Furthermore, finding suitable datasets based on different selection criteria such as subject topic, size, licensing, publisher, language etc. is not supported. To facilitate this, interoperable metadata about the different aspects or facets of datasets is needed, and faceted search (also called view-based search) [27, 14, 18] can be used to provide an alternative paradigm for string-based search.

This chapter presents a solution approach along these lines for creating, publishing, and finding datasets based on metadata. In contrast to systems like CKAN[7], a

---

[2] http://linkeddata.org/

[3] http://www.data.gov/ and http://data.gov.uk/

[4] http://swse.org/

[5] http://swoogle.umbc.edu/

[6] http://watson.kmi.open.ac.uk/WatsonWUI/

[7] http://www.ckan.net/

widely used system for publishing metadata about datasets, our approach is ontology based, using controlled vocabularies with RDF-based semantics. We make use of the Linked Data oriented VoiD[8] (Vocabulary of Interlinked Datasets) metadata schema [2] with some extensions for describing the datasets. Furthermore, many property values are taken from a set of shared domain ontologies, providing controlled vocabularies with clearly defined semantics. Content is annotated using a web-based annotation tool SAHA3[9] [22] connected to ONKI ontology services[10] [33, 31] that publish the domain ontologies. SAHA3 has been integrated with the lightweight multifaceted search engine HAKO[11] [22], which facilitates automatically forming a faceted search and browsing application for taking in and discerning the datasets on offer. As a proof of concept, the system has been applied to describing the LOD cloud datasets as well as the datasets in the Finnish Open Data Catalogue Project[12] complementing the linked open governmental datasets on a national level. The demonstration system called DATAFINLAND is available online[13]—it received the first prize of the "Apps4–Doing Good With Open Data" competition[14] in the company application series in 2010.

We will first present the general model and tools for creating and publishing metadata about (linked) datasets, and then discuss the VoiD metadata schema and ontology repository ONKI presenting a controlled vocabulary. After this, the annotation tool SAHA3 for distributed semantic content creation is presented along with the faceted publication engine HAKO. Finally, we will provide a review of related work in the area of publishing, searching, and exploring metadata about open datasets including the widely used CKAN registry for open data packages.

5.2 Overview of the Publication Process

Figure 5.1 depicts the generic components and steps needed for producing and publishing metadata about datasets. In the figure, we have marked the tools and resources used in our proof-of-concept system DATAFINLAND in parentheses, but the process model itself is general.

The process begins with the publication of a dataset by its provider (upper right hand corner). Metadata for the dataset is produced either by its original publisher or by a third party, using an annotation tool, in the case of DATAFINLAND the editor SAHA3. A metadata schema, in our case modified voiD, is used to dictate for the distributed and independent content providers the exact nature of the metadata

---

[8] http://www.w3.org/TR/void/

[9] http://www.seco.tkk.fi/services/saha/

[10] http://www.onki.fi/

[11] http://www.seco.tkk.fi/tools/hako/

[12] http://data.suomi.fi/

[13] http://demo.seco.tkk.fi/saha3sandbox/voiD/hako.shtml

[14] http://www.verkkodemokratia.fi/apps4finland

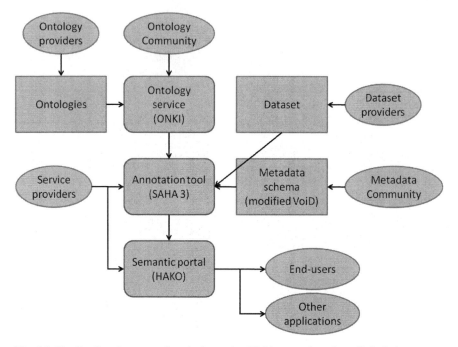

Fig. 5.1 The distributed process of producing and publishing metadata about (linked) datasets

needed according to community standards. Interoperability in annotation values is achieved through shared ontologies that are used for certain property values in the schema (e.g., subject matter and publisher resources are decribed by resources (URIs) taken from corresponding ontologies). The ontologies are developed by experts and provided for the annotation tool as services, in our case by the national ONKI Ontology Service, or by the SAHA3 RDF triple store itself that also implements the ONKI APIs used. Finally, the metadata about the datasets is published in a semantic portal capable of using the annotations to make the data more accessible to the end-user, be that a human or a computer application. For this part, the faceted search engine HAKO is used, with its SPARQL end-point and other APIs. Based on the SPARQL end-point, HAKO can also be used by itself for creating semantic recommendation links from one data instance to another.

5.3 Ontologies

A common practice in community-based annotation is to allow the users to create the needed terms, or tags, freely when describing objects. This facilitates flexibility in annotations and makes it easier for novice users to describe things. On the other hand, in the professional metadata world (e.g., in museums, libraries, and archives) using shared pre-defined thesauri is usually recommended for enhancing interoperability between annotations of different persons, and enhancing search precision and recall in end-user applications. Both approaches are usually needed, and can also be supported to some extent by e.g. suggesting the use of existing tags. For example, in the domain of open datasets, CKAN uses free tagging, but always also suggests using existing ones by autocompletion. This has the benefit that new tags are easy to add but, at the same time, there is a possibility for sharing them. However, the problem with traditional tag-based systems is that it is easy to end up with several different tags that mean the same thing, and in turn a single tag may end up denoting several different things, because the meaning in tags in not explicitly defined anywhere. This is problematic from both a human and a machine use point of view.

The traditional approach for harmonizing content indexing is to use keyword terms taken from shared vocabularies or thesauri [12, 1]. A more advanced approach is to use ontologies [29] where indexing is based on language-free concepts referred to by URIs, and keywords are labels of the actual underlying concepts. Defining the meaning behind the index terms in an explicit way, and furthermore by describing the relations between the different concepts, allows for better interoprability of contents and their use by machines. This is important in many application areas, such as semantic search, information retrieval, semantic linking of contents, and automatic indexing. With even a little extra work, e.g. by just systematically organizing concepts along subclass hierarchies and partonomies, substantial benefits can be obtained [20].

In order to make the use and sharing of ontologies easier, various ontology repositories have been developed [32, 25, 8]. The main idea behind these repositories is to offer a centralized location from which users and applications can find, query and utilize the ontologies. Repositories can also facilitate interoperability, allowing the mapping of concepts between different ontologies and guiding the user in choosing the most appropriate ontology [3].

For DATAFINLAND we used the ONKI Ontology service, which provides a rich environment for using ontologies as web services [21] as well as for browsing and annotation work. ONKI offers traditional web service (WSDL and SOAP) and AJAX APIs for easy integration to legacy applications, such as cataloging systems and search engines, and provides a robust platform for publishing and utilizing ontologies for ontology developers. The simplest way to use ONKI in providing controlled vocabularies for an application is through the Selector Widget. It is an extended HTML input field widget that can be used for mash-ups on any HTML page at the client side with two lines of Javascript code. The widget could be added to, for example, the CKAN web browser based editor, providing then the new possibility of using ontology references as tags in annotations. The ONKI widget provides its user ready-to-use ontology browser functionalities, such as concept finding, semantic disambiguation, and concept (URI) fetching. It can be configured to provide access to a selected ontology or a group of them, possibly on different ONKI-compatible servers [34], to support the use of different languages on the human interface, and so on.

In DATAFINLAND the subject property of a given dataset was connected to the ONKI instance of the General Finnish Ontology (YSO)[15] with some 25,000 concepts, because a major use case of the system is Finnish open datasets. In a similar way, any other ontology such as WordNet[16] or even DBpedia[17] could have been used through ONKI APIs.

5.4 Annotation Schemas

A note on terminology: the word vocabulary can be used to refer to the annotation terms as well as to the annotation schemas in the sense that a vocabulary defines the properties used in the annotations. Here we use the word vocabulary to refer to the terms and the word schema to refer to the annotation structure. Also of note here is that RDF schema (without the capital 'S') refers to a schema made in RDF as opposed to the RDF Schema language.

Aside from using a controlled vocabulary for describing the open datasets, another important consideration is the choice of annotation schemas that are used. If ontologies define the vocabulary, the schemas can be seen as the topics in the description outlining the information that should be recorded. The aim is to provide a concise, machine usable description of the dataset and how it can be accessed and used.

For DATAFINLAND, we chose the Vocabulary of Interlinked Datasets (VoiD), an RDF schema for describing linked datasets [2], as the starting point for our schema. One of the guiding principles behind the design of VoiD was to take into account clear accessing and licensing information of the datasets resulting in efficient discovery of datasets through search engines. Furthermore, VoiD realized effective dataset selection through content, vocabulary, and interlinking descriptions, and, finally, query optimization through statistical information about the datasets.

The basic component in VoiD is the dataset, a meaningful collection of triples, that deal with a certain topic, originate from a certain source or process, are hosted on a certain server, or are aggregated by a certain custodian. The different aspects of metadata that VoiD collects about a given dataset can be classified into the following three categories or facets:

1. *Descriptive metadata* tells what the dataset is about. This includes properties such as the name of the dataset, the people and organizations responsible for it, as well as the general subject of the dataset. Here VoiD reuses other, established vocabularies, such as `dcterms` and `foaf`. Additionally, VoiD allows for the recording of statistics concerning the dataset.

2. *Accessibility metadata* tells how to access the dataset. This includes information about the SPARQL endpoints, URI lookup as well as licensing information so

---

[15] http://www.yso.fi/onki/yso/

[16] http://wordnet.princeton.edu/

[17] http://dbpedia.org/

that potential users of the dataset know the terms and conditions under which the dataset can be used.

3. *Interlinking metadata* tells how the dataset is linked to other datasets through a linkset resource. If dataset :DS1 includes relations to dataset :DS2, a subset of :DS1 of the type `void:Linkset` is made (:LS1) which collects all the triples that include links between the two datasets (that is, triples whose subject is part of DS1 and whose object is part of :DS2).

In an unmodified state, VoiD supports only RDF datasets, so in order to facilitate annotating also non-linked open datasets, we made some extensions to VoiD. Using VoiD as the baseline has the benefit of retaining the usability of existing VoiD descriptions and making interoperability between the original and the extended VoiD simple.

The most important of these extensions was a class for datasets in formats other than RDF:

- `void-addon:NonRdfDataset` is similar to the `void:Dataset` but does not have the RDF-specific properties such as the location of the SPARQL endpoint.

The addition of this class resulted in modifications to most of the VoiD properties to include `void-addon:NonRdfDataset` in their domain specifications.

Another addition to the basic VoiD in our system was `dcterms:language` that facilitates multi-language applications.

In order to simplify annotation, we also defined two non-essential classes:

- `void-addon:Organization` is for including metadata about the organization or individual responsible for a given dataset, with properties `rdfs:label`, `dcterms:description`, and `dcterms:homepage`.
- `void-addon:Format` is the class for file formats and holds only the name of format under the property of `rdfs:label`.

These classes are useful in that organizations with multiple datasets can refer to the same class instance without the need to describe it again every time they annotate a new dataset. The same is true for format instances.

In order to define the format for the datasets, a new property was needed. One possibility would have been `dcterms:format` but that is normally associated with Internet Media Types and can also include information about size and duration, so we decided on a more limited property:

- `void-addon:format` records the file format of the dataset having `void-addon:Format` as the range of the property.

For annotation work, the property `dcterms:subject` was connected to the ONKI instance of the General Finnish Ontology (alternatively, this could be any other suitable, widely-used ontology) and the property `dcterms:license` to the ONKI instance of Creative Commons licenses. It is also possible for annotators to define their own licenses using the annotation tool SAHA3, which is described in the next section.

5.5 Annotation Tools

This section discusses requirements for a semantic annotation tool for DATA-
FINLAND and presents a solution for the task.

5.5.1 Requirements

In our application scenario, content creators are not literate in semantic web technologies, and annotate datasets in different, distributed organizations on the web.
For this task, a human-friendly metadata editor that hides the complexities of RDF
and OWL is needed. The editor should also allow for many simultaneous users
without creating conflicts, and the results of annotations, e.g. creating a new organization instance or modifying an existing one, should be instantly seen by every
other user. Otherwise, for example, multiple representations and URIs for the same
object could be easily created.

For DATAFINLAND we used and developed further the SAHA3 metadata editor
[22], which is easily configurable to different schemas, can be used by multiple
annotators simultaneously, and works in a normal web browser, therefore needing
no special software to be installed. The support for multiple annotators is made in
a robust way with synchronization and locks which guarantee that the annotators
don't interfere with each other's work. The tool also includes a chat channel, if
online dicussions between annotators is needed. SAHA3 is available as open source
at Google Code[18].

5.5.2 Initialization Process

The initialization process for a new SAHA3 project consists of two parts. First, the
project is created by importing a metadata schema along with any available initial
data conforming to that schema. The structure of the schema is important, since the
behavior and views of SAHA3 are based on the RDFS and OWL constructs found in
the schema. The classes defined serve as the types of resources that are annotated,
the properties in the domain of those classes are offered in the annotation forms
by default, and range definitions control what type of values a resource property
field accepts. In general, the SAHA3 interface makes use of any applicable schema
construct it can recognize and acts accordingly, and is often ready to be used without
any further configuration. Additional RDF files can later be imported to the project
—they are simply appended to the project's existing RDF model along with any
schema information the new model might contain.

---

[18] http://code.google.com/p/saha/

Second, the SAHA3-specific configuration of the project is done through a separate configuration view. This is for configuration aspects that only concern SAHA3 and not the data in general, such as the order in which the properties are listed, the external ontology services used by certain properties and if a property should be hidden from the interface. Since this information is not usually interesting outside the context of SAHA3, it is not included in the project's RDF model but is rather stored in a separate XML configuration file. This kind of configuration is class specific, so distinct classes can have different orderings for their properties even if the properties themselves are the same.

5.5.3 Annotation Process

The annotation process is simple using SAHA3. When a SAHA3 project has been initialized and configured, the annotator is shown the main view of the project[19], giving a general overview of the annotation project. On the left side, there is a list of all metadata items that can be created, in this case format types, license types, LOD datasets, non-RDF datasets, and organizations. On the schema level, these types are represented as classes (i.e., instances of the meta class owl:Class). After the class type, one can see a number in parantheses representing the count of how many instances of that class exist in the project. In the figure, for example, metadata descriptions of 88 LOD datasets have been created. The instances can be viewed or new ones created by clicking on the corresponding type name opening up the list of instances shown.

When clicking on the name of a metadata instance, such as a dataset in our case, an item page is opened showing the basic overview of an annotated resource. Such a resource can be, for example, the metadata about the Linked Open Data dataset BBC Music[20]. In an item page like this, all property values of the resource are listed, except those that are configured to be hidden. The page also contains an [edit] button under the main title: clicking on it takes the user to the annotation page, in which the metadata can be edited.

When editing a metadata item (i.e., an instance of an owl:Class instance in the schema) on an annotation page, the annotator is provided with a number of editable fields that correspond to the properties of the class instance at hand (i.e., properties whose domain matches the class of the instance in the underlying schema are made editable) —for example, the annotation page corresponding to the BBC Music dataset[21]. Depending on the range of a given property in the schema, the field takes in either free text or instances of classes. In the latter case, the instances can be either ones defined internally in the current SAHA3 project or chosen from external resources on the web implementing the ONKI ontology web service API [31].

In DATAFINLAND, ontologies in the National Ontology Service ONKI[22] are used. Also the massive RDF triple store of the CultureSampo semantic portal [24], including e.g. DBPedia, could be used here via the ONKI API. In all cases, (semantic) autocompletion[19][16] can be used to aid the annotator.

A nice feature of the SAHA3 editor is its generality, based on RDF(S) and OWL standards, and independence of application domain. Basically, one can put in any simple RDF/OWL schema, conforming to certain generic contraints of SAHA3, and the end-user inferface and other services are automatically created online. For example, the source RDF of the project becomes available for download online, a HAKO search engine application can be created by the push of a button [22], and APIs, such as a SPARQL end-point and ONKI API are created automatically. The end-user interface can then be modified interactively according to an application's specific needs, such as ordering the metadata fields in a certain order, or hiding internal properties from the annotator.

If the metadata has already been recorded elsewhere, the resulting RDF can also be easily uploaded into an existing SAHA3 project by an interactive tool, or by simply making a union of the RDF decription files. This means that the metadata can be collected from various sources and as long as it can be transformed to conform to the shared schema in use, all the harvested data can be included for publishing.

5.5.4 Implementation

On an implementation level, we have paid special attention to the design of the underlying search index system, with performance and simplicity as the main goals. Especially global text searches and other operations that require extensive lookup can be quite slow even with contemporary triple store systems. To speed them up, the index is divided into two parts: a regular triple store (based on Jena TDB[23]) that houses all of the actual RDF data, and a full-text index (based on Apache Lucene[24]), to which most of the search operations are made. The system scales up to at least hundreds of thousands of instances.

The architecture and data flow of SAHA3 can be seen in Figure 5.2. The user interface uses both the full-text index and the triple store through page loads and asynchronous Direct Web Remoting (DWR)[25] calls, while external APIs, such as the SPARQL end-point based on Joseki[26], directly query the triple store. Business logic between the UI and the indices controls the search logic and index synchronization.

A major challenge in using multiple indices for the same data is to keep them syncronized bringing both stability and performance concerns. Fortunately, in a manual

---

[22] http://www.onki.fi/

[23] http://openjena.org/TDB/

[24] http://lucene.apache.org/

[25] http://directwebremoting.org/dwr/index.html

[26] http://www.joseki.org/

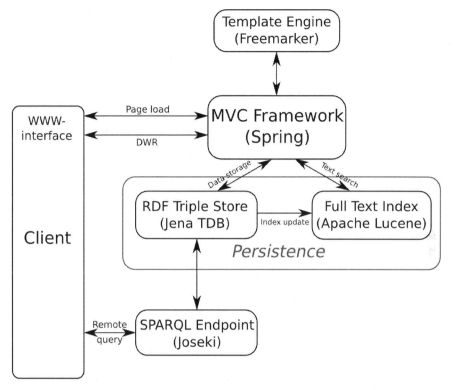

Fig. 5.2 Data flow and system architecture of SAHA 3

editing environment such as SAHA3, most write operations on an RDF graph are simple adds and deletes which are quite efficient in triple-based data. In practice their effect on performance is insignificant when compared to the speed boost given to the read operations by a fast search index.

5.6 Publishing

The final part in the publication process is the actual publishing of the datasets and the associated metadata. Ideally, the metadata about different datasets is gathered into a central repository. Since the datasets have been annotated using RDF properties and ontologies, a natural choice for exposing the metadata to human users is to use a semantic portal [28], featuring powerful semantic search and browsing capabilities, distributed content management, and direct machine-usability of the content.

In DATAFINLAND, we used HAKO, a faceted search engine, to publish the metadata recorded in the SAHA3 project as a readily usable portal [22]. The RDF data produced in SAHA3 is directly available for HAKO, which is integrated over the same index base as SAHA3.

Publishing a SAHA3 project as a HAKO application can be performed easily and interactively. First, the publisher clicks the HAKO button in SAHA3, seen in the upper right corner of the SAHA3 main view. After this, a page is opened[27] where the publisher selects the classes whose instances are to be used as search objects of the final application. All the classes explicitly defined (i.e., used as a subject) in the data model are offered as choices on the left side of the view.

On the same page, the facets corresponding to the properties of the selected classes in the search engine are selected. Similarly to the classes, all object properties (defined by being of type `owl:ObjectProperty`) present in the data are offered as facet choices. After selecting the instances and facets, clicking the link 'start hako' on the right end in the figure starts the application.

The result is a semantic portal for human end-users supporting faceted search (cf. Figure 5.3, the facets are on the left). In addition, a complementary traditional free text search engine is provided. The search input field and button is seen in Figure 5.3 below the title DataSuomi (Data in Finnish).

For machine use, SAHA3-HAKO has a SPARQL endpoint[28] which can be used to access the metadata from the outside as a service, in addition to accessing the HAKO portal via the human interface. The SPARQL interface can be used also internally in SAHA3 for providing, e.g., semantic recommendation links between data objects on the human interface.

Since HAKO and SAHA3 are built on the same index, the search engine is fully dynamic: changes made to the data in SAHA3 are immediately visible in HAKO. This is useful for making real time changes to the data, such as creating new search instances, or updating old metadata, such as the license of a dataset or its other descriptions.

In DATAFINLAND, HAKO is configured to search for both RDF and non-RDF datasets, and to form the search facets based on the license, language, format and subject properties. This way the end-user can, for example, constrain search to cover only Linked Open datasets by choosing the RDF format. In Figure 5.3, the user has selected from the facets on the left RDF datasets concerning music in the English language. Out of the seven results provided by HAKO, the user has chosen BBC Music to see its metadata.

5.7 Discussion

In the section, contributions of the chapter are summarized, related work discussed, and some future directions for development outlined.

---

[27] http://www.seco.tkk.fi/linkeddata/datasuomi/hakoConf.png

[28] http://demo.seco.tkk.fi/saha/service/data/voiD/sparql?query={query}

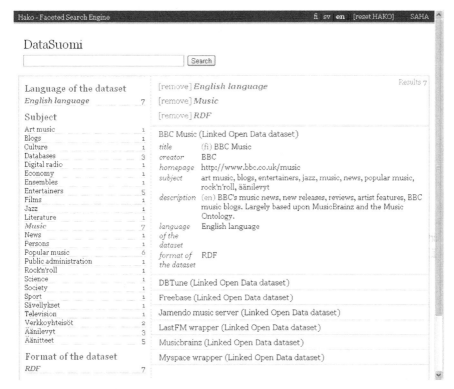

Fig. 5.3 HAKO faceted search portal

5.7.1 Contributions

Making data open and public enhances its (re)use and allows for the development of new and innovative applications based on the data. To facilitate this, the data must be made easily findable for the developers. This paper argues that metadata based on ontologies can play here a crucial role for both human and machine end-users. Annotations created in a distributed environment can be made interoperable by using shared ontologies and ontology services, and the resulting RDF repository can be used for semantic search and browsing in human user interfaces, such faceted search in DATAFINLAND. Using SPARQL and other RDF-based APIs means easy access for applications that wish to make use of the metadata.

A major bottleneck for creating such systems is the production, updating and editing of the metadata. It should all be as effortless as possible, and annotation tools should be easy to use, hiding e.g. the complexities of RDF from the annotators, and support collaborative, distributed work.

DATAFINLAND provides an easy-to-use environment facilitating both semantic content creation (SAHA3) and search/browsing (HAKO) into a seamless whole. The system works in common web browsers and does not need the installation of any specialized software. SAHA3 annotation editor can be used easily with RDFS-based metadata schemas, such as the extended VoiD presented in the paper. It allows for both RDF and non-RDF datasets to be annotated in a way that is readily compatible with the existing VoiD metadata. Connected to the ONKI ontology service, SAHA3 provides a powerful annotation environment featuring controlled vocabularies that are always up to date. Finally, HAKO can be used to publish the dataset metadata in a semantic portal that is accessible, with little configuration, to both human and machine users.

5.7.2 Related Work

At the moment, the most widely used system for annotating and publishing datasets is CKAN[29] by the Open Knowledge Foundation[30]. DATAFINLAND differs from CKAN by being based on semantic web technologies, facilitating more accurate machine processable annotations, semantic interoprability in distributed content creation, semantic search and browsing for human end-users, and RDF-based APIs for machines. The free tagging method of annotation used in CKAN, as well as in some commercial dataset repositories such as Infochimps[31] and Socrata[32] leads to various problems such as semantic ambiguity of tags as well as having several tags with the same meaning.

Concurrently to our development of the DATAFINLAND metadata schema, an alternative approach to the schema was taken by Maali et al. for their dcat vocabulary schema [23]. Here existing data catalogues were considered, and the common properties used to describe the datasets in them were identified. Furthermore they evaluated the metadata consistency and availability in each of the data catalogues, and based on this survey, they developed their own RDF Schema vocabulary called dcat. After having defined dcat, they performed a feasibility study proving the cross-catalogue query capabilities of their system. It should be noted, however, that no matter what specific schema is chosen, mapping between different schemas should be relatively straightforward because of the fairly simple application domain, datasets. This means that it is possible to change schemas wihout too much difficulty, and that compatibility across metadata recorded according to different schemas should be fairly easy to achieve.

A special feature of DATAFINLAND is its use of external ontology services. Aside from ONKI, there is a number of other possibilities for ontology repositories, such as BioPortal [26], which hosts a large number of biomedical ontologies. It features many advanced features, such as comprehensive mappings between ontologies and automatic indexing of the metadata for online biomedical data sets. However, at the

---

[29] http://ckan.org/

[30] http://okfn.org/

[31] http://www.infochimps.com/

[32] http://www.socrata.com/

moment the domain of the vocabularies is bio-focused and so not suitable for a big part of governmental datasets. Another recently developed ontology repository is Cupboard [9], where the central idea is that user's create ontology spaces which host a number of ontologies that are then mapped to one another. For searching purposes, each ontology uploaded to Cupboard is automatically indexed using the Watson[33] search engine, which has both a human UI as well as access mechanisms for machine use. Finally, there is the Open Ontology Repository project [3] that is being developed but is not yet in use.

There are also various desktop applications suited for browsing and searching for datasets, as an alternative to the web browser based solutions, An example of these is Freebase Gridworks, an open-source application used for browsing tabular datasets annotated according to the dcat schema in [7]. Through some modifications, Gridworks is able to provide a faceted interface and text search in a native UI over the dataset metadata, with tabular datasets being openable.

The approach taken by the Callimachus project[34] is somewhat similar to SAHA3, but even more general: it provides a complete framework for any kind of data-driven application. Through its custom templates and views, a similar system to SAHA3 could be constructed. However, since SAHA3 is more focused in its application area, additional tailor-made features can be utilized, such as the use of external ontology services described above. Additionally, SAHA3 is designed through simplicity to be immediately usable also for less technically oriented annotators.

5.7.3 Future Development

A problem of faceted search with wide-ranging datasets is that facets tend to get very large, which makes category selection more difficult. A solution to this is to use hierarchical facets. However, using the hierarchy of a thesaurus or an ontology intended originally for annotations and reasoning, may not be an optimal facet for information retrieval from the end-user's perspective [30]. For example, the top levels of large ontologies with complete hierarchies can be confusing for the end-users. Our planned solution in the future is to provide the annotators with a simple tool for building hierarchies for the facets as part of the annotation process. Another possible solution would be to use some kind of an all-inclusive classification system as the top level of the facets. There has been some discussion of a classification schema for open datasets in the Linked Data community, but no clear standard has risen yet. A possibility in our case could be using the Finnish Libraries' classification system that is based on the Dewey Decimal Classification.

---

[33] http://watson.kmi.open.ac.uk/

[34] http://callimachusproject.org/

Acknowledgements

We would like to thank Jussi Kurki for his work on SAHA3, Kim Viljanen and Jouni Tuominen for their work on ONKI ontology repository, Tuomas Palonen for his annotation work on the datasets for the DataFinland demonstration, and Petri Kola and Antti Poikola for fruitful discussions on publishing open datasets. The work on DATAFINLAND was conducted as part of the National Semantic Web Ontology project in Finland[35] (FinnONTO, 2003–2012), funded mainly by the National Technology and Innovation Agency (Tekes) and a consortium of 35 public organizations and companies.

References

1. Aitchison, J., Gilchrist, A. and Bawden, D. *Thesaurus construction and use: a practical manual.* Europa Publications, London, 2000.
2. Alexander, K., Cyganiak, R., Hausenblas, M. and Zhao, Jun. Describing linked datasets - on the design and usage of void, the 'vocabulary of interlinked datasets'. In *Linked Data on the Web Workshop (LDOW 09), in conjunction with 18th International World Wide Web Conference (WWW 09)*, 2009.
3. Baclawski, K. and Schneider, T. The open ontology repository initiative: Requirements and research challenges. In *Proceedings of Workshop on Collaborative Construction, Management and Linking of Structured Knowledge at the ISWC 2009*, Washington DC., USA, October 2009.
4. Berners-Lee, T. 2006. http://www.w3.org/DesignIssues/LinkedData.html.
5. Bizer, C., Cyganiak, R. and Heath, T. How to publish linked data on the web, 2007.
6. Bizer, C., Heath, T. and Berners-Lee, T. Linked data - the story so far. *International Journal on Semantic Web and Information Systems (IJSWIS)*, 2009.
7. Cyganiak, R., Maali, F. and Peristeras, V. Self-service linked government data with dcat and gridworks. In *Proceedings of the 6th International Conference on Semantic Systems*, I-SEMANTICS '10, pages 37:1–37:3, New York, NY, USA, 2010. ACM.
8. d'Aquin, M. and Lewen, H. Cupboard - a place to expose your ontologies to applications and the community. In *Proceedings of the ESWC 2009*, pages 913–918, Heraklion, Greece, June 2009. Springer–Verlag.
9. d'Aquin, M. and Lewen, H. Cupboard - a place to expose your ontologies to applications and the community. In *Proceedings of the ESWC 2009*, pages 913–918, Heraklion, Greece, June 2009. Springer–Verlag.
10. dÁquin, M. and Motta, E. Watson, more than a semantic web search engine. *Semantic Web – Interoperability, Usability, Applicability*, 2011.
11. Finin, T., Peng, Yun, Scott, R., Cost, J., Joshi, S.-A., Reddivari, P. Pan, R., Doshi, V. and Li, Ding. Swoogle: A search and metadata engine for the semantic web. In *In Proceedings of the Thirteenth ACM Conference on Information and Knowledge Management*, pages 652–659. ACM Press, 2004.
12. Foskett, D.J. Thesaurus. In *Encyclopaedia of Library and Information Science, Volume 30*, pages 416–462. Marcel Dekker, New York, 1980.
13. Hausenblas, M., Halb, W., Raimond, Y. and Heath, T. What is the size of the semantic web? In *Proceedings of I-SEMANTICS '08*, 2008.

[35] http://www.seco.tkk.fi/projects/finnonto/

14. Hearst, M., Elliott, A., English, J., Sinha, R., Swearingen, K. and Lee, K.P. Finding the flow in web site search. *CACM*, 45(9):42–49, 2002.
15. Heath, T. and Bizer, C. *Linked Data: Evolving the Web into a Global Data Space*. Morgan & Claypool, San Francisco, USA, 2011.
16. Hildebrand, M., van Ossenbruggen, J., Amin, A., Aroyo, L., Wielemaker, J. and Hardman, L. The design space of a configurable autocompletion component. Technical Report INS-E0708, Centrum voor Wiskunde en Informatica, Amsterdam, 2007.
17. Hogan, A., Harth, A., Umrich, J. and Decker, S. Towards a scalable search and query engine for the web. In *WWW '07: Proceedings of the 16th international conference on World Wide Web*, pages 1301–1302, New York, NY, USA, 2007. ACM.
18. Hyvönen, E., Saarela, S. and Viljanen, K. Application of ontology-based techniques to view-based semantic search and browsing. In *Proceedings of the First European Semantic Web Symposium, May 10–12, Heraklion, Greece*. Springer–Verlag, 2004.
19. Hyvönen, E. and Mäkelä, E. Semantic autocompletion. In *Proceedings of the First Asia Semantic Web Conference (ASWC 2006), Beijing*. Springer–Verlag, 2006.
20. Hyvönen, E., Viljanen, K., Tuominen, J. and Seppälä, K. Building a national semantic web ontology and ontology service infrastructure—the FinnONTO approach. In *Proceedings of the ESWC 2008, Tenerife, Spain*. Springer–Verlag, 2008.
21. Hyvönen, E., Viljanen, K., Tuominen, J., Seppälä, K., Kauppinen, T., Frosterus, M., Sinkkilä, R., Kurki, J., Alm, O., Mäkelä, E. and Laitio, J. National ontology infrastructure service ONKI. Oct 1 2008.
22. Kurki, J. and Hyvönen, E. Collaborative metadata editor integrated with ontology services and faceted portals. In *Workshop on Ontology Repositories and Editors for the Semantic Web (ORES 2010), the Extended Semantic Web Conference ESWC 2010, Heraklion, Greece*. CEUR Workshop Proceedings, http://ceur-ws.org/, June 2010.
23. Maali, F., Cyganiak, R. and Peristeras, V. Enabling interoperability of government data catalogues. In Maria Wimmer, Jean-Loup Chappelet, Marijn Janssen, and Hans Scholl, editors, *Electronic Government*, volume 6228 of *Lecture Notes in Computer Science*, pages 339–350. Springer Berlin / Heidelberg, 2010.
24. Mäkelä, E. and Hyvönen, E. How to deal with massively heterogeneous cultural heritage data—lessons learned in culturesampo. *Semantic Web – Interoperability, Usability, Applicability*, under review, 2011.
25. Noy, N.F., Shah, N.F., Whetzel, P.L., Dai, B., Dorf,M. Griffith, N., Jonquet, C., Rubin, D.L., Storey, M.-A., Chute, C.G. and Musen, M.A. BioPortal: ontologies and integrated data resources at the click of a mouse. *Nucleic Acids Research*, 37(Web Server issue):170–173, 2009.
26. Noy, N.F., Shah, N.H., Whetzel, P.L., Dai, B., Dorf, M., Griffith, N., Jonquet, C., Rubin, D.L., Storey, M.-A., Chute, C.G. and Musen, M.A. BioPortal: ontologies and integrated data resources at the click of a mouse. *Nucleic Acids Research*, 37(Web Server issue):170–173, 2009.
27. Pollitt, A.S. The key role of classification and indexing in view-based searching. Technical report, University of Huddersfield, UK, 1998. http://www.ifla.org/IV/ifla63/63polst.pdf.
28. Reynolds, D., Shabajee, P. and Cayzer, S. Semantic information portals. In *Proceedings of the 13th international World Wide Web conference on Alternate track papers & posters*, WWW Alt. '04, pages 290–291, New York, NY, USA, 2004. ACM.
29. Staab, S. and Studer, R., editors. *Handbook on ontologies (2nd Edition)*. Springer–Verlag, 2009.
30. Suominen, O., Viljanen, K. and Hyvönen, E. User-centric faceted search for semantic portals. Springer–Verlag, 2007.
31. Tuominen, J., Frosterus, M., Viljanen, K. and Hyvönen, E. ONKI SKOS server for publishing and utilizing skos vocabularies and ontologies as services. In *Proceedings of the 6th European Semantic Web Conference (ESWC 2009)*. Springer–Verlag, 2009.

Matias Frosterus, Eero Hyvönen, and Joonas Laitio

32. Viljanen, K., Tuominen, J. and Hyvöen, E. Ontology libraries for production use: The Finnish ontology library service ONKI. In *Proceedings of the 6th European Semantic Web Conference (ESWC 2009)*. Springer–Verlag, 2009.
33. Viljanen, K., Tuominen, J. and Hyvönen, E. Ontology libraries for production use: The Finnish ontology library service ONKI. In *Proceedings of the ESWC 2009, Heraklion, Greece*. Springer–Verlag, 2009.
34. Viljanen, K., Tuominen, J., Salonoja, M. and Hyvönen, E. Linked open ontology services. In *Workshop on Ontology Repositories and Editors for the Semantic Web (ORES 2010), the Extended Semantic Web Conference ESWC 2010*. CEUR Workshop Proceedings, http://ceur-ws.org/, June 2010.

Chapter 6

StdTrip: Promoting the Reuse of Standard Vocabularies in Open Government Data

Percy Salas, José Viterbo, Karin Breitman, and Marco Antonio Casanova

Abstract Linked Data is the standard generally adopted for publishing Open Government Data. This operation requires that a myriad of public information datasets be converted to a set of RDF triples. A major step in this process is deciding how to represent the database schema concepts in terms of RDF classes and properties. This is done by mapping database concepts to a vocabulary, which will be used as the base for generating the RDF representation. The construction of this vocabulary is extremely important, because it determines how the generated triples interlink the resulting dataset with other existing ones. However, most engines today provide support only to the mechanical process of transforming relational to RDF data. In this chapter, we discuss this process and present the StdTrip framework, a tool that supports the conceptual modeling stages of the production of RDF datasets, promoting the reuse of W3C recommended standard RDF vocabularies or suggesting the reuse of non-standard vocabularies already adopted by other RDF datasets.

6.1 Introduction

The focus of Open Government Data (OGD) lies on the publication of public data in a way that it can be shared, discovered, accessed and easily manipulated by those desiring such data [2]. The Semantic Web provides a common framework that allows data to be shared and reused across applications, enterprises, and community boundaries. Particularly, for representing open data, W3C recommends the Linked Data standard [10], which is based on the representation of data in the form of sets of RDF triples. This approach requires the conversion of a myriad of public information datasets, stored in relational databases (RDB) and represented by database schemas and their instances, to RDF datasets. A key issue in this process is deciding

Correspondance author: Percy Salas, Departamento de Informática, Pontifícia Universidade Católica do Rio de Janeiro, R. Mq. de S. Vicente, 225, Rio de Janeiro/RJ, 22451-900, Brazil, e-mail: `psalas@inf.puc-rio.br`. See the List of Contributors for full contact details.

how to represent database schema concepts in terms of RDF classes and properties. This is done by mapping database concepts to an RDF vocabulary, to be used as the base for generating the RDF triples. The construction of this vocabulary is extremely important, because the more one reuses well known standards, the easier it will be to interlink the result to other existing datasets [13]. This approach greatly improves the ability of third parties to use the information provided by governments in ways not previously available or planned, such as the creation of data mashups, i.e., the merge of data from different data sources, in order to produce comparative views of the combined information [1].

There are applications that provide support to the mechanical process of transforming relational data to RDF triples, such as Triplify [4], D2R Server [11] and OpenLink Virtuoso [26]. However, they offer very little support to users during the conceptual modeling stage. In this chapter, we present the StdTrip process, which aims at guiding the users in the task of converting relational data to RDF, providing support in the stage of creating a conceptual model of the RDF datasets. Based on an *a priori* design approach, StdTrip promotes the reuse of standard — W3C recommended — RDF vocabularies, when possible, suggesting the reuse of vocabularies already adopted by other RDF datasets, otherwise.

The rest of this chapter is organized as follows. In Section 6.2, we discuss the process of publishing relational databases as RDF triples and tools that support this operation. In Section 6.3, we discuss the interoperability problems and explain the *a priori* matching approach. In Section 6.4, we present the StdTrip process to be used in the conceptual modeling stages of the process. Finally, in Section 7.6, we conclude discussing some limitations of our approach and the challenges to be met in the future.

6.2 RDB-to-RDF Conversion Tools

The publication of relational databases as RDF is known as the RDB-to-RDF approach [37]. This operation takes as input a Relational Database (schema and data) and produces as output one or more RDF graphs [37]. This process may be divided in two independent tasks: the mapping and the conversion. The mapping is a fundamental step in the RDB-to-RDF process and consists in defining how to represent database schema concepts in terms of RDF classes and properties. This definition — represented in a mapping file using specific languages and formats — is used as the base for the conversion, which consists in the generation of the set of RDF triples containing each instance stored in the database. The consumer of the RDF Graph (virtual or materialized) can access the RDF data in three different ways [37]:

- **Query access.** The agent issues a SPARQL query against an endpoint exposed by the system, receives and processes the results (typically the result is a SPARQL result set in XML or JSON);
- **Entity-level access.** The agent performs an HTTP GET on a URI exposed by the system, and processes the result (typically the result is an RDF graph);

- **Dump access.** The agent performs an HTTP GET on dump of the entire RDF graph, for example in Extract, Transform, and Load (ETL) processes.

A survey on existing RDB-to-RDF approaches [40], points out that researchers and practitioners have provided different mechanisms with which to tackle the RDB-to-RDF conversion process. It is important to note, however, that the current RDB-to-RDF approaches provide different, proprietary, mapping languages for the mapping process. Due to this fact, there are initiatives towards establishing standards to govern this process. Such is the case of the W3C RDB2RDF Working Group[1], which is currently working on a standard language to express relational database to RDF mappings called R2RML [39]. A standard RDB to RDF mapping language will allow vendors to compete on functionality and features. The most relevant RDB-to-RDF approaches are summarized ahead.

- **Triplify.** Auer et al. [4] describe Triplify, a simplified approach based on mapping HTTP-URI requests onto relational database queries. Triplify motivates the need for a simple mapping solution through using SQL as mapping language, for transforming database query results into RDF triples and Linked Data. The mapping is done manually. It uses the table-to-class and column-to-predicate approach for transforming SQL queries results to the RDF data model. This transformation process can be performed on demand through HTTP or in advance (ETL). The approach promotes the reuse of mapping files, through a collection of configurations files for common relational schemata. It can be easily integrated and deployed with numerous popular Web applications such as WordPress, Gallery and Drupal. Triplify also includes a method for publishing update logs to enable incremental crawling of linked data sources. The approach was tested with 160 GB of geographical data from the OpenStreetMap project, showing high flexibility and scalability.
- **D2RQ.** Bizer et al. describe D2RQ [11], which generates the mapping files automatically, using the table-to-class and column-to-predicate approach. D2RQ uses a declarative language, implemented as Jena graph [14], to define the mapping file. The approach allows relational databases to offer their contents as virtual RDF graphs without replication of the RDB in RDF triples. The tool can also provide the RDF dump of the relational database if required. In the virtual access the mapping file is largely used for translating SPARQL to SQL queries. The mapping file may be customized by the user, thereby allowing the ontology reuse in the mapping process.
- **Virtuoso RDF View.** Erling et al. [26] describe the virtuoso RDF View, which uses the table-to-class approach for automatic generation of the mapping file. The mapping file, also called RDF view, is composed by several declarations called "quad map patterns", which specify how the table column values are mapped to RDF triples. Similarity to D2RQ [11], Virtuoso RDF View allows to map arbitrary collections of relational tables, into "SPARQL accessible RDF" without having to convert the whole data into RDF triples. It is important to note

---

[1] http://www.w3.org/2001/sw/rdb2rdf/

that quad map patterns can be stored as triples, and are, therefore, queryable via SPARQL.

- **DB2OWL.** In [20] the authors present the DB2OWL tool, which maps a relational database to a single, local ontology. The DB2OWL mapping file uses the XML based language R2O [5] to describe relationships between database components and a local ontology. This mapping language is used to either execute the transformation in response to a query or to create an RDF dump, in batch mode. The DB2OWL tool adopts the table-to-class and column-to-predicate approach with some improvements, the more significant of which is the identification of object properties.

- **RDBtoOnto.** In [18], Cerbah proposes the RDBtoOnto tool and discusses how to take advantage of database data to obtain more accurate ontologies. The RDBtoOnto is a tool that guides the user through the design and implementation of methods for ontology acquisition using information stored in relational databases. It also supports the data transformation to populate the ontologies. The RDBtoOnto uses the table-to-class and column-to-predicate approach to create an initial ontology schema, which is then refined through identification of taxonomies hidden in the data.

- **Ultrawrap.** Sequeda et al. [43] present the automatic wrapping system called Ultrawrap, which provides SPARQL querying over relational databases. The Ultrawrap tool defines a triple representation as an SQL view in order to take advantage of the optimization techniques provided by the SQL infrastructure. The ontology, which is the basis for SPARQL queries, is generated following the table-to-class approach with First Order Logic, introduced by Tirmizi et al. in [45].

- **Automated Mapping Generation for Converting Databases into Linked Data.** Polfliet et al. [36] propose a method that automatically associates database elements with ontology entities in the mapping generation process. This method uses schema matching approaches, mainly string-based ones, to align RDB elements with ontology terms. D2RQ [11] is used to create the initial ontology schema. This approach provides a rudimentary method for linking data with other datasets, based on SPARQL queries and *rdfs:label* tags.

6.3 The Interoperability Problem

The RDB-to-RDF mapping operation results in the definition of a generic ontology that describes how the RDB schema concepts are represented in terms of RDF classes and properties. The sheer adoption of this ontology, however, is not sufficient to secure interoperability. In a distributed and open system, such as the Semantic Web, different parties tend to use different ontologies to describe specific domains of interest, raising interoperability problems.

Ontology alignment techniques could be applied to solve heterogeneity problems. Such techniques are closely related to schema matching approaches, which consist of taking two schemata as input and producing a mapping between pairs of elements that are semantically equivalent [38]. Matching approaches may be classified as syntactic vs. semantic and, orthogonally, as *a priori* vs. *a posteriori* [15]. Both syntactic and semantic approaches work *a posteriori*, in the sense that they start with existing datasets, and try to identify links between the two. A third alternative — the *a priori* approach — is proposed in [15], where the author argues that,"when specifying databases that will interact with each other, the designer should first select an appropriate standard, if one exists, to guide design of the exported schemas. If none exists, the designer should publish a proposal for a common schema covering the application domain".

The same philosophy is applicable to Linked Data. In the words of Bizer, Cyganiak and Heath [9]: *"in order to make it as easy as possible for client applications to process your data, you should reuse terms from well-known vocabularies wherever possible. You should only define new terms yourself if you can not find required terms in existing vocabularies".*

As defined by W3C, ontologies can serve as the global schema or standard for the *a priori* approach. The authors in [15] list the following steps to define a common schema for an application domain

- Select fragments of known, popular ontologies such as WordNet [2] that cover the concepts pertaining to the application domain;
- Align concepts from distinct fragments into unified concepts; and
- Publish the unified concepts as ontology, indicating which are mandatory and which are optional.

According to [30], it is considered a good practice to reuse terms from well-known RDF vocabularies whenever possible. If the adequate terms are found in existing vocabularies, these should be reused to describe data. Reuse of existing terms is highly desirable, as it maximizes the probability of the data being consumed by applications tuned to well-known vocabularies, without further processing or modifying the application. In the following list we enumerate some vocabularies that cover a widespread set of domains and are used by a very large community. As such, to ensure interoperability, these vocabularies should be reused whenever possible [9].

- **Dublin Core Metadata Initiative (DCMI)**[3]. Defines general metadata attributes such as title, creator, date and subject.
- **Friend-of-a-Friend (FOAF)**[4]. Defines terms for describing people, their activities and their relations to other people and objects.
- **Semantically-Interlinked Online Communities (SIOC)**[5]. Describes aspects of online community sites, such as users, posts and forums.

---

[2] http://wordnet.princeton.edu/

[3] http://dublincore.org/documents/dcmi-terms/

[4] http://xmlns.com/foaf/spec/

[5] http://rdfs.org/sioc/spec/

- **Description of a Project (DOAP)**[6]. Defines terms for describing software projects, particularly those that are Open Source.
- **Programmes Ontology**[7]. Defines terms for describing programmes such as TV and radio broadcasts.
- **Good Relations Ontology**[8]. Defines terms for describing products, services and other aspects relevant to e-commerce applications.
- **Creative Commons (CC)**[9]. Defines terms for describing copyright licenses in RDF.
- **Bibliographic Ontology (BIBO)**[10]. Provides concepts and properties for describing citations and bibliographic references (i.e., quotes, books, articles, etc.).
- **OAI Object Reuse and Exchange**[11]. Used by various library and publication data sources to represent resource aggregations such as different editions of a document or its internal structure.
- **Review Vocabulary**[12]. Provides a vocabulary for representing reviews and ratings, as are often applied to products and services.
- **Basic Geo (WGS84)**[13]. Defines terms such as latitude and longitude for describing geographically-located things.

Matching two schemata that were designed according to the *a priori* approach, is an easier process as there is a consensus on the semantics of terminology used, thus avoiding possible ambiguities. Unfortunately, this is not what happens in practice. Most teams prefer to create new vocabularies — as do the vast majority of tools that support this task —, rather than spending time and effort to search for adequate matches [32]. We believe that this fact is mainly due to the distributed nature of the Web itself, i.e., there is no central authority one can consult to look for a specific vocabulary. Semantic search engines, such as Watson, works as an approximation for such mechanism. Notwithstanding, there are numerous standards that designers can not ignore when specifying triple sets, and publishing their content.

Only if no well-known vocabulary provides the required terms, the data publishers should define new — data source-specific — terminology [9]. W3C provides a set of guidelines to help users in publishing new vocabularies [8], such as, "if new terminology is defined, it should be made self-describing by making the URIs that identify terms Web dereferenceable. This allows clients to retrieve RDF Schema or OWL definitions of the terms as well as mappings to other vocabularies".

---

[6] http://trac.usefulinc.com/doap

[7] http://purl.org/ontology/po/

[8] http://purl.org/goodrelations/

[9] http://creativecommons.org/ns#

[10] http://bibliontology.com/

[11] http://www.openarchives.org/ore/

[12] http://purl.org/stuff/rev#

[13] http://www.w3.org/2003/01/geo/

6.4 The StdTrip Process

The StdTrip process aims at guiding users during the conceptual modeling stages of the task of converting relational databases into RDF triples. Most tools that support this task do that by mapping relational tables to RDF classes, and attributes to RDF properties, with little concern regarding the reuse of existing standard vocabularies [4] [26]. Instead, these tools create new vocabularies using the internal database terminology, such as the table and attribute names. We believe that the use of standards in schema design is the only viable way for guaranteeing future interoperability [12] [16] [33]. The StdTrip process is anchored in this principle, and strives to promote the reuse of standards by implementing a guided process comprised by six stages: conversion, alignment, selection, inclusion, completion and output. These stages are detailed in the following subsections. To illustrate our description we are going to use the publication database depicted in Figure 6.1 throughout the next sections.

It is important to note that we make the implicit assumption that the input database is fully normalized. That is, we assume that the input data is a relational database in the third normal form (3NF). Furthermore, we assume that the user that follows this approach has some knowledge about the application domain of the databases.

6.4.1 Conversion

This stage consists in transforming the structure of the relational database in an RDF ontology. It takes as input the relational database schema (Figure 6.1), which contains the metadata of the RDB. This stage is comprised by two major operations. In the first operation, we transform the relational database schema into an Entity-Relationship (ER) model. In the second operation, we transform the Entity-Relationship model, resulting from the previous operation, into an OWL ontology.

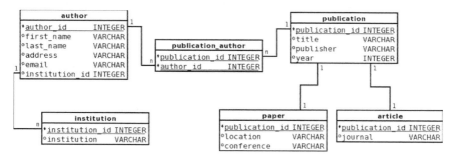

Fig. 6.1 Author-Publication relational schema.

The reason for splitting the conversion stage in two separate operations is that mapping the relational database model directly to OWL would not properly map some of the attributes, such as a binary relationship, to object properties. Using a direct RDB to OWL mapping approach, the table *publication_author* (Figure 6.1) would result in the Class *Publication_author* with *publication_id* and *author_id* as subjects, while the RDB to ER to OWL approach would correctly result in two object properties *publication_author* and the inverse property *has_publication_author*.

In the following subsections we describe each operation in more detail, starting with the mapping from relational database model to entity-relationship followed by the conversion process from entity-relationship to OWL.

6.4.1.1 Relational model to Entity-Relationship

The relational data model, as originally conceived by Codd [19], leaves practically all semantics to be expressed by integrity constraints. Therefore the use of relations as the sole data structure makes the model conceptually and semantically very simple. In order to solve this lack of semantics, we convert the relational database schema into an Entity-Relationship model, which provides a high-level conceptualization to describe the database.

This operation is a combination of ideas and mapping rules proposed by [6], [17], and [31]. This process can be characterized as a reverse engineering process, because the input of this process is the implementation model, and the expected result is a conceptual model. According to [31] the transformation process has the following major steps:

1. **Identification of ER elements for each table:** Each relation (table) in the relational model represents an entity, a relationship or a weak entity in the entity-relationship model. The following mapping rules, extracted from [17] and [31], are the ones we elected in our implementation of the RDB to ER mapping.

   - **Entity:** Corresponds to every primary key that is not composed by foreign keys. In other words, if a relation does not reference other relation schemes, the relation represents an Entity. For instance, in the example depicted in Figure 6.1, the table *author* with the primary key *author_id* has no foreign keys. Thus the table *author* is an *Entity*.
   - **Relationship:** A table that has a primary key composed by multiple foreign keys represents a relationship element between the tables referenced by these foreign keys. For instance, in the same example, the table *publication_author* has the columns *publication_id* and *author_id* composing a primary key. Both columns are foreign keys referencing the tables *author* and *publication*. Thus the table *publication_author* is a *Relationship* between the tables *author* and *publication*.
   - **Weak Entity or Specialized Entity:** The table whose primary key intersects with the foreign key represents a weak entity or a specialization of the entity referenced by this foreign key. For instance, the table *article* has

publication_id as primary key, which is also a foreign key to the table *publication*. Thus we can state that the table *article* is a *Weak Entity* that depends on — or is a specialization of — the *publication* entity.

2. **Definition of relationship cardinality:** The cardinality of a relationship can be 1-n, 1-1 or n-n. Heusler, in [31], states that in order to classify the cardinality of a given relationship we need to verify the data stored in the tables. With the purpose of systematizing this step, we adopted the following rules.

   - **Cardinality n-n:** Every relationship mapped directly from a table has the n:n cardinality. The table *publication_author*, in our example illustrates, such case.
   - **Cardinality 1-1:** This cardinality is found in relationships between an entity and its specialized entity. The tables *article* and *publication* are examples of 1-1 mappings.
   - **Cardinality 1-n:** This cardinality is frequently found in columns that represent foreign keys, but are not part of the primary key. For instance, the column *institution_id* from the table *author* generates a new relationship with 1-n cardinality.

3. **Definition of attributes:** According to [31], in this step every column of a table that is not a foreign key should be defined as an attribute of the entity or the relationship.

4. **Definition of entities and relationships identifiers:** The final major step in the transformation process deals with the entities and relationship identifiers. Heusler in [31] stated that every column that is part of the primary key, but is not a foreign key, represents an entity or a relationship identifier. The table *institution*, in our running example, with its column *institution_id* as primary key, functions as entity identifier for the *institution* entity.

Before starting the ER to OWL mapping operation, we recommend modifying the internal database nomenclature (codes and acronyms) to more meaningful names, i.e, names that better reflect the semantics of the ER objects in question. In our example, the *publication_author* relationship could by modified to *hasAuthor*, that better describes this relationship between *Publication* and *Author*. Compliance to this recommendation will be very useful in later stages of the StdTrip process.

6.4.1.2 Entity-Relationship to OWL mapping

In order to obtain an RDF representation of the database schema, we have to apply some mapping rules to convert the entity-relationship model, just obtained. The mapping rules used to transform the entity-relationship model are straightforward, due to the fact that we start from a conceptual, entity-relationship model, with the adequate level of database semantics. The transformation rules listed below are a compendium from the work of [29] and [34] adapted for our specific scenario.

- Map each **entity** in the ER to a class in the OWL ontology. For instance, the entity *author* is mapped to the class *Author*.
- Map each **simple attribute of entity** in the ER to a functional datatype property. Domain of the datatype property is the entity, and range is the attribute datatype. For instance, the attribute *address* of the entity *author* is mapped to the datatype property *address* with *author* as domain and *XSD:String* as range.
- Map each **identifier attribute of entity** in the ER to a datatype property tagged with functional and inverse functional. For instance, the identifier attribute *author_id* of the entity *author* is mapped to a functional datatype property *author_id* with *author* as domain and *XSD:Integer* as range.
- Map each **specialized entity** in the ER to a Class tagged with *subClassOf* indicating the owner Class. For instance, the entity *article* is mapped to the class *Article* and the property *subclassOf* related to the class *Publication*.
- Map each **binary relationship without attributes** into two object properties between the relationship entities. One corresponding to the relationship as represented in the ER, and the second as an inverse property of the former one. For instance, the relationship *publication_author* is mapped to a object property with the same name and an inverse object property *isAuthorOf*.
- Map each **binary relationship with attributes** to a class with datatype corresponding to the relationship attribute, and two pairs of inverse object property between the new class and the relationship entities.
- Map the **relationship cardinality** into max and min cardinality restrictions.

The output of the conversion stage corresponding to our example is illustrated in Figure 6.2. It is important to note that the resulting ontology is a model that simply mirrors the schema of the input relational database depicted in Figure 6.1.

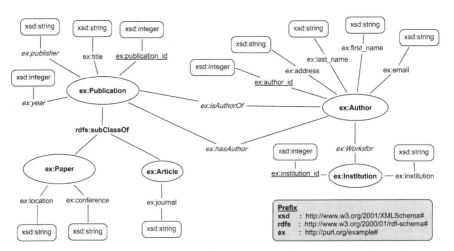

Fig. 6.2 Ontology representing the output of the conversion stage in the Author-Publication example

6.4.2 Alignment

The alignment stage is where lies the essence of our approach. As the name suggests, is in this stage that we apply existing ontology alignment algorithms. We aim at finding correspondences between a generical ontology — obtained in the previous stage — and standard well-known RDF vocabularies. The alignment operation is supported by the *K-match* ontology alignment tool, which is based on a collaborative approach to find matches between ontology terms. This tool was inspired by the work of Do Hong Hai [23], in which he presents a composite matching approach for schema matching.

Better than proposing "yet another ontology matching tool", *K-match* capitalizes from years of collaborative research and results obtained by the Semantic Web community, particularly during the OAEI contest [27] [28]. The collaborative aspect of the *K-match* tool comes from the characteristics of the Web 2.0 itself, as the tool is a mashup application that uses and combines functionalities from several alignment tools already available in the form of APIs[14] in the Web. Therefore, the *K-match* tool allows us to use different alignment applications (matchers) — with the option of including new ones — and applies different strategies to combine the results.

The *K-match* tool takes as input two OWL ontologies and produces a mapping indicating which elements of the inputs correspond to each other. In the StdTrip context, the ontology obtained in the previous stage is one of the input ontologies, while the second input ontology is one of a list of common RDF vocabularies (enumerated in Section 6.3), alternated automatically during repeated executions of the tool. After each execution, a set of matching results is generated. Each result is comprised of a set of mapping between elements, together with similarity values ranging from 0 to 1, eveluating the similarity degree between the mapped elements.

The alignment process is comprised by three steps: the first step consists in the execution of different matchers, the second step combines the results of the previous step applying aggregation strategies, and the final step applies one of several selected strategies to choose the match candidates for each ontology term [24]. The steps of the *K-match* alignment process are depicted as follows.

1. **Matchers execution.** In this step we use three top ranked matchers of the OAEI 2009[15] contest, namely Lily [47], Aroma [22] and Anchor-Flood [42]. Most of them are syntactic matchers, mainly due to the lack of instances stored in standard vocabularies hosted in the Web, a fact that hinders the adoption of semantic, instance-based approaches[16]. The result of the execution of the matcher with K matchers, N elements from the source ontology and M elements from the target ontology is a $K \times N \times M$ cube of similarity values. It is important to note that we applied a directional match, since the goal is to find all match

---

[14] API : Application Programming Interface

[15] http://oaei.ontologymatching.org/2009/

[16] This is a limitation of existing tools, not of the *K-match* framework, which may be extended to include new matchers in the future.

candidates just for the ontology target. For instance, Table 6.1 presents the similarity values from a partial alignment between the Friend of a Friend (FOAF) vocabulary, now called ontology source *O1*, with the single term *ex:last_name*, from the generic ontology obtained in the previous step of the StdTrip process (Figure 6.2), now called ontology target *O2*.

Table 6.1 Similarity Cube: Similarity values from a partial alignment between *O1* and *O2* for the term *ex:last_name*, from the Author-Publication example

Matcher *(K)*	Ontology Source *(N)*	Similarity Value
Lily	**foaf:**first_name	0.5
	foaf:familyName	0.5
	foaf:givenName	0.5
Aroma	**foaf:**first_name	0.6
	foaf:familyName	0.8
	foaf:givenName	1.0
Aflood	**foaf:**first_name	0.3
	foaf:familyName	1.0
	foaf:givenName	1.0

2. **Combination strategies.** In this step we combine the matching results of the *K* matchers, executed in the former step and stored in the *similarity cube*, in a unified *similarity matrix* with *M X N* result elements. In other words, after applying the aggregation strategy, each pair of ontology terms gets a unified similarity value. For instance, Table 6.2 presents the combined similarity values obtained for the term *ex:last_name*. The following aggregation strategies are provided by the *K-match* tool to combine individual similarity values for pairs of terms into a unified value:

   - **Max.** This strategy returns the maximal similarity value of any matcher. It is optimistic, in particular in case of contradictory similarity values.
   - **Weighted.** This strategy determines a weighted sum of the similarity values and needs relative weights for each matcher, which should correspond to the expected matchers importance.
   - **Average.** This strategy represents a special case of the *Weighted* strategy and returns the average similarity over all matchers, i.e., considering all them equally important.
   - **Min.** This strategy uses the lowest similarity value of any matcher. As opposed to *Max*, it is pessimistic.
   - **Harmonic mean.** This strategy returns the harmonic mean over the matchers, with values greater than zero.

3. **Selection of match candidates.** The final step is to select possible matching candidates from the similarity matrix obtained in the previous step. This

Table 6.2 Similarity Matrix: Similarity values combined from Table 6.1 for the term *ex:last_name*, from the Author-Publication example

Ontology Source *(N)*	Similarity Value
foaf:first_name	0.47
foaf:familyName	0.77
foaf:givenName	0.83

is achieved applying a selection strategy to choose the match candidates for each ontology term. For selecting match candidates, the following strategies are available:

- **MaxN.** The *n* elements from the source ontology with maximal similarity are selected as match candidates. Having n=1, i.e., Max1, represents the natural choice for 1:1 correspondences. Generally, n>1 is useful in interactive mode to allow the user to select among several match candidates.
- **MaxDelta.** The element from the source ontology with maximal similarity is selected as match candidate, together with all elements with a similarity degree differing by at most a given tolerance value *d*, which can be specified either as an absolute or relative value. The value *d* is set by the user. The idea is to return multiple match candidates when there are several source ontology elements with the same or almost the same similarity value.
- **Threshold.** All elements from the source ontology with a similarity value higher than a given threshold *t* are returned. The value *t* is set by the user.
- **Max-Threshold.** This strategy represents a special case of the previously strategy, and returns the source ontology element with the maximal similarity above a given threshold *t*. Again, value *t* is fixed by the user.

To illustrate this step, we applied the *Threshold* strategy in the partial result depicted in Table 6.2, with $t = 0.6$. The result was the choice of **foaf:***familyName* and **foaf:***givenName* as match candidates for **ex:***last_name*.

6.4.3 Selection

In this stage, human interaction plays an essential role. Ideally, the user should know well the application domain, because he or she will have to choose the vocabulary elements that best represent each concept in the database. The user will select each vocabulary element from a list of possibilities, listed in decreasing order of similarity value obtained as the result of the previus stage.

For instance, in the case of the term *ex:last_name* the user will have to decide between the terms *foaf:givenName* and *foaf:lastName* with 0.83 and 0.77 of similarity value respectively. Figure 6.3 shows the OWL ontology after the execution of this stage. In cases where there were two or more choices of matching RDF vocabulary terms, we opted always for the ones with higher similarity values.

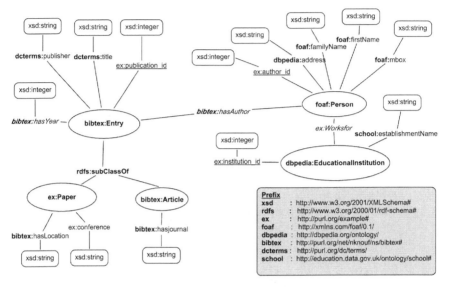

Fig. 6.3 OWL ontology after the *Selection* stage

6.4.4 Inclusion

There are cases where the selection stage does not yield any result, i.e., either there is no element in the known vocabularies that matches the concept in the database, or none of suggestions in the list is considered adequate by the user. For such cases we provide a list of terms from other, vocabularies in the web that might be possible matches. The choice of these vocabularies is domain-dependent, and the search, based on keywords, is done using a semantic web searching tools. The rationale is the following, "if your concept is not covered by any of the known standards, look around and see how others dealt with it. By choosing a vocabulary in use, you will make your data more interoperable in the future, than by creating a brand new vocabulary."

This stage is accomplished with the aid of existing mechanisms for searching semantic documents offered by Semantic Web searchers, namely Watson[17] [21], which executes a keywords based search. In order to improve the quality of the results, it is crucial to follow some *"tuning"* and configuration guidelines to get the

---

[17] http://kmi-web05.open.ac.uk/WatsonWUI/

best out of this type of service. The following list is a compendium of the guidelines that we adopt:

- Restrict the exploration space, searching just for terms belonging to domain ontologies directly related to the database domain.
- Filter expected results specifying the type of term — classes or properties —, i.e., if we are searching for a class, every property will be excluded.
- Extract the term description, if available, and apply similarity algorithms to reduce ambiguity as much as possible.

6.4.5 Completion

If, for some terms, none of the previous stages was able to provide appropriate RDF mapping, the user will have to define a new vocabulary. During this stage, we help users providing recommendations and best practices on how his or her vocabulary should be published on the Web, how choose an appropriate URI namespace, and its constituent elements (classes and properties). The following list is a collection of best practices for this specific scenario, compiled from [8], [7], [41], [30] and [3].

- **Do you own the domain name?** The URI namespace you choose for your vocabulary should be a URI to which you have write access, so that you will be able to mint URIs in this namespace.
- **Keep implementation-specific out of your URIs:** URIs should not reflect implementation details that may need to change at some point in the future.
- **How big you expect your vocabulary to become?**
    - **Small vocabularies and stable sets of resources,** may be more conveniently served if the entire vocabulary is retrieved in a single Web access. Such a vocabulary would typically use a hash namespace. *Good Relations*[18] is an example of a vocabulary that uses a hash namespace. For instance, the following URI identifies a Class in this vocabulary.

    *http://purl.org/goodrelations/v1#***ProductOrServiceModel**

    - **Large vocabularies, to which additions are frequently,** should be arranged to ease the extension of terms in the vocabulary. Therefore, terms must be retrieved through multiple Web accesses. Such a vocabulary would typically use a slash namespace. *Friend of a Friend (FOAF)*[19] is an example of a vocabulary that uses a slash namespace. For instance, the following URI identifies a class in this vocabulary.

    *http://xmlns.com/foaf/0.1/***Person**

---

[18] http://purl.org/goodrelations/v1

[19] http://xmlns.com/foaf/0.1/

- **Name resources in CamelCase:** CamelCase is the name given to the style of naming in which multiword names are written without any spaces but with each word written in uppercase, e.g., resource names like *rdfs:subClassOf* and *owl:InverseFunctionalProperty*.

  - **Start class names with capital letters,** e.g., class names *owl:Restriction* and *owl:Class*.
  - **Start property names in lowercase,** e.g., property names *rdfs:subClassOf* and *owl:inverseOf*.

- **Name resources with singular nouns,** e.g. classes names *owl:DatatypeProperty* and *owl:SymmetricProperty*.

The actual process of publishing a new RDF vocabulary is outside of the scope of the StdTrip process. By providing these guidelines we hope that users understand the value of making the semantics of their data explicit and, more importantly, reusable.

6.4.6 Output

This is not properly a stage, rather the output of the StdTrip process, which produces two artifacts.

1. **A mapping specification file.** This artifact serves as the core parameterization for a RDB-to-RDF conversion tool. The specification file format can be easily customized for several approaches and tools that provide support to the mechanical process of transforming RDB into a set of RDF. Among them, there are the formats used by Triplify [4], Virtuoso RDF views [26] and D2RQ [11], and also R2RML [39], the new standardized language to map relational data to RDF. For instance, the code below shows a fragment of the mapping specification file for the Triplify tool [4] corresponding to the Author-Publication example.

```
$triplify['queries']=array(
'article'=> "SELECT
        publication_id as 'id'
      , journal as 'bibtex:hasJournal'
    FROM article",
 'author'=> "SELECT
        author_id as 'id'
      , institution_id as 'ex:worksFor'
      , first_name as 'foaf:firstName'
      , last_name as 'foaf:familyName'
      , address as 'dbpedia:address'
      , email as 'foaf:mbox'
    FROM author",
  ...);

$triplify['classMap']=array(
```

```
            "article" => "bibtex:Article",
            "author" => "foaf:Person",
...);

$triplify['objectProperties']=array(
        "ex:worksFor" => "institution",
        "bibtex:hasAuthor" => "author");
...
```

2. **"Triples Schema"**. The second artifact is an ontology representing the original database schema, with the corresponding restrictions, and maximizing the reuse of standard vocabularies. The code below is a "Triples Schema" fragment of the Author-Publication, running example.

```
<rdf:RDF xmlns:rdf="http://www.w3.org/1999/02/22-rdf-syntax-ns#"
        xmlns:bibtex="http://purl.org/net/nknouf/ns/bibtex#"
        xmlns:foaf="http://xmlns.com/foaf/0.1/"
...
<rdfs:Class rdf:about="http://purl.org/net/nknouf/ns/bibtex#Article">
    <rdfs:label xml:lang="en">Article</rdfs:label>
</rdfs:Class>
...
<rdf:Description rdf:about="http://purl.org/net/nknouf/ns/bibtex#
Article">
    <rdfs:subClassOf rdf:resource="http://purl.org/net/nknouf/ns/
    bibtex#Entry"/>
</rdf:Description>
...
<owl:DatatypeProperty rdf:about="http://purl.org/net/nknouf/ns/
bibtex#hasJournal">
    <rdfs:domain rdf:resource="http://purl.org/net/nknouf/ns/bibtex#
    Article"/>
    <rdfs:range rdf:resource="http://www.w3.org/2001/XMLSchema#
    string"/>
    <rdfs:label xml:lang="en">hasJournal</rdfs:label>
</owl:DatatypeProperty>
...
<owl:ObjectProperty rdf:about="http://purl.org/example#worksFor">
    <rdfs:domain rdf:resource="http://xmlns.com/foaf/0.1/Person"/>
    <rdfs:range rdf:resource="http://dbpedia.org/ontology/Educational
    Institution"/>
    <rdfs:label xml:lang="en">worksFor</rdfs:label>
</owl:ObjectProperty>
...
```

6.5 Conclusion

In this chapter, we introduced StdTrip, a tool that emphasizes the use of standard-based, *a priori*, design of triples, in order to promote interoperability, the reuse of vocabularies and to facilitate the integration with other datasets in the Linked Data cloud. StdTrip was initially conceived to serve as an aid in a training course on Publishing Open Government Data in Brazil. The course was an initiative of W3C Brasil to promote the adoption of the Linked Data technology by Brazilian government agencies. Target audiences were assumed to have no familiarity with Semantic

Web techniques in general, nor with RDF vocabularies, in particular. To promote vocabulary and standards reuse, we designed a tool that "has it all in one place", i.e., supports all the operations needed to create conceptual model. The StdTrip approach served as an educational tool by "reminding" — or by introducing new — RDF vocabulary concepts to users.

We believe our approach can be further improved as follows. First of all, as we discussed in Section 6.4.1, typically the terminology used to describe the relational database, including table and column names, is inappropriate to be externalized. To examplify this, we could think of a relationship element named *country_id* that relates *City* and *Country*, an acronym *tb_cust* that could represent a table *Customer* or, even worst, an attribute *Ir675F* representing an ISBN code. In such cases, the StdTrip process tackles this lack of semantics with the following techniques:

- A domain expert (e.g. database administrator) first defines an external vocabulary, i.e., a set of terms that will be used to identify the data materialized to Web users. Artificially generated primary keys, the foreign keys that refer to such primary keys and attributes with domains that encode classifications or similar artifacts, when selected for the StdTrip process, should have their internal names replaced by more meaningful names, best suited for external use.
- A common user could replace the inappropriate terminology by consulting documents that fully describe the data represented in the database (e.g. glossary, data dictionary).

It is important to note that, currently, none of these techniques is supported by an automatic or even semi-automatic mechanism during the StdTrip process, making this operation practically unfeasible in the absence of a domain expert or a document that fully describes the database domain. In future work, we plan to add semi-automatic techniques in order to help the user to decide the most adequate terms that characterize the nature of the data itself in the following ways:

- We can take advantage of instance based approaches, such as the one proposed by [46], to suggest suitable names based on the data stored in the dataset. For example, an attribute named *Ir675F*, in the format XXX-XXXXXXXXXX (where Xs are numbers) may be easily identified as ISBN numbers automatically.
- Taking into consideration that the relationships in the ER model — derived from the relational model — often lack proper names, we can use the semantics of the elements related by these relationships and apply Natural Language Processing algorithms to suggest terms that better describe such relationships. For example, a relationship attribute named *country_id*, which relates the entities *City* and *Country*, can be replaced by *isPartOf*, in order to obtain an statement *City isPartOf Country*.
- Following the work of [44], we plan to use Wordnet extensions to expand and normalize the meaning of database comments, using such comments as a source for additional semantics.

Secondly, as we mentioned in Section 6.4, we assume that the input of the StdTrip is a relational database in third normal form (3NF). This assumption has some drawbacks in practice, as many databases might not be well normalized. Without support for database normalization, users might be tempted to directly take the databases as input even if badly designed. We plan to resolve this drawback in the following ways:

- Following the approach of [25] and [48], we plan to automate the process of finding functional dependencies within data, in order to eliminate data duplication in the source tables, and to algorithmically transform a relational schema to third normal form. Please note that there are cases where the third normal form is not possible, e.g. the U.S. Environmental Protection Agency's Facilities Registry System dataset available as CSV on data.gov that model much meaningful data as plain literal strings.
- We also plan to offer more input options, such as W-Ray [35], in which a set of database views, capturing the data that should be published, is manually defined. In this sense, another interesting and helpful input option could be a valid SQL query against the input database.
- We noticed that many relational databases use autonumbered columns to set tables identifiers (primary key). This autonumber does not work properly as identifier for well-known entities such as people, institutions or organizations. Therefore we plan to include the option of replacing the table primary key, whenever possible, for a more suitable column that better identifies what is represented in the table. For example, a table *Person* that uses as primary key an autonumber column *person_id*, could have this key replaced by a column *SSN* (security social number), which would better identify the data stored in the table *Person*.

Finally, as users are likely to be confronted with more than one choice during the StdTrip process, e.g., *foaf:Person* or *foaf:Agent*, we plan to include a mechanism for capturing rationale to register design decisions during the modeling process (stages discussed in Sections 6.4.3 and 6.4.4). A what-who-why memory would be a beneficial asset, allowing the reuse of previous mapping files that could be rapidly updated to adapt to future modifications, improvements and redesign of the dataset.

Acknowledgements The authors would like to thank the reviewers for their contributions. This research was made possible by grants E-26/170028/2008 from FAPERJ and 557.128/2009-9 from CNPq, at the Brazilian Web Science Institute.

References

1. Improving access to government through better use of the web (2009). URL http://www. w3.org/TR/egov-improving/
2. Publishing open government data (2009). URL http://www.w3.org/TR/gov-data/
3. Allemang, D., Hendler, J.: Semantic Web for the Working Ontologist: Effective Modeling in RDFS and OWL. Morgan Kaufmann (2008)

4. Auer, S., Dietzold, S., Lehmann, J., Hellmann, S., Aumueller, D.: Triplify: light-weight linked data publication from relational databases. In: WWW '09: Proceedings of the 18th international conference on World wide web, pp. 621–630. ACM, New York, NY, USA (2009). DOI http://doi.acm.org/10.1145/1526709.1526793

5. Barrasa, J., Corcho, O., Gómez-Pérez, A.: R2O, an extensible and semantically based database-to-ontology mapping language, vol. 3372 (2004)

6. Batini, C., Ceri, S., Navathe, S.B.: Conceptual database design: an Entity-relationship approach (1991)

7. Berners-Lee, T.: Cool uris don't change. Retrieved January 10, 2010, from http://www.w3.org/Provider/Style/URI (1998)

8. Berrueta, D., Phipps, J.: Best practice recipes for publishing rdf vocabularies – w3c working group note. Retrieved December 14, 2010, from http://www.w3.org/TR/swbp-vocab-pub/ (2008)

9. Bizer, C., Cyganiak, R., Heath, T.: How to publish linked data on the web. Retrieved December 14, 2010, from http://www4.wiwiss.fuberlin.de/bizer/pub/LinkedDataTutorial/ (2007)

10. Bizer, C., Heath, T., Ayers, D., Raimond, Y.: Interlinking Open Data on the Web (Poster). In: In Demonstrations Track, 4th European Semantic Web Conference (ESWC2007) (2007)

11. Bizer, C., Seaborne, A.: D2RQ-treating non-RDF databases as virtual RDF graphs (2004)

12. Breitman, K., Casanova, M.A., Truszkowski, W.: Semantic Web: Concepts, Technologies and Applications (NASA Monographs in Systems and Software Engineering). Springer-Verlag New York, Inc., Secaucus, NJ, USA (2006)

13. Breslin, J., Passant, A., Decker, S.: The Social Semantic Web. Springer Publishing Company, Incorporated (2009)

14. Carroll, J.J., Dickinson, I., Dollin, C., Reynolds, D., Seaborne, A., Wilkinson, K.: Jena: implementing the semantic web recommendations, pp. 74–83 (2004)

15. Casanova, M.A., Breitman, K., Brauner, D., Marins, A.: Database conceptual schema matching. IEEE Computer **40**(10), 102–104 (2007)

16. Casanova, M.A., Lauschner, T., Leme, L.A.P., Breitman, K., Furtado, A.L., Vidal, V.: A strategy to revise the constraints of the mediated schema. In: Proc. of the 28th Int'l. Conf. on Conceptual Modeling, *Lecture Notes in Computer Science*, vol. 5829, pp. 265–279. Springer (2009). DOI 10.1007\/978-3-642-04840-1_21

17. Casanova, M.A., de Sá, J.E.A.: Mapping uninterpreted schemes into entity-relationship diagrams: two applications to conceptual schema design. IBM Journal of Research and Development **28**, 82–94 (1984). DOI http://dx.doi.org/10.1147/rd.281.0082

18. Cerbah, F.: Learning highly structured semantic repositories from relational databases. The Semantic Web: Research and Applications pp. 777–781 (2008)

19. Codd, E.F.: A relational model of data for large shared data banks. Communications of the ACM **13**, 377–387 (1970). ACM ID: 362685

20. Cullot, N., Ghawi, R., Yétongnon, K.: DB2OWL: A Tool for Automatic Database-to-Ontology Mapping, pp. 491–494 (2007)

21. d'Aquin, M., Sabou, M., Dzbor, M., Baldassarre, C., Gridinoc, L., Angeletou, S., Motta, E.: Watson: A gateway for the semantic web (2007)

22. David, J.: AROMA results for OAEI 2009 (2009)

23. Do, H.H.: Schema matching and mapping-based data integration (2006). URL http://lips.informatik.uni-leipzig.de/?q=node/211

24. Do, H.H., Rahm, E.: COMA: a system for flexible combination of schema matching approaches, pp. 610–621. VLDB '02. VLDB Endowment (2002). URL http://portal.acm.org/citation.cfm?id=1287369.1287422. ACM ID: 1287422

25. Du, H., Wery, L.: Micro: A normalization tool for relational database designers. Journal of Network and Computer Applications **22**(4), 215–232 (1999). DOI 10.1006/jnca.1999.0096

26. Erling, O., Mikhailov, I.: Rdf support in the virtuoso dbms. Networked Knowledge-Networked Media pp. 7–24 (2009)

27. Euzenat, J., Ferrara, A., Hollink, L., et al.: Results of the ontology alignment evaluation initiative 2009. In: Proc. 4th of ISWC Workshop on Ontology Matching (OM) (2009)
28. Euzenat, J., Shvaiko, P.: Ontology matching. Springer-Verlag, Heidelberg (DE) (2007)
29. Fahad, M.: Er2owl: Generating owl ontology from er diagram. Intelligent Information Processing IV pp. 28–37 (2008)
30. Heath, T., Bizer, C.: Linked Data. Morgan & Claypool Publishers (2011)
31. Heuser, C.A.: Projeto de banco de dados. Sagra Luzzatto (2004)
32. Kinsella, S., Bojars, U., Harth, A., Breslin, J.G., Decker, S.: An interactive map of semantic web ontology usage. In: IV '08: Proceedings of the 2008 12th International Conference Information Visualisation, pp. 179–184. IEEE Computer Society, Washington, DC, USA (2008). DOI http://dx.doi.org/10.1109/IV.2008.60
33. Leme, L.A.P., Casanova, M.A., Breitman, K., Furtado, A.L.: Owl schema matching. Journal of the Brazilian Computer Society **16**(1), 21–34 (2010). DOI 10.1007/s13173-010-0005-3
34. Myroshnichenko, I., Murphy, M.C.: Mapping ER Schemas to OWL Ontologies, vol. 0, pp. 324–329. IEEE Computer Society (2009). DOI http://doi.ieeecomputersociety.org/10.1109/ICSC.2009.61
35. Piccinini, H., Lemos, M., Casanova, M.A., Furtado, A.: W-Ray: A Strategy to Publish Deep Web Geographic Data. In: Proceedings of the 4th International Workshop on Semantic and Conceptual Issues in GIS (SeCoGIS 2010), to appear (2010)
36. Polfliet, S., Ichise, R.: Automated mapping generation for converting databases into linked data. Proc. of ISWC2010
37. Prud'hommeaux, E., Hausenblas, M.: Use cases and requirements for mapping relational databases to rdf. Retrieved December 18, 2010, from http://www.w3.org/TR/rdb2rdf-ucr/ (2010)
38. Rahm, E., Bernstein, P.A.: A survey of approaches to automatic schema matching. The VLDB Journal **10**(4), 334–350 (2001). DOI http://dx.doi.org/10.1007/s007780100057
39. S., D., S., S., R., C.: R2rml: Rdb to rdf mapping language. w3c rdb2rdf working group. Retrieved December 15, 2010, from http://www.w3.org/TR/r2rml/ (2010)
40. Sahoo, S.S., Halb, W., Hellmann, S., Idehen, K., Thibodeau Jr, T., Auer, S., Sequeda, J., Ezzat, A.: A survey of current approaches for mapping of relational databases to rdf. W3C RDB2RDF Incubator Group report (2009)
41. Sauermann, L., Cyganiak, R.: Cool uris for the semantic web. Retrieved January 18, 2010, from http://www.w3.org/TR/cooluris/ (2008)
42. Seddiqui, M.H., Aono, M.: Anchor-Flood: Results for OAEI-2009
43. Sequeda, J.F., Depena, R., Miranker, D.P.: Ultrawrap: Using sql views for rdb2rdf. Proc. of ISWC2009
44. Sorrentino, S., Bergamaschi, S., Gawinecki, M., Po, L.: Schema normalization for improving schema matching. In: Proc. of the 28th International Conference on Conceptual Modeling (ER '09), pp. 280–293. Springer-Verlag, Berlin, Heidelberg (2009). DOI http://dx.doi.org/10.1007/978-3-642-04840-1_22
45. Tirmizi, S., Sequeda, J., Miranker, D.: Translating sql applications to the semantic web, pp. 450–464 (2008)
46. Wang, J., Wen, J.R., Lochovsky, F., Ma, W.Y.: Instance-based schema matching for web databases by domain-specific query probing. In: Proc. of the 13th international conference on Very large data bases (VLDB '04), pp. 408–419. VLDB Endowment (2004)
47. Wang, P., Xu, B.: Lily: Ontology alignment results for OAEI 2009 (2009)
48. Wang, S.L., Shen, J.W., Hong, T.P.: Mining fuzzy functional dependencies from quantitative data, vol. 5, pp. 3600–3605 vol.5 (2000). DOI 10.1109/ICSMC.2000.886568

Chapter 7
Official Statistics and the Practice of Data Fidelity

Richard Cyganiak, Michael Hausenblas, and Eoin McCuirc

Abstract Official statistics are the "crown jewels" of a nation's public data. They are the empirical evidence needed for policy making and economic research. Statistics offices are also among the most data-savvy organisations in government and often have a strong history of publishing data in electronic form. There is hardly any analytical task involving government data that doesn't require some statistical data, such as population figures or economic indicators. At the same time, the handling of statistical data as Linked Data requires particular attention in order to maintain its integrity and fidelity. This chapter gives an introduction to the field of official statistics, discusses the modelling of statistical data in RDF including its integration with other kinds of government data, tools for data conversion and publishing of statistics as Linked Data, and methods for using statistical data in queries, reports, and visualisations.

7.1 The world of statistics

Statistics pervade our modern society. There are a world of bean counters out there, of all different shapes and sizes, counting every and any type of bean. There are serious statistics of economic and social indicators monitoring the likes of population size, inflation, trade and employment. Less serious statistics, unless you are a fan, on football, ice hockey, music, movies and box office statistics and absurd statistics like "74.1% of all statistics are made up on the spot". Of course there are statistics on statistics too. Accurate and reliable statistics provide a basis for making informed judgements about people, products and society.

In this chapter we provide an introduction to the field of official statistics from the Linked Data perspective. First, we will have a look at characteristics of statistics

Correspondance author: Richard Cyganiak, DERI, NUI Galway IDA Business Park, Lower Dangan Galway, Ireland, e-mail: `richard.cyganiak@deri.org`. See the List of Contributors for full contact details.

and formats for representing and disseminating them. Then, in Section 7.2, we motivate the use of Linked Data as a technology for representing statistics. Section 7.3 describes the modelling of statistics as data cubes. Section 7.4 presents a representation of data cubes in the Resource Description Framework (RDF). Section 7.5 guides the reader through tools for converting statistics to Linked Data formats as well as showing how to consume the data, and eventually we conclude this chapter in Section 7.6.

7.1.1 The producers of statistics

The more serious statistics tend to be produced by official national and international agencies. National statistics offices, government departments and other public bodies collect and disseminate statistics at national level. These statistics are collected, collated and disseminated by international agencies to generate a world view of economic and social indicators. To ensure quality and accuracy common methodologies, standards and classifications are used in collecting, classifying (using standardised code lists), processing and publishing statistics. Professional statisticians oversee the work. This work is guided by the UN Fundamental Principles of Official Statistics [1]. This attempts to ensure each bean counter is counting the same kind of beans in the same way.

Statistics can take the form of a snapshot of a point in time like a census where everyone is counted on a particular day or a trend where we compare different periods over time as in the rate of unemployment i.e. a time series. Again statistic can be based on counting the complete population as in a census or by taking a sample and estimating the population based on the sample as in a household survey. Counting a complete population is more accurate but more expensive. The larger the sample the more accurate but the more costly it generally is to produce the statistic. The statistics themselves can be either descriptive and describe data or inferential which reach beyond the data to draw conclusions or forecast beyond the immediate data. How many beans have I got today, how does this compare with last week or last year, do I count them all again, how many will I have next year?

Another key factor is the timeliness of the statistics. To be useful a statistic has to be relevant, accurate and timely. If we get the statistics on all the horses and jockeys in a race after the race is run, it is too late to help us predict a winner.

So for each statistic there is a cost, quality and time aspect. The value of the statistic depends on its relevance, accuracy and timeliness. Each of these attributes comes with a cost. Is it worth compiling the statistic at all? Should we count the beans, plant them or just eat them?

7.1.2 The users of statistics

The users of the statistic are another important consideration. Users can be classed into three categories: tourists, farmers and miners. The tourist users are the general public and interested in information, e.g. tonnes of beans produced. Farmers are the subject matter experts interested in a wide range of statistics usually at aggregate level, e.g. bean harvest over time, by region and variety of bean. Miners are statisticians, researchers and analysts who delve deeply into a particular area of interest at the *microdata* level, e.g. why particular farmers decide to grow a variety of bean. Each different user has preferences on how the statistical data is presented and the actual data itself. Tourist like, tables, graphs, stories and visualisation in paper and online that help them understand the data. Hans Rosling[1] has become a favourite among them for his highly engaging presentations of demographic trends. Farmers prefer datasets, series of aggregate data over time, classified and formatted and easily accessible to computer driven processes, such as the Eurostat database portal[2]. Miners prefer to get as close as possible to the raw data and view the data in a format that facilitates digital analysis, for example, anonymised microdata from a census.

7.1.3 Dissemination formats

Statistics are nowadays typically produced in relational databases, where previously, for example, historical data was published as tables or obtained from microfilm. The raw data captured is cleaned as well as validated, and clean unit records are stored in data tables, which are aggregated ensuring the confidentiality of individuals and entities. Aggregate data is stored and commonly disseminated in *data cubes*. The advantage of data cubes is twofold, first allowing a user to "slice and dice" the cube to pick their area of interest and second allowing the user to pivot the cube to present the data as required.

Our bean example could be a cube of data, by time, country of origin and variety of bean, showing national figures for the value and volume of imports and exports of each variety of bean. Slicing and dicing makes it possible to get data for imports, for a particular year and a specific variety of bean. Pivoting allows the presentation of data by year, bean variety and imports/exports.

Statistics for publication can be disseminated using various media. Paper releases and publications are still common, while the Web is more and more the de facto means of dissemination. Data is disseminated as HTML pages and PDF documents; tables, graphs, visualisations, descriptive text and data cubes are commonly used on the Web. Methodological reports, quality statements, statements of accuracy, sam-

---

[1] Professor of International Health at the Karolinska Institute as well as co-founder and chairman of the Gapminder Foundation.

[2] http://epp.eurostat.ec.europa.eu/portal/page/portal/statistics/search_database

Rating	Meaning	Example
★	On the Web, under an open licence	PDF document containing tables
★★	As above, but in structured format	Excel sheet, PC-Axis
★★★	As above, but in non-proprietary format	CSV, SDMX
★★★★	As above, and observations, etc. have URIs	RDF/XML
★★★★★	As above, and links to other datasets for context	RDFa with out-bound links

Table 7.1 Examples of statistics dissemination formats along the 5-star plan for Open Data.

pling techniques classification, metadata descriptors and codes list used are all uploaded to the Web. Interactive maps, Wikis, online bulletins, animation and video make data more meaningful, while social media like Twitter, Flickr, YouTube and Facebook make it more accessible.

Dissemination formats can be understood along the " plan for Open Data" [6], introduced by Tim Berners-Lee. The Table 7.1 lists respective examples for statistical data and formats.

7.1.4 Major data sets

The Table 7.2 shows major providers of statistic data sets on the international level. Additionally, governmental agencies at all levels, from local authorities such as counties and cities to nation-level bodies [2] typically produce and disseminate official statistics.

Publisher	Coverage	Access
Eurostat	Economy, Population, Industry, Transport, etc.	browse, download
Factbook	History, People, Government, Geography, etc,	browse, download
IMF	Finance	browse, download/pay-wall
OECD	Aid, Economy, Education, Health, Unemployment, etc.	browse, download
UN	Crime, Education, Energy, Environment, Food, Labour, etc.	browse, download, tools
WHO	Health	browse
World Bank	Agriculture, Infrastructure, Labor, Economy, Education, etc.	browse, download, API

Table 7.2 Major providers of statistic data sets, worldwide.

7.2 Why linked statistics?

In the following we will argue that *linked statistics* on the one hand sits on the sweet-spot in the "cost vs. data fidelity" curve, delivering rich and straight-forward to consume data, in a standardised format. Secondly, the ability to enrich the statistics with contextual data turns out to be a major win. We will motivate and discuss these two aspects in greater detail now.

7.2.1 Costs vs. data fidelity

Putting together statistics is a labours task; disseminating them can be as well: quite often the need arises to deliver custom statistics, for example, a local authority such as a county council needs to report to an up-stream entity like the national government, which typically involves a person manually assembling the report, including a selection of relevant statistics along with interpretations. While the state of the art in disseminating official statistics still seems to focus on carefully laid out PDF documents, this seems to be sub-optimal in the light of Tim Berners-Lee's " plan for Open Data". Obviously, re-using data that is locked-up in PDF documents is hard. Additionally, automating (at least parts of the workflow) seems not possible.

With the rise of special-purpose, domain-specific formats such as PC-Axis or SDMX, which are at time of writing more and more deployed in national and international statistics agencies, re-using data certainly is more straight-forward possible. However, with the complexity introduced by these formats, the barrier for consuming the data is raised as well. On the other hand, general-purpose formats such as Microsoft's Excel or CSV are very widely deployed and a number of tools and libraries in any kind of programming language one could possibly think of exist to process them. The down-side of these formats is equally obvious: as much of the high-quality annotations and metadata (how to interpret the observations at hand) is not or only partially captured, the data fidelity suffers. Even worse, using these formats, the data and metadata typically gets separated.

To illustrate the situation we are facing with today's formats, consider Eurostat's bulk download facility[3] that offers the data in TSV (Tab Separated Values, a CSV variant) and SDMX format. So, one has the choice between using SDMX and a rather simple tabular representation in TSV. Let's imagine we go for the second option: in order to being able to use the data, one needs to i) consult the table of contents that includes the list of the datasets available to figure what datasets are available and where they are located, and ii) by using the "dictionaries" of all the coding systems used in the datasets gain an understanding how to interpret them. Not only is the data (TSV) separated from the metadata (table of contents and dictionaries)

---

[3] http://epp.eurostat.ec.europa.eu/portal/page/portal/statistics/
bulk_download

but also does the latter not come in a standardised format, meaning interoperability issues and additional burden on the consumer.

With linked statistics, that is, statistic data in Linked Data format, one can leverage the existing infrastructure[4]—hundreds of tools and libraries in several major programming languages—as well as retaining metadata along with the data, yielding high data fidelity, consumable in a standardised, straight-forward way.

In all fairness, one has to point out that for the foreseeable future, Linked Data formats will not simply replace Excel sheets and the like. The reason being that the majority of the developers and also end-users are very familiar with these formats, which also happen to offer great support for visualisation as well as integration, for example Microsofts Office suite or Google Docs. However, we reckon that, in the next couple of years, the advances concerning plug-ins as well as the integration into existing applications—for example, cf. how to use Microsoft's Pivot as an interface for the visual exploration of Linked Data[5]—will eventually compensate this shortcoming.

7.2.2 Context

In this section we will have a closer look at the second important aspect we pointed out earlier, delivered through applying the fourth Linked Data principles and ultimately being rewarded with five stars in Tim Berners-Lee's "5-star plan for Open Data": putting the statistics into a context.

Providing identifiers for every observation, code, dimension, etc. allows for fine-grained documentation and annotation, and makes everything citable. For example, if the URI of an observation is known, one can make assertions about it on a global scale; this could include provenance, trust or belief assertions [9].

Going beyond the operations of slicing, filtering and visualising statistics data requires typically out-of-band information to *combine statistical data with other kinds of data*. For example, in a business intelligence application, demographical statistics might be required to be presented along with facts about the region, such as what political party is in charge at a given time. This contextual information is not found in the statistics data itself. An archetypical work-around might be as follows: assuming the statistics data is available in a spreadsheet and one of the column headings reads `city`, a human could, for example, look up the respective column values (like, "Dublin", "Galway", etc.) in Wikipedia to (manually) integrate the information about who rules the respective city. Having explicit links from the statistics data—in the case at hand, it could be a link to DBpedia along the city-dimension—would allow a program to directly integrate the aspired contextual information, such as found in the *European Digital Competitiveness Report* [3].

---

[4] http://www.w3.org/2001/sw/wiki/Tools

[5] http://lists.w3.org/Archives/Public/public-lod/2010Mar/0229.html

Another benefit linked statistics provide and in fact enable are *queries across datasets*. Given the dimensions are linked, one can learn from a certain observation's dimension value, other provided dimension values, enabling the automation of cross-dataset queries. For example, consider the case where one has two statistics at hand: one that covers product sales by countries over the past ten years, and a second one (likely from an official statitics agency) that represents demographics per country (distribution of male, female, age groups, etc.). In order to answer a question like: *what sort of product do women between 20 and 30 prefer?* one surely needs to consult both statistics. Now consider the linked statistics case where the country instances in the sales statistics are interlinked with the ones in the demographics statistics. It is plain to see that, once both statistics are available in Linked Data format and in fact interlinked, one can execute a query that pulls in the related data from across the datasets, hence cutting down integration costs and delivering results quicker.

7.3 From tables to data cubes: Modelling of statistical data

The most familiar representation of statistical data might be the lowly table, perhaps with countries down the page, years increasing from left to right, and figures for agricultural exports in each cell. But statistical data rarely only has two dimensions. Once a third dimension is added, for example if the exports are subdivided by agricultural product, then we already have a data cube. This can be thought of as stacking multiple tables, one for each product, above each other. Data cubes are not limited to three dimensions; four or more dimensions are common.

A two-dimensional table can be derived from a high-dimensional cube by repeatedly applying two operations. First, one can "flatten" or "roll up" the cube by summing up or averaging all the values along one dimension, e.g., by considering the total of all products. Second, one can Òslice through the cube across one dimension, picking only a single value of interest, e.g., a single product or a single country.

Data cubes are characterised by their *dimensions*, its *measures*, and possibly by additional *attributes*. Each "cell" in the cube is called an *observation*.

7.3.1 Dimensions

The *dimensions* of a statistical data cube tell us what each observation in the cube is all about. In a cube of agricultural trade statistics, the dimensions might be: *country*, *product*, *time period*, and *trade activity*. An individual observation is associated with a unique value along each of these dimensions. A single observation might tell us exactly how many tons of lentils (*product*) were imported (*trade activity*) in 2009 (*time period*) into the Republic of Ireland (*country*).

Many data cubes include time as a dimension. Any such cube is known as a *time series*.

7.3.2 Code lists

The possible values for each dimension are taken from a *code list*, also known as a *classification*. A code list could be a list of countries, or a list of agricultural products. (Code lists are equivalent to what's called a controlled vocabulary in other fields. Some code lists are hierarchical, and thus can be considered small taxonomies.)

The design, maintenance and standardisation of such code lists is an important activity in statistics-producing organisations. Does the code for the common bean subsume kidney beans, or is there a separate code for those? Should the same code be used for pre-unification West Germany and post-unification Germany, or separate codes? Is the UK one country or four? Is "2009" the calendar year or the fiscal year? Such questions can usually be answered in a pragmatic way depending on the purpose of the statistic and its collection methodology. But once made, the decision has to be documented and applied consistently.

Code lists are especially valuable if they are shared between multiple data cubes, or even between multiple statistics-producing organisations, because this makes different statistics directly comparable. One can imagine using agricultural import statistics together with demographic statistics to predict economic trends.

7.3.3 Measures

The *measure* represents the phenomenon being observed. What kind of quantity is being measured or counted in an observation?

Cubes may contain one or multiple measures. Multi-measure cubes are often organised by adding another dimension frequently, the measure dimension. The measure dimension of an agricultural statistics cube might tell us that a number measures "export", "import", or "production".

7.3.4 Attributes

Finally, observations may have attached attributes. Attributes help us interpret the observation value. Is it measured in tons, units, or US$? If it is measured in US$, then is there a unit multiplier (thousand, million)? What level of precision is used?

One particularly important attribute in many cubes is the observation status: Is this number preliminary? Is it an estimate? Attributes are often coded (possible values are taken from a code list, such as a list of units of measurement), but can be free text as well (footnotes).

This model of organising statistical gives us many advantages:

- All observations within a data cube can be readily compared,
- Statements of completeness can be made about a cube,
- There are well-defined and documented code lists,
- Individual observations can be annotated with attributes.

Next we will explore the expression of these statistical concepts–code lists, observations, dimensions, data cubes–in RDF.

7.4 Data cubes in RDF

In this section, we will explore how to describe a data cube in RDF, starting with its code lists, followed by the structure of a data cube, and finally we will express individual observations.

7.4.1 URI sets and concept schemes

A code list is a collection of codes. Each code represents a certain concept or entity such as a country, a time period, or an agricultural product.

Some of these entities are important for information management far beyond the area of statistics. For example, administrative areas such as countries, counties and electoral divisions are relevant for many kinds of government data. Defining standard URIs as identifiers for these entities is an important part of many Linked Government Data activities. The report *Designing URI Sets for the UK Public Sector* [8] provides good rationale and practical recommendations for the design and management of such URIs. URIs defined according to such guidelines, grouped together into a *URI set* by a shared RDFS/OWL class, make excellent code lists.

Where standard identifiers have not been defined for the entities in a code list, we can use the the *Simple Knowledge Organization System (SKOS)* [10] to represent the code list in RDF. provides classes and properties for representing different kinds of knowledge organization schemes, including controlled vocabularies, in RDF.

When translating a code list to SKOS, the concept behind each code becomes an instance of the skos:Concept class. As always with RDF, best practice is to mint a globally unique, persistent and authoritative URIs for each skos:Concept.

The actual code string, such as "IE" for the Republic of Ireland, becomes a skos:notation value of that concept and the code list itself becomes a skos:ConceptScheme. SKOS provides rich terms for documenting a code list, including skos:definition, skos:scopeNote, and skos:changeNote.

Where possible, URI sets and SKOS concept schemes for code lists should be re-used between different data cubes. Where this is not practical, SKOS provides terms for mapping between different concept schemes. This allows the expression of equivalencies between codes in different code lists, and the publication of such mappings on the Web.

7.4.2 Describing data cube structures with the Data Cube Vocabulary

Now that we have the code lists for our data cube expressed in RDF, we can move on to the structure of the cube itself. In the following we will use a data set extracted from a StatsWales report [5] describing life expectancy broken down by region, age and time to illustrate the steps. This example statistic is shown in Table 7.3.

	2004-6		2005-7		2006-8	
	Male	**Female**	**Male**	**Female**	**Male**	**Female**
Newport	76.7	80.7	77.1	80.9	77.0	81.5
Cardiff	78.7	83.3	78.6	83.7	78.7	83.4
Monmouthshire	76.6	81.3	76.5	81.5	76.6	81.7
Merthyr Tydfil	75.5	79.1	75.5	79.4	74.9	79.6

Table 7.3 Example statistic excerpt from StatsWales.

Every data cube conforms to a certain *data structure definition (DSD)*. The DSD characterizes the data cube by specifying its dimensions, measure and attributes. A DSD can be defined in RDF using the *Data Cube Vocabulary* [6].

The Data Cube Vocabulary is based on the *SDMX Information Model (SDMX-IM)* [4], an abstract model for the representation of statistical data and metadata. SDMX-IM is part of the SDMX suite of standards[7], a widely accepted industry standard in the statistics field that also includes the XML-based SDMX-ML format and a web service specification for accessing statistical data. The Data Cube Vocabulary is intended as a companion to SDMX that represents the core of the SDMX-IM in RDF, and hence allows the publishing and querying of SDMX-compatible data in a Linked Data context.

An outline of the Data Cube Vocabulary is shown in Figure 7.1. A cube structure is defined as an instance of the `qb:DataStructureDefinition` class. Each of its *components*–a collective term for dimensions, measures and attributes–is defined with the help of an instance of `qb:ComponentSpecification`, which connects the DSD to the actual component.

---

[6] http://linked-statistics.org/datacube/

[7] http://sdmx.org/

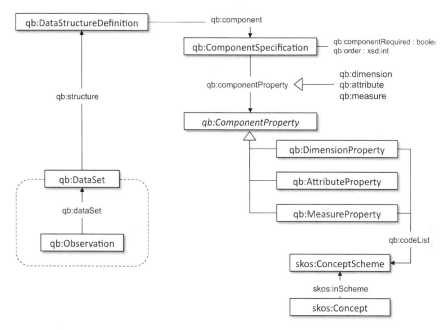

Fig. 7.1 An outline of the Data Cube Vocabulary. Terms for defining data structure definitions to the top and right; terms for expressing a data cube and its observation to the bottom left.

Components (dimensions, measures and attributes) are defined as RDF properties in the Data Cube Vocabulary. As we will see in the next subsection, this allows for very compact representation of actual observations.

Components may be marked as optional with the `qb:componentRequired` property, which takes an `xsd:boolean` value (true or false). A required component must be present on every observation. Dimensions are never optional, as they are necessary to uniquely define an observation's position within the cube. Measures are usually required. Attributes are often optional.

Components can be coded or uncoded. A coded component takes its values from a limited set of possible values, expressed as a code list. An uncoded component can take any value. Most dimensions are coded, with the time dimension sometimes an exception. The measure is usually uncoded, as its value is the measured number or quantity. Attributes are sometimes coded (e.g., observation status) and sometimes uncoded (e.g., a free-text footnote).

As described in the previous section, a code list is usually described in RDF as a `skos:ConceptScheme` or as an RDF class that represents a URI set. A coded property is linked to its code list via the `qb:codeList` property.

7.4.3 Expressing observation data in RDF

The final, and bulkiest, part of a cube that can be expressed in RDF is the actual observation data, the numbers in the cells (see Figure 7.1, lower left).

While an instance of `qb:DataStructureDefinition` defines a re-usable structure for cubes, a concrete cube is an instance of `qb:DataSet`. It is connected to the DSD that defines its schema through the `qb:structure` property.

Each observation is represented as an instance of `qb:Observation`. It is connected to the `qb:DataSet` resource through the `qb:dataSet` property.

The other properties of an observation instance are the dimensions, the measure, and the attributes. This is why these components were defined as RDF properties in the previous section: this allows them to be directly used as properties of the observation instance. There must be exactly one value for every required component. There may be zero or one value for the optional components. Typically, these are:

- Exactly one value for each dimension property, taking a value from the dimension's associated code list,
- exactly one value for the measure property, taking a numeric value,
- possibly additional values for the attribute properties.

This completes the simple representation of an entire statistical dataset in RDF.

7.5 Tools of the trade

In this section we discuss methods and tools to convert statistics to Linked Data formats as well as show how to consume the data, especially in terms of query and visualisation.

Most statistical data is produced in professional statistics packages that already support the creation and management of code lists and data cube structures. However, currently no such package has the capability of directly exporting RDF or publishing in Linked Data format. Therefore, a typical workflow involves the conversion of data exports from these packages to RDF.

7.5.1 Conversion

Depending on the original format there are different options available to convert 1-star to 3-star statistics data to 4/ data.

From Excel or CSV. Google Refine is a tool for understanding and manipulating tabular data, such as CSV, TSV or Excel. While Google Refine has rich import and export capabilities, it does not have an intuitive way to export RDF data. The RDF Extension for Google Refine [12] enables reconciliation against RDF data sources as well as exporting the data in an RDF serialisation.

The export functionality is based on describing the shape of the desired RDF through a skeleton detailing what resources and literals to include in the RDF graph, what relations to set between them and what URIs to use for resources. The skeleton design is supported through a GUI[8]. The exporter iterates through the project rows and evaluates *Google Refine Expression Language* (GREL) expressions in the skeleton based on the cell's content to produce a sub-graph corresponding to each row. The final RDF graph is the result of merging all the row sub-graphs.

Another alternative is XLWrap [11]. It is a spreadsheet-to-RDF wrapper capable of transforming spreadsheets (Microsoft Excel, OpenDocument, CSV, TSV, Google Spreadsheets, etc.) to arbitrary RDF graphs based on a mapping specification. It can load local files or download remote files via HTTP. XLWrap is able to execute SPARQL queries, and since it is possible to define multiple virtual class extents in a mapping specification, it can be used to integrate information from multiple spreadsheets. Compared to Google Refine, XLWrap shines when many spreadsheets have to be converted according to a common reproducible process. The effort for converting an individual spreadsheet is significantly higher though.

From relational databases. For statistics data that originates from relational databases, D2R Server [7] can be used to perform the conversion. D2R Server is a tool for publishing the content of relational databases as Linked Data through a declarative mapping that specifies how resources are identified and how property values are generated from database content. Based on this mapping, D2R Server allows Web agents to retrieve RDF as well as HTML representations of resources and to query non-RDF databases using SPARQL.

From other formats. Conversion from other formats, such as PC Axis or SDMX-ML, still requires custom coding as general tools for converting from these formats are not yet available.

7.5.2 Publishing and Enrichment

Once data has been converted to RDF, it is typically loaded into a SPARQL store. This enables fine-grained queries of the statistics, as well as the creation of custom applications and visualisations.

Linked Data publishing. The Linked Data principles call for the use of resolvable HTTP URIs as identifiers in RDF data. *Linked Data Pages*[9] is a template-based framework that exposes data from a SPARQL endpoint both for humans and in RDF serialisations. An exemplary screen-shot is shown in Fig. 7.2. The framework currently supports the navigation of the data and identification of URIs of entities and schema items for SPARQL queries. A number of templates for rendering certain well-known entities (such as people or places) is in preparation at time of writing.

---

[8] http://lab.linkeddata.deri.ie/2010/grefine-rdf-extension/

[9] https://github.com/csarven/linked-data-pages

Link discovery. The use of HTTP URIs as identifiers for codes in code lists enables a light-weight integration of datasets via links. These links are qualified with the type of the relation between linked resources that they express, such as equality represented with `owl:sameAs` or `skos:closeMatch`. A tool to set the typed links in RDF dataset is the Silk Link Discovery Framework [13].

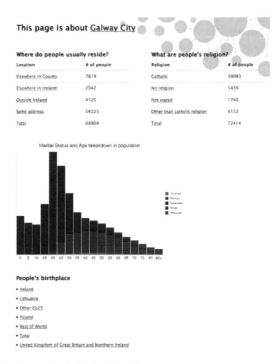

Fig. 7.2 Rendering of statistics in Linked Data Pages.

7.5.3 Consumption

From a consumer perspective, statistics data in RDF has a number of advantages but also challenges. Exploring a dataset is typically straight-forward and assisted through the self-descriptive nature of the data. Depending on the application that consumes the linked statistics a data dump and/or the availability of a SPARQL endpoint can be beneficial. Utilising a SPARQL endpoint, one can build powerful visualisations and provide context-rich navigation. On page 149 we show an example SPARQL query against statistics data in Fig. 7.3 along with an excerpt of the result set for the subject `d:75-79` in the Table 7.4.

```
PREFIX qb: <http://purl.org/linked-data/cube#>

SELECT ?observation ?property ?value
FROM <http://geo.data-gov.ie/city/galway.rdf>
WHERE {
    ?observation a qb:Observation ;
                 ?property ?value .
}
```

Fig. 7.3 Exemplary SPARQL query against DataCube data.

observation	property	value
d:75-79	rdf:type	<http://purl.org/linked-data/cube#Observation>
d:75-79	sdmxd:refPeriod	<http://reference.data.gov.uk/id/year/2006>
d:75-79	sdmxd:sex	<http://purl.org/linked-data/sdmx/2009/code/sex-F>
d:75-79	qb:dataSet	<http://stats.data-gov.ie/data/persons-by-gender-age-and-marital-status>
d:75-79	dg:age2	<http://stats.data-gov.ie/codelist/age2/75-79>
d:75-79	dg:geoArea	<http://geo.data-gov.ie/city/galway>
d:75-79	dg:maritalStatus	<http://stats.data-gov.ie/codelist/marital-status/divorced>
d:75-79	dg:population	"8"^^xsd:integer

Table 7.4 Result of the exemplary SPARQL query from Fig. 7.3.

Note that for readability reasons, we have used prefixes in the results with the following mapping:

```
d: http://stats.data-gov.ie/data/persons-by-gender-age-and-marital-status/2006/galway-city/F/divorced/
sdmxd: http://purl.org/linked-data/sdmx/2009/dimension#
dg: http://stats.data-gov.ie/property/
```

A prototypical DataCube rendering application[10] is depicted in Fig. 7.4, aiming to provide a fine-grained navigable interface for statistical Linked Data expressed in the DataCube vocabulary.

Fig. 7.4 Rendering of statistics represented in DataCube.

7.6 Conclusion

In this chapter we have provided an introduction to the field of official statistics from the Linked Data perspective. We have discussed characteristics and formats of statistics data as well as the modelling of statistical data in RDF including its integration with other kinds of government data. We have reviewed tools for data conversion and publishing of statistics as Linked Data, and presented a selection of methods for using statistical data in queries, reports, and visualisations.

One take-away message is that code lists are vital and that, once they are available on the Web, in a standard format (SKOS), the consumers greatly benefit from it. We did not cover the ability of DataCube to represent slices and aggregates as well as other advanced topics, such as publication schedules or how to describe relationships between datasets (such as derived-from, etc.), essentially representing provenance. Further topics worthy being explored are microdata and with it confidentiality issues.

The main barrier today is, in our experience, that the conversion tools from SDMX, PC-Axis and the like to Linked Data formats are not widely available and mature enough for production use. This is also true for tools that allow one to interact with the data, for example a solid and powerful DataCube viewer.

---

[10] http://code.google.com/p/human-readable-data-cube-interface/

References

1. Fundamental Principles of Official Statistics.   `http://unstats.un.org/unsd/` `methods/statorg/FP-English.htm`.
2. Statistics Finland: Producers and publishers of statistics, 2010. `http://www.stat.fi/` `tup/tilvir/index_en.html`.
3. European Commission: European Digital Competitiveness Report, 2011.   `http:` `//ec.europa.eu/information_society/digital-agenda/documents/` `edcr.pdf`.
4. SDMX Information Model: UML conceptual design.   Sdmx 2.1 technical specification, SDMX Initiative, April 2011. `http://sdmx.org/wp-content/uploads/2011/` `04/SDMX_2-1_SECTION_2_InformationModel.zip`.
5. StatsWales: Report number 003311, 2011. `http://www.statswales.wales.gov.` `uk/TableViewer/tableView.aspx?ReportId=3816`.
6. Berners-Lee, T.   Linked Data–Design Issues, 2006.   `http://www.w3.org/` `DesignIssues/LinkedData.html`.
7. Bizer, C. and Cyganiak, R. D2R server - publishing relational databases on the semantic web. In *Poster at the 5th International Semantic Web Conference*, 2006.
8. Davidson, P.   Designing URI Sets for the UK Public Sector.   A report from the Public Sector Information Domain of the CTO CouncilÕs cross-Government Enterprise Architecture, Cabinet Office, October 2009. `http://www.cabinetoffice.gov.uk/` `resource-library/designing-uri-sets-uk-public-sector`.
9. Hausenblas, M.   Linked Open Data star scheme by example, 2010.   `http://lab.` `linkeddata.deri.ie/2010/star-scheme-by-example/`.
10. Isaac, A. and Summers, E. SKOS Simple Knowledge Organization System Primer. W3C Working Group Note, World Wide Web Consortium, August 2009. `http://www.w3.org/` `TR/skos-primer/`.
11. Langegger, A. and Wöss, W. XLWrap - Querying and Integrating Arbitrary Spreadsheets with SPARQL. In *8th International Semantic Web Conference (ISWC2009)*, 2009.
12. Maali, F., Cyganiak, R. and Peristeras, V. Re-using Cool URIs: Entity Reconciliation Against LOD Hubs. In *WWW 2011 Workshop: Linked Data on the Web (LDOW2011), (Hyderabad, India)*, 2011.
13. Volz, J., Bizer, C., Gaedke, M. and Kobilarov, G. Silk â A Link Discovery Framework for the Web of Data. In *WWW 2009 Workshop: Linked Data on the Web (LDOW2009)*, Madrid, Spain, 2009.

Part III
Consuming Linked Government Data

Linked Data is only useful if it can be used. Users of governmental content may be inter- or intra-agency in nature or from the general public. All of those categories are addressed in this part.

Pierre Desrochers describes the merging of traditional information and Linked Data techniques to the problems of visualization within the Government of Canada. Qing Liu and her colleagues report on their progress tying together many inter-agency, disparate data sets for sustainability science in Australia. Lastly, DiFranzo et al record their experiences creating mashups on governmental Linked Data for public consumption.

Chapter 8
Visualizing Open Government: Case Study of the Canadian Recordkeeping Approach

Pierre Desrochers

Abstract This chapter highlights the necessity of raising societal awareness of what is available to citizens in terms of government information. *What is not known cannot be made known.* It provides an overview of the organizational structure and information resources context within government organizations as part of linked government data initiatives. It examines some practical approaches used in governments underpinning the persistence and discoverability of information and discusses pro-disclosure schemes for government information as a means to facilitate the collection and dissemination of information following linked data principles. The chapter is supported by a case study from the Government of Canada's implementation of recordkeeping. It provides best practices for an up-front assessment of information resources based on criteria of value that can facilitate the identification, collection and dissemination of government data in a linked form. Visualization techniques are presented as a means to encourage greater understanding of the context for disclosure of information resources of business value through linked government data and information tools and techniques explored in other chapters.

8.1 Introduction

To Know and Be Known. This is the title of the Report from the 1969 Canadian Federal Task Force on Government Information chaired by D'Iberville Fortier[17], which set the context and tone for nearly twenty-five years of subsequent discussion on the development and emergence of access to information legislation in Canada, finally passed in 1983. Forty years later, the concepts embedded in the title of this Report continue to resonate in our emerging and evolving digital society and the growing expectations for access to public sector information.

Correspondance author: Pierre Desrochers, Library and Archives Canada, 550 Boul. de la Cité, Gatineau, QC, K1A 0N4, e-mail: pierre.desrochers@bac-lac.gc.ca.

Over the past few decades, governments have recognized that effective and efficient management of documents, records, data and information[1] constitutes a fundamental component of successful public administration[45, pp.3-6].This chapter establishes the relative relationship of linked government data to foundational principles of "openness", and in particular and most importantly, **to the necessity of raising societal awareness of what is available to citizens**.

Essential to this chapter is the understanding that open data is not necessarily, nor does it equate with, open government. Open government goes beyond concepts of open data, concepts of open innovation from government, or the usage or opportunities offered by the use of new forms of information and communication technologies. The concepts of open government are well defined by the OECD [42, p.28], i.e., as foundational principles for good governance; of transparent, accountable decision-making processes of the government under the rule of law necessary for the effective and efficient delivery of programs and service by governments.

Structurally, this chapter is presented in three parts. The first two parts are context setting sections that provide a foundation for the application of the visualization technique explored in Part III. Part I provides a literature review and examines the practical approaches used by documentary heritage institutions to address some of the information resource management and development issues related to the application of linked data and publication of government information to the Web. The main focus on this part is the fundamental role standards have in creating and maintaining linkages across government information holdings. The literature review provided is by no means exhaustive, however it provides relevant references for researchers, academics and documentary heritage professionals interested in pursuing further research.

Part II describes pro-disclosure schemes for government information and their subsequent disclosure through a "Whole of Government Information Publication Scheme" model. It outlines the use of publication schemas for governments holdings, which evolved through the use of Freedom of Information legislation in Australia, the United Kingdom, and in Canada, and can be repurposed for use in linked government data initiatives.

---

[1] The concepts of records, documents, data and information are shaped by an understanding of these terms by a diverse field of experts, the expansion and reformulation of legislative instruments, and by the gradual adoption and study of new forms of information processing. These terms have different meanings based on contextual understanding from within the field of experts or users, such as for business managers as well as recordkeeping, information management and information technology specialists. For the purpose of the Government of Canada, these are defined in the Treasury Board Secretariat's Directive on Recordkeeping[49]:

Information resources (*Ressources documentaires*): Any documentary material produced in published and unpublished form regardless of communications source, information format, production mode or recording medium. Information resources include textual records (memos, reports, invoices, contracts, etc.), electronic records (e-mails, databases, internet, intranet, data etc.), new communication media (instant messages, wikis, blogs, podcasts, etc.), publications (reports, books, magazines), films, sound recordings, photographs, documentary art, graphics, maps, and artefacts.

Part III uses a case study of the development of a recordkeeping regime in the Government of Canada (GC) to demonstrate the applicability of an up-stream assessment of information resources based on criteria of value for the express purpose of deciding their continuing persistence, preservation or disposition. This part documents the benefits of applying information visualization techniques to represent the linkages across the business enterprises of government, essentially the pancorporate business and information architecture of the GC. This approach and visualization technique can serve as a means to describe an organizational ontology essential to the provision of linked government data initiatives.

8.2 Part I - Information Resource Management

The following section provides a brief literature overview of international standards in library and information science underpinning the discoverability, provenance, and persistence of government information. The aim is to provide an overview of the role that normative or non-normative standards have in creating and maintaining linkages across information domains, to support collaboration and interoperability initiatives. In terms of practical solutions, the US Government Printing Office's (GPO) Federal Digital System (FDsys) repository demonstrates the applicability of a persistent identifier system for government information that can serve as a foundational element for linked government data.

The need for reliable, accurate and timely information for decision-makers requires that information resources are created, captured and stored and that their structure, context and content is intact. Canadian government employees are asked to

> [. . .] document actions and decisions in support of government programs and activities, and maintain information so that it is accessible to anyone who is authorized to have access, including those individuals exercising their rights to access information under the Access to Information Act and the Privacy Act. Managing information to support transparency and accountability also means reporting on performance in ways that are clear to Canadians and Parliament.[51]

The need for information to be discoverable. That it is what it purports to be (authentic, reliable). That its origin can be ascertained (provenance). And that it can be retrieved for long as is needed (persistence), requires standardized principles and approaches by business enterprise and business managers, and by society at large. Past approaches and principles based on analogue published material, and previously represented in flat-like structure, differs from information presented dynamically on the Web. Conversely, the standards which were once used to describe and organize information in a printed form are no longer necessarily relevant to the hyper structured forms of information now found on the Web[18, p.42]. The following perspectives in this section are based on linked-data publishing to the Web. They do not cover methods, techniques, and standards for sources of structured information that are not available on the web, or in what is commonly called the "deep web" (large sources of unstructured information).

8.2.1 Persistence and Provenance of Government Information

With respect to provenance, a number of observations can be made based on the fact that government publishing is still operating in an analogue publishing model (i.e., information flows from the government to media and citizens alike). Likewise, the social transformations within society have gradually shifted this relationship to one where government has become a platform for collaboration and innovation. Consequently, ascertaining and validating that the information is what it purports to be becomes fundamental for segments of society charged with preserving a society's documentary heritage.

Making persistent URIs for information resources is an arduous and resource intensive task in government, especially for those responsible for preserving a society's documentary heritage. On the need for persistent locators for information resources, Tim Berners-Lee in his statement on Linked Data Design Issues stated that "URIs identify any kind of object or concept"[10]. He specifically mentions that derivatives of the URI scheme such as Digital Object Identifier (DOI) as problematic. In contrast, John Erickson and others[25, 26, 46], have articulated the specific value in DOI, as well as addressed some of the concerns brought about by Tim Berners-Lee. Chu, in her book on "Information Representation and Retreival in the Digital Age"[18, pp.44-45] provides an overview of the DOI system as a means to provide a seamless, uniform permanent linking mechanism. Likewise, Zeng and Qin provide in their book on metadata[63] provide an overview of the various metadata standards used in archival and preservation environments that address some of the challenges and opportunities in providing persistence to information resources over time. These include Encoded Archival Description (EAD) and the Metadata Object Description Schema (MODS) and the MAchine-Readable Cataloging (MARC) family. Recently, the W3C Linked Library Data Incubator Group[59] have investigated various issues surrounding the use of linked data techniques for library data, including resources for describing library and museum authorities as Linked Data.

In an presentation at the Library of Congress on November 16, 2010, Kate Zwaard from U.S. Government Printing Office's provided an overview of the suite of tools and services that helps GPO preserve and provide long-term access to the digital publications of the US Federal government[38]. To quote the LoC overview of the event[38]:

> And while the FDsys is a modern software environment, the roots of the issues it was designed to solve go back to the early days of GPO. The FDLP [Federal Depository Library Program] worked remarkably well for print publications for over a century, but as agencies opted to host more and more publications on their websites instead of printing them, it became more difficult for users to find what they were looking for. Instead of going to a library or a catalog and looking for an item, you had to know what organization (or sub-organization) was responsible for producing the documents and where they were posted on

the web. More importantly, no federal government entity looked after preservation of the content for public access. Material could be put on a webpage and taken down the next day, or accidentally corrupted, or rendered unusable by obsolescence of technology.

The FDsys is the U.S. Government Printing Office Electronic system which provides electronic access to Federal electronic information, and is an example of systems that demonstrate the use of persistent identifier systems for government. This system provides online access free of charge to official publications of the U.S. Federal Government. These can include, amongst others, presidential papers, congressional papers, Congressional Bills, hearings and records, and other foundational government information. It also provides an ability to provide this information in standard XML formats as well as the ability to download the content and the metadata in a compressed file format (encapsulating the content and metadata together for long-term preservation and persistence).

8.2.2 Discoverability of Government Information

Locating information across business domains of activity within government in the past involved library and information science techniques. These same techniques have now transposed themselves to the inner workings of linking government data. Recently, the W3C's Library Linked Data incubator group [59] articulated[60] that:

> A re-orientation in the library perspective on information interoperability is needed, building on existing Web architecture and standards, in order to bring this content to the Web. A lot of structured data is already available within library systems and could be released as Linked Data, using Semantic Web technologies. Cultural heritage institutions could be a major provider of authoritative datasets (persons, topicsÉ) for the Linked Data Web.

This is not new, Hjartarson and Hudon[31] provide a historical perspective on the establishment of government wide thesauri by the Canadian and UK governments, as well as work on the creation of "metathesauri" to support the ongoing operations of government and how these can be used to "increase semantic interoperability"[31, p.49].

One problem surfaced by Hjartarson and Hudon was that across these systems, it proved difficult to capture the language of each business domain via term-based definitions. What was one term for specialists working in one business domain in government did not necessarily equate to a similar term used by another business domain. To facilitate this retrieval, documentary heritage professionals within government have been engaged in the process of developing controlled vocabularies such as subject heading schemes, classification schemes and thesauri to be applied to information resources. Some of the most well-known of these are the Library of Congress Subject Headings (LCSH), the Dewey Decimal Classification (DDC), and the Library of Congress Classification (LCC). Canadian examples include the Canadian Subject Headings (CSH) or the Répertoire de vedettes-matière (RVM), the GC Core Subject Thesaurus (CST) and the GC Records Management

Metadata Standard (GCRMMS). The W3C[58] considers that these examples, when used to browse collections, catalogues, or other structured forms of data are representations of knowledge organization systems (KOS). Miles and Pérez-Agüera[40] provide Simple Knowledge Organization System (SKOS) as an example of a formal language representing controlled vocabularies that can be used for sharing and linking knowledge organization systems to the Web. Thomas Baker and Johannes Keizer[48] also provide an overview of the application of SKOS in a Resource Description Framework (RDF).

In effect, controlled vocabularies are used for describing and managing resource discovery metadata by information creators so that search engines, and information systems can retrieve and locate the information more efficiently and effectively. As defined by Library and Archives Canada (LAC)[36] the terms "controlled vocabulary" and "thesaurus" are described thus:

- "Controlled vocabulary" is a general term for a list of standardized terms used for indexing and information retrieval usually in a defined information domain. It is characterized by consistent format, syntax and may include synonyms and cross-references. In a controlled vocabulary, one of a set of possible terms representing a concept is chosen as the representative term for that concept (preferred term). Consequently, all resources about that particular concept, within a body of information resources, can be indexed using the representative term.
- A "thesaurus" is a tool used for vocabulary control. Using a thesaurus improves search results. A thesaurus is a sub-set of the language we use in daily life. It includes information about the relationships of words and phrases (i.e. broader terms, narrower terms, preferred terms, non-preferred, or related terms). A thesaurus is normally restricted to a specific subject field (e.g. health, education, government documents). It allows searchers to use terminology they are familiar with to find the most relevant information.

In the Terminology Registry Scoping Study at UKOLN[29], Golub and Tudhope describe terminology registry systems as mechanisms for locating suitable vocabularies that can provide the necessary metadata schemes for exposing information resources for information navigation and retrieval. These lists can also contain information about terms, concepts and relationships, and can serve for automated classification, as well as for semantic knowledge representation.

As a specific example, in the GC, the Treasury Board's Standard on Metadata[56] requires that the controlled vocabulary be used when describing information resources on the Web. Specifically, under section 8.2.2, the standard identifies the GC Controlled Vocabulary Registry system, managed by LAC, to be the registrations system for controlled vocabularies. Likewise, the standard also identifies under section 8.2.1 that the GC Core Subject Thesaurus, again managed by LAC, is the preferred controlled vocabulary. Devey, and others[23] provides an overview of the evolution of the metadata schemes founded on the Dublin Core classification scheme used in the GC. The implementation and approach of the Dublin Core metadata scheme for incorporating metadata within pages on the web can be found in ISO 15836:2003, "Information and documentation Ð The Dublin core metadata element set".

Recently, as part of ongoing commitments to "open data, open information and open dialogue"[15] and the potential for linked data, LAC published on their website a downloadable version of the GC Core Subject Thesaurus in a SKOS/RDF, XML, and delimited text file version[37]. Table 1 provides an extract of the RDF version of the Thesaurus for Aboriginal affairs.

```
<?xml version="1.0" encoding="utf-8"?>
<rdf:RDF
xmlns:rdf="http://www.w3.org/1999/02/22-rdf-syntax-ns#"
xmlns:skos="http://www.w3.org/2004/02/skos/core#"
>
<skos:Concept rdf:about="http://my.site.com/#
Aboriginal%20affairs">
<skos:prefLabel>Aboriginal affairs</skos:prefLabel>
<skos:French>Affaires autochtones</skos:French>
<skos:UsedFor>Aboriginal issues</skos:UsedFor>
<skos:RelatedTerm>Aboriginal rights</skos:RelatedTerm>
<skos:RelatedTerm>Land claims</skos:RelatedTerm>
<skos:SubjectCategory>GV Government and Politics
</skos:SubjectCategory>
<skos:SubjectCategory>SO Society and Culture
</skos:SubjectCategory>
</skos:Concept>
```

Table 8.1 Extract of SKOS/RDF for Government of Canada Core Subject Thesaurus

The field SubjectCategory in the SKOS is populated with the following nineteen terms found in Table 2. This approach used by the GC also satisfies 4 stars out of Tim

AA Arts; Music; Literature	AG Agriculture	EC Economics and Industry
ET Education and Training	FM Form descriptors	GV Government and Politics
HE Health and Safety	HI History and Archaeology	IN Information and Communications
LB Labour	LN Language and Linguistics	LW Law
MI Military	NE Nature and Environment	PE Persons
PR Processes	SO Society and Culture	ST Science and Technology
TR Transport		

Table 8.2 CST subject categories

Berners Lee's 5 star rating for open government data[10]. Potentially, a crosswalk could link these subject terms to the GC's government-wide outcomes in the following spending areas: Economic Affairs, Social Affairs, International Affairs, and Government affairs. This could further facilitate the discoverability of information resources in the GC by domain of government activity, as reported to Parliament and citizens in a results-based management framework, instead of broad subject based terms. This crosswalk would have potential if applied in pro-disclosure publication schemes in a linked government data approach.

8.3 Part II - Pro-Disclosure Publication Schemes

Pro-disclosure schemes for government information and their subsequent disclosure through a "Whole of Government Information Publication Scheme" model evolved through the use of Freedom of Information legislation in Australia, the United Kingdom, and in Canada. These schemes provide an efficient and effective method to discover what is available to citizens in terms of government information. More importantly, it provides citizens with ways and means to assess the value of the information resources, and to identify them for further use and re-use, such as through linked government data initiatives.

8.3.1 Australian Information Publication Schemes

The concept of an Information Publication Scheme is not new, having been used within Queensland, Australia, and also in Great-Britain. As noted by one Senator contributing to the final report of the Government 2.0 Taskforce Secretariat, in relation to Project Report 7[8, p.26]. The whole of Government Information Publication Scheme will:

> [...] not only encourage, but mandate, agencies to publish what they can lawfully publish forcing a change of attitude for agencies to think about what they should be publishing rather than what they are obliged to. [...] In other words, the publication scheme and the Information Commissioner's role in overseeing and ensuring compliance with it, aim to change the emphasis from agencies defining their publication of information by what is required, to a culture of openness where information is made available unless it is against the public interest to do so.

Drawing on a report prepared by the UK Campaign for Freedom of Information 2004 on government publication schemes, the Project 7 final report emphasizes that an information publication scheme is not a facet of proactive disclosure, rather it seeks to maximize the use and re-use of public information[8, p.27]:

> The purpose of the PS [publication scheme] is to ensure that a large amount of information is readily available to members of the public, i.e. without the need for specific consideration under the FOI Act, and to inform the public of the extent of material that is available.

The Australian Government announced during the 2007 election that it would reform the Freedom of Information Act 1982 (FOI Act)[4], in order to "end the culture of secrecy"[47] and promote pro-disclosure across the Government and greater openness in government. Recently, the Australian Information Commissioner Act 2010[6], and the Freedom of Information Amendment (Reform) Act 2010[5] passed through the Parliament on 13 May 2010, received Royal Assent on 31 May 2010 and came into force on the 1st November 2010. With the introduction of these new legislative instruments and their coming into force, a new statutory agency, the Office of the Australian Information Commissioner (OAIC), now reports to the Prime Minister and Cabinet. As reported by the Government of Australia on the 8th of June 2010[3]:

> The OAIC will bring together the functions of information policy, privacy protection and freedom of information into the same agency for the first time, ensuring the development of a consistent workable information policy across all Australian Government agencies.

As reported by the Australian Department of Prime Minister and Cabinet[9], new measures introduced by this legislation will have the following implementation dates:

- 1 May 2011: the Information Publication Scheme (new Part II of the FOI Act) This Whole of Government Information Publication Scheme, modelled on the UK, enables agencies and departments to disseminate government information on a set schedule and provides for default presumption of open access.
- 1 May 2011: a requirement for agencies to publish information where access has been given under Part III of the FOI Act (new section 11C FOI Act)
- 1 January 2011: changes to bring forward the Ôopen access period' in the Archives Act 1983 for most records from 30 years to 20 years (i.e., for records created in 1980 or 1981) will be phased in over a ten year period so that a record created in 2000 will be in the open access period on 1 January 2021; and
- 1 January 2011: changes to bring forward the 'open access period' in the Archives Act for Cabinet notebooks from 50 years to 30 years will be phased in over a ten year period, so that a Cabinet notebook created in 1990 will be in the open access period on 1 January 2021.

Of note are the Recommendations of the Government Response to the Report on the Government 2.0 Taskforce[7]. Recommendation 6 tasks the new OAIC in making public sector information more open, accessible and reusable. It also proposes that creative commons licensing be applied to government information, as opposed to Crown copyright schemes in recommendation 6.4:

> Use of more restrictive licensing arrangements should be reserved for special circumstances only, and such use is to be in accordance with general guidance or specific advice provided by the proposed OIC.

Recommendation 8.1 also endorses the:

> Development, management and implementation of a [whole of] government information publication scheme.

Within Canada, the concept of a publication scheme differs to that of the GC's "Info Source", i.e., a series of publications containing information about and/or collected by the GC. Rather, an Information Publication Scheme intends to publish accurate, up-to-date and complete information on what is created, acquired, captured, managed in Australian agencies, including operational information, e.g., those that assist the agency to perform or exercise the agency's functions or powers in making decisions or recommendations affecting members of the public (or any particular person or entity, or class of persons or entities).

8.3.2 Canadian Info Source

The GC produces a series of publications named Info Source that contains information collected, stored or managed by the GC. The purpose of the Info Source publications is to assist Canadians in exercising their rights, under the Federal Access to Information Act and the Privacy Act. Treasury Board Secretariat's Access to Information Policy[53], facilitates this fundamental access to records and information held by public bodies, and enshrines it in the policy's introduction:

> The Government of Canada recognizes the right of access by the public to information in records under the control of government institutions as an essential element of our system of democracy. The government is committed to openness and transparency by respecting both the spirit and requirements of the Access to Information Act, its Regulations and its related policy instruments.

In Appendix A of the Implementation Report No. 112[54], published by the Treasury Board Secretariat in March 2009, instructions for producing the Info Source material for government departments changed to align to the Program Activity Architecture (PAA) Structure as per the requirements of the Management, Resources and Results Structure (MRRS) Policy from Treasury Board Secretariat. This significant change aligned the source of government information to the business activities, programs and services as reported to Parliamentarians.

8.3.3 Results Based Management: Management, Resources and Results Structure

In the GC, the business mission, strategy, line of business, organization structure, business process models, and business function through business performance requirements, are defined through a department's PAA, under the MRRS Policy, and through the requirements of the GC Management Accountability Framework (MAF).

In section 3.1 of the MRRS Policy, the instrument indicates that it "supports the development of a common government-wide approach to the identification of programs and to the collection, management, and reporting of financial and non-financial information relative to those programs."[57] It is with this policy that each department in government is required to link their financial and non-financial information across government. Central to the policy is the requirement for departments to develop a PAA for their activities:

Program activity architecture (*Architecture des activités de programmes*) - Is an inventory of all the program activities undertaken by a department. The program activities are depicted in their logical relationship to each other and to the strategic outcome(s) to which they contribute. The program activity architecture is the initial document for the establishment of a Management, Resources and Results Structure.

The PAA takes the form of a high-level outline of departmental accountabilities aligned to the enabling business processes/activities that a department undertakes to perform its functions/mandated program activities and to deliver on its strategic outcomes. In effect, the PAA describes each government department's Strategic Outcome, or more depending on the complexity of departments' activities. Each subsequent Strategic Outcome is linked to a Program Activity, Program Sub-activity, etc., level that describe the activities, services or programs that support these Strategic Outcomes. In effect, the PAA allows Parliament, the ultimate recipient of this information, to re-align any possible government activities and resources to Strategic Outcomes, and not departmental business lines.

The MRRS policy expresses the business context, goals and expected results for Program Activities and their administration within government institutions and comprises the reporting mechanism to support them: "A description of the current governance structure, which outlines the decision-making mechanisms, responsibilities and accountabilities of the department."[57]

This results-based management approach is, in effect, technology agnostic in its application, and represents an emerging element of new public administration. This approach can be found in reporting mechanisms, such as the publication of "Canada's Performance", to the Canadian Parliament at a whole-of-government level. This publication is an annual report to Parliament on the federal government's contribution to Canada's performance as a nation in terms of Pan-Corporate Strategic Outcomes in the following spending areas: Economic Affairs, Social Affairs, International Affairs, and Government affairs[55].

8.4 Part III - Case Study: Applying Information Visualization Techniques to GC's Pan-Corporate Strategic Outcomes

Documentary heritage institutions, such as libraries, archives and museums serve as a location of authentic state memory and have the mandated role within society for the long-term preservation of enduring or historical information resources created or acquired by these governments. These same government institutions have an implicit mandate to understand the pan-corporate view of the information resources development and management for all government activities, services and programs in order to carry out its legislated mandate.

Consider the viewpoint of a business manager in policy research to understand the difficulties for a documentary heritage institution in comprehending the complexity of the pan-government business activities – those across all government institutions and departments. For example, policy research for food products at

Agriculture Canada can overlap policy research undertaken at Health Canada for pharmaceutical applications. Both of these areas follow similar business activities, they create public sector information in the form of data sets, and produce reports, or other derivative information resources. In fact, in the United States, President Obama, in his 2011 State of the Union address[41], provides a pointed overview of how vexing this multi-jurisdictional approach to policy-making can be in governments:

> We live and do business in the Information Age, but the last major reorganization of the government happened in the age of black-and-white TV. There are 12 different agencies that deal with exports. There are at least five different agencies that deal with housing policy. Then there's my favorite example: The Interior Department is in charge of salmon while they're in fresh water, but the Commerce Department handles them when they're in saltwater. (Laughter.) I hear it gets even more complicated once they're smoked. (Laughter and applause.)

Besides the public administration challenges and issues of jurisdictional mandates, one of the underlying challenges for business managers in government is the availability of reliable, timely, and relevant information necessary for decision-making. The GC brought this to the forefront for the requirement for a modern management regime through the 1979 Royal Commission on Financial Management and Accountability[16], by associating accountability with the existence of information: "accountability relies on a system of connecting links - a two-way circuit involving a flow of information that is relevant and timely, not only for managers but for those who must scrutinize the decisions and deeds of managers." This Royal Commission recognized that the computerized systems which were designed to meet the accounting and financial requirements of Parliament, did not adequately meet the informational needs required by Governments to properly plan, make decisions, budget, control and evaluate the expenditures of Government. This was not construed to be an Electronic Data Processing systems design failure, but rather a much more deeply situated issue within the wider organizational culture, one which did not properly document its decisions, nor make the necessary connecting links across the various policy domains (such as, for example, creating provisions to share data and information with other federal government departments, other governments, or non-governmental organizations).

These past issues provide a backdrop for today's discussions on open data, open government, and their related initiatives. They are however exacerbated by the proliferation of information at the desktop, generally outside of corporate control, and by new uses of technologies by employees – such as, social media, mobile, video, and the cloud.

Within this context, and as a result of internal modernization activities, LAC has recently undertaken some fundamental and thoughtful views into its current traditional, theories and approaches that are used to provide an understanding of the management and the development of Canada's documentary heritage in a digital age. These views[21, 20, 44] are reflected in this chapter.

As a documentary heritage institution, LAC is mandated to ensure that the best possible account of Canadian life is captured through acquiring, preserving and making known the essential documentary heritage available to Canadians[20]. In order to better facilitate this mandate, it acts as a central agency department[1] for Recordkeping within the GC. Furthermore, as per its legislated mandate, LAC authorizes the disposition[34] of information resources in the GC.

During the implementation of the GC's Recordkeeping Regime Initiative in 2008 to 2009[50], a GC enterprise visualization approach for recordkeeping was proposed in order to leverage an enterprise approach to documentation standards[19, 43]. This approach would enable LAC to generate a graphical view of the GC business architecture and thereby facilitate the disposition of these information resources as a core function of the institution's mandate. It was further postulated that, at a high level, it offered possible venues for a greater understanding of society's infosphere – as seen through the interventions of Government. More broadly, it provided an innovative and efficient method and strategy to obtain a greater understanding of Government's documentary output, as well as leveraging visualization technique as a means of providing an efficient and macro perspective of the complex relationships between agencies and individuals. In essence, it provided an ontological view of the federal government's organizational structure based on the business of government, and not on its Weberian hierarchal organizational structures.

For the past fifteen years, documentary heritage professionals employed in the GC have used macroappraisal as a method, theory and process intertwined[35] and ensconced in bureaucratic rules[61] to enable LAC to carry out its roles and responsibilities related to the disposition of information resources from the GC[12, 35]. Under the authority of the LAC act, Section 12, Canadian government institutions are authorized to dispose of records and information, provided that they have meet the regulatory instruments "Disposition Authorities" enabling them to do so, and as stated by LAC[45] that they :

- do not have continuing business value to organizations under a records retention and disposal plan supporting business needs;
- are not subject to a legal hold under processes of audit, investigation or litigation; or
- are not subject to statutory provisions or regulatory obligations requiring the retention of records for periods of time over and above their internal business utility assessment.

These regulatory instruments issued by the Librarian and Archivist of Canada to government institutions serve two primary purposes: to provide for the orderly disposal (which can encompass a variety of actions[2]) of information resources by government institutions under an authorized process; and to provide for the preservation of information resources having enduring or historical value.

Since the advent of a modern bureaucratic state, the primary purpose of documentary heritage professionals is to have an understanding of the evolution of

---

[2] Such as immediate physical destruction; retention for a further period within the business unit; and various transfers actions such as to storage areas or medium under control of organizations, or another organization that has assumed control for that business activity, or provider, to an organizational archive or external archives authority see ISO 15489:2001[32] for a complete overview.

government institutions (the administrative history), their subsequent organizational structures, reporting relationships, and other functionality that helps to situate the information, records or data within context of an institutional framework. With the introduction of results-based management, new public management and new forms of digital era governance[24], the properties of organizational structures and functions have shifted from a hierarchal command and control structure (where hierarchies are well defined, i.e., where authority, information and accountabilities are clearly defined and flow from top to bottom) –a Weberian state – to one where an organization exists and interacts in a network with other institutions in order to achieve strategic outcomes.

Furthermore, with new forms of citizen-state interactions new forms of relationships and reciprocal relations of social structures in society (institutions) – and how individuals interact with them – are formulated. In this new context, it becomes more difficult for these same government professionals to ascertain traditional concepts of information resource's structure, context, and content. In a modern networked age, the previous approaches based a Weberian state for organizational structures becomes cumbersome and obsolete and are no longer applicable to linked government data initiatives.

8.4.1 Linked Government Data, and the Emergence of Open Government

A graphical view GC business architecture that visualizes the pan-corporate strategic overview of the spending areas of government, and linking them to the business and information architectures would enable a strategic overview on the GC's business, with input into organizational structure, business process models, and business functions. This in turn, would provide insight into information resources of business value that are captured, created, used and managed by government departments and agencies to accomplish their legislative mandate and vision to parliamentarians and citizens.

Linkages between program activities and the creation and management of information resources by business functions can eventually lead to predict their potential information creation, as documentary output, over time. Insight into this documentary output is based on discussions[39] held during the Recordkeeping Symposium in 2008 at LAC with Government Consulting Services of Public Works and Government Services Canada. Furthermore, insights into this research, are based on, in an expanded form, the methodology and approach for the intellectual appraisal for the historical and archival records and information in the GC. It follows the concept, articulated by the American archivist Margaret Cross Norton, "that records follow, relate to and support business functions"[35].

8.4.2 Approach

Pan-corporate strategic outcomes from the MRRS[52] are presented in an activity tree model, by spending areas (and policy areas): economic affairs, social affairs, international affairs, and governmental affairs. As such, by demonstrating the complex data relationships in a hierarchical viewpoint, between the MRRS (prescriptive accountability requirements such as the reports on plans and priorities, the departmental performance reports, and other reports to Parliament) and program activity requirements (such as business process analyses, workflow documentation and recordkeeping requirements), a greater understanding of the relationships between these activities could be ascertained, as well as providing for linkages across government programs, and strategic outcomes.

This research was conducted using the following software:

1. OWL2Prefuse, a Java package which creates Prefuse graphs and tree data structures.[30]
2. XML TreeML, an XML (Extensible Markup Language) Document Type Definition (DTD) format for representing branch/leaf tree structures.[28]
3. ValidateXML, version 1.1., a simple XML validation tool that allows validating against DTD.[62]

One of the methods demonstrating linkages is through repurposing the domain analysis of the government-wide outcomes in four spending areas: economic affairs, social affairs, international affairs and government affairs. This can be accomplished by linking specific GC spending areas (i.e., Economic Affairs) to their respective outcome areas (i.e., Strong economic growth) using the following data extraction steps using the above mentioned software.

The first step requires obtaining the raw data held by Treasury Board Secretariat. This data is provided on their website in a spreadsheet format, organized by spending areas: economic affairs, social affairs, international affairs, and government affairs, as found in Table 3 for Government Affairs. An XML format for this information is not available (either in 2008, or as this was under press via the data.gc.ca domain).

Government Affairs - Outcome Areas for 2008-2009		
Institution	**Strategic Outcomes**	**Program Activities**
Canada Revenue Agency	Eligible families and individuals receive timely and correct benefit payments.	Benefit Programs
Status of Women Canada	Gender equality and the full participation of women in the economic, social, cultural and political life of Canada	Build Knowledge and Organizational Capacity on Gender Equality
Office of the Superintendent of Financial Institutions Canada	Regulate and supervise to contribute to public confidence in Canada's financial system and safeguard from undue loss.	Regulation and Supervision of Federally Regulated Private Pension Plans
Office of the Superintendent of Financial Institutions Canada	Contribute to public confidence in Canada's public retirement income system.	Office of the Chief Actuary

Table 8.3 Spreadsheet for Government Affairs

The linkages are then established by spending areas, then GC outcomes, then departments listed under each GC outcomes (this maybe in multiples, as departments report on different Strategic Outcomes to various spending areas).

Parliament	Economic Affairs
Parliament	International Affairs
Parliament	Social Affairs
Parliament	Government Affairs
Economic Affairs	Income Security and Employment for Canadians
Economic Affairs	Strong Economic Growth
Economic Affairs	An Innovative and Knowledge Based Economy
Economic Affairs	A Clean and Healthy Environment
Economic Affairs	A Fair and Secure Marketplace
International Affairs	A Safe and Secure World Through International Cooperation

Table 8.4 Linkages between spending areas and GC Outcomes

The second step involves repurposing this master document to create an XML data tree using a small set of UNIX utilities like grep and sort, and drop down data filters found within spreadsheet software, and to parse this information into an TreeML[28] data structure. Two instances were created. The first for an XML validation using validation software[62], the second for visual testing within PrefuseOWL.

Fig. 8.1 PrefuseOWL tree visualization of Whole of Government Canada's Spending Areas

The Tree structure is based on branches, and leafs[27], branches are nested within branches, and can contain leaves, but leaves cannot be nested. This has for consequence that the lowest level of the tree node is represented by a business process, a sequence of activities, or an individual data node. The top level branch for this tree node, or trunk, is Parliament, each spending area is also a branch, and so forth until the lowest aggregate business process.

This simplistic tree structure is based on a more complex organizational ontology reflected in the MRRS, and described above. The tree structure is a representation the business of government, it is not intended to serve as a data model, or "systems" model or meta-model approach in defining the relationships between information architecture and other elements of a potential enterprise architecture. Furthermore, the traditional relationships identified in hierarchal Weberian command and control structure are slowly being identified as interactions within networks of institutions which share similar expected results. As a result, the traditional concepts of institutions, and their decomposition into sub-institutions and groups are slowly being replaced with networks of institutions in a networked governance model.

The third step involves compiling the TreeML file into the Prefuse toolkit, see Figure 2.

```
<tree>
 <declarations>
  <attributeDecl name="name" type="String"/>
 </declarations>
 <branch>
 <attribute name="name" value="Parliament"/>
 <branch>
 <attribute name="name" value="Economic Affairs"/>
  <attribute name="name" value="Canada Revenue Agency"/>
  </branch>
  <branch>
  <attribute name="name" value="Status of Women Canada"/>
  </branch>
```

Fig. 8.2 TreeML OWL data structure

This toolkit also allows attributes to be added to the tree structure, and map to the screen. This can include additional information, such as images or ancillary information for each tree node. For the purpose of this approach, additional information was not added.

Information from Treasury Board Secretariat was represented graphically using PrefuseOWL. Figure 3 also presents a tree view representing a pan corporate strategic overview of the policy and spending areas of government reporting to Parliament with an expanded view of the Economic spending area of government.

This allows us to explore business process models and program activity diagrams by drilling down from government-wide outcomes by spending areas and eventually linking them to departmental business processes.

It is to be noted that this provides a different perspective than traditional enterprise architecture models. In some of these traditional models, an enterprise architecture can provide a high level blueprint -or overview- of an organizations operations and systems and facilitates the integration of its underlying dependencies between processes, information, people, locations, applications, data and technology elements. This current visualization technique intends to be technological neutral,

Fig. 8.3 PrefuseOWL tree visualization of departments linked to Government Affairs in 2008

and if at all possible, technologically agnostic, i.e., does not provide an overview of the technologies, in the form of databases or repositories, used to define the information needs and processes[33]. This visualization technique takes a *documentation standards* and *recordkeeping* view and viewpoint[33, pp. 3-4].

In *documentation standards* and *recordkeeping* view and viewpoints, business architectures are compulsory to support the achievement of program goals and to support accurate performance reporting. An information architecture, aligned to the business architecture is supported by recordkeeping standards and practices. As a result, a record or document "known as an information resource of business value" are generated by business activities. The definition of information resource of business value is taken from section 3.3 of Treasury Board Secretariat's Directive on Recordkeeping[49] in which information resources of business value include:

> published and unpublished materials, regardless of medium or form, that are created or acquired because they enable decision making and the delivery of programs, services and ongoing operations, and support departmental reporting, performance and accountability requirements. An information resource identified as having business value and placed into a repository enables effective decision making and provides reliable evidence of business decisions, activities and transactions, for program managers, deputy heads, ministers, and Canadian citizens.

Recordkeeping focuses on the point of creation or acquisition of information resources of business value and their formal capture in a departmental recordkeeping repositories. Recordkeeping establishes a link between:

- The business functions and activities undertaken by a department to meet its legislated mandate;
- The information resources of business value created or acquired to support these functions, and;
- How those information resources of business value are managed within the business value continuum, for as long as they are of use to the department.

In this respect, recordkeeping strengthens the relationship between program delivery and information management within government departments, facilitating business requirements, ongoing operations, decision-making, and the delivery of programs and services.

Under section 6.1.1 and 6.1.3 of the Recordkeeping Directive, departments are required to:

- Identify information resources of business value, based on an analysis of the department's business context within and across the GC, (and which is understood to be based on the department's Program Activity Architecture, developed under the Management, Resources, and Results Structure Policy).
- Based on the analysis, specify the information resources of business value that must be created or acquired, and captured in a department's repositories to enable or support the department's legislated mandate.

The Recordkeeping Directive therefore repurposes existing business process models and workflow diagrams that visualize the various business process steps that constitute a Program Activity where information resources of business value are created, or need to be created, to operate the business process to its completion as a business transaction, business output, or business result[45].

A visualization technique, linked to a business architecture, provides an understanding of how information resources of business value form an integral part of the business of government, and how an individual interacts within this government process. These information resources of business value can be visualized and modelled or mapped to the wider GC business context. This provides the means to establish the relationships across the government's high level business objectives and provides for accountability, transparency and greater administrative and business coherence across government. These steps identified above provide an infrastructure where information resources of business value can be used to facilitate decision making and the efficient delivery of government programs and services; to meet program delivery, legislated, and accountability requirements. Moreover, they ensure LAC meets the requirements of its mandate for the preservation of information of enduring or historical value. Recent recasting and revisions to the macroappraisal methodology for identifying information resource of enduring value are currently under review[12] and will benefit from repurposing the GC's program activity or business architecture.

This visualization technique, and tree data structure, provides an overview of organizational structure and information resources context at whole-of-government level. It supports linked government data initiatives in providing organizational context, content and structure for the information resources (which include data) across a number of functional domains (human, financial and people resources).

8.5 Conclusions and Further Work

In this chapter we explored the dependance between an effective and efficient management of documents, records, data, and information and the success of linked
government data initiatives. To put it simply,*What is not known cannot be made
known.*

We proposed that creating an information visualization of the pan-corporate
strategic outcomes can be repurposed to provide an overview of organizational
structure and information resources context at whole-of-government level. These
pan-corporate strategic outcomes are expressed and linked to each departments or
agencies program activity architecture or business architecture, and as such will
most likely be captured within recordkeeping requirements as identified in the *Directive on Recordkeeping*[49]. The ancillary benefit of this information visualization technique is also to demonstrate the linkages between program activities, and
subsequently to visualize and eventually to create linkages across the various information holdings of government. This, in turn, provides for greater administrative
and business coherence within government and encourages disclosure of information resources of business value as a source of Public Sector Information (PSI) for
society as a whole.

The application of pro-disclosure schemes for government information can provide an efficient and effective method to discover what is available to citizens in
terms of government information. It provides citizens with ways and means to assess the value of the information resources, and to identify them for further use and
re-use, such as through linked government data initiatives.

The application of terminology registry systems can assist in the identification
and discovery of relevant information found in the pro-disclosure schemes published
to the web. In the GC, the application of the GC Controlled Vocabulary Registry system, managed by LAC, could provide the necessary metadata schemes for exposing
information resources for information navigation and retrieval and leverage linked
government data initiatives.

We highlighted the significance in the shift occurring as the result of the introduction of results-based management, new public management and now forms of digital era governance to principles of linked **government** data initiatives. These have
shifted the relationships that existed in traditional organizational ontologies where
hierarchies are well defined, i.e., where authority, information and accountabilities
are clearly defined and flow from top to bottom. Our viewpoint of organizational
structures from this view also needs to shift. These structures need to incorporate
various other perspectives, such as **societal agents, structures, and systems**. These
are the individuals, groups, organizations, institutions, networks, communities, and
other entities from the state, private and civil spheres who contribute to the development of society. These are the new forms of citizen-state interactions where new
forms of relationships and reciprocal relation of social structures in society (institutions) – and how individuals interact with them – are formulated. Our view of organizational structures of government, as approached in an Weberian state, needs to
evolve for linked government data initiatives. Would the introduction of new struc-

tural analysis and domain analysis facilitate this discussion of the networks emerging within governments? Could some of the answer to this question be found in the understanding and repurposing how governments organize themselves, and report to Parliament in a results based management framework?

8.5.1 Further Work

Our main findings and recommendations can be summarized as follows. First, that information obtained from Treasury Board Secretariat can be repurposed using information visualization techniques for making sense of complex relationships across GC spending areas. Second, that an XML export of the data from Treasury Board Secretariat is a preferred format over that of proprietary formats (Microsoft Excel), as found in section 4.2. This would satisfy the 3 star rating system of Tim Berners Lee's 5 star rating for open government data. The application of other techniques, tools and methods to represent non-RDF datasets using RDF descriptions can be found in the chapter by Frosterius *et al.*, and also the proposal by Alan Dix for descriptions of CSV dumps[2]. These proposals can provide meaningful ways and means to bridge existing government data using linked data principles. Third, and of highest importance, as stated in the opening paragraph of this chapter by D'Iberville Fortier, information must be made known by business managers, and the public, for them to be eventually disclosed, linked and used within society. It is in line with this context that on the 22nd of March 2011, the GC launched the Open Data Pilot Project[13] which set out to "create socio-economic opportunities and promote informed participation by the public by expanding access to federal government data."[14]

Potentially, a crosswalk could link subject terms in the GC Core Subject Thesaurus to the GC's government-wide outcomes in the following spending areas: Economic Affairs, Social Affairs, International Affairs, and Government affairs could facilitate the discoverability of information resources in the GC by domain of government activity. This crosswalk would have potential if applied in pro-disclosure publication schemes in a linked government data approach.

The publication of the PAA in an SKOS/RDF and XML format would leverage the provenance of the information contained in the pro-disclosure schemes, and could be applied for organization ontologies. Further work would need to explored in organizational ontologies, leveraging the work already started by Dave Reynolds in his Organizational Ontology[22].

8.5.2 Emerging Trends

Further work on the various aspects of an up-front assessment of information resources based on criteria of value, manifested as self-conscious acts and outcomes of deliberate and deliberative documentation by business managers, will emerge as governments introduce various ways and means to implement Open Government, and Open Data initiatives. Invariably, the issue of the quality of the government data being linked will be highlighted. Recently, Jerry Brito, Senior Research Fellow at the Mercatus Center at George Mason University appeared before the United States Congress on the recent Open Government initiatives[11]. In his testimony, Mr. Brito highlights that accountability has yet to be observed with Open Government:

> [...] despite the Obama Administration's technological efforts and Congressional legislation like the Federal Funding Accountability and Transparency Act (FFATA), whether government is performing effectively is still not completely transparent. That's because the vast majority of newly available data is not about government activity, and disclosures that are about government tend to report its activities, not data on program outcomes. When program outcomes are reported, they are suspect because they are self-measured and self-reported by program managers.

Mr. Brito also highlights the fact that while the Obama administration is taking great strides in publishing datasets on Data.gov, these are mostly about government regulating industry, and not about disclosing what government does:

> But if disclosure works for regulated industries, it should work for government, too. To me that is what open government is about government disclosing its own actions, not simply the actions of those it regulates. [...] A quick scan of the remaining 1,500 datasets [found on Data.gov] reveals that only 200 to 300 report on the activities or performance of government, not the activities of some other entity. There is plenty of smoke, but little fire.

Indeed, the public utility of the datasets themselves is anticipated to become a contentious issue as progress is made on Open Government, and linked government data. In sum, to reiterate the opening words of the 1969 Canadian Federal Task Force on Government Information, forty years on, there is still a need *To Know and Be Known*.

Acknowledgements The author is grateful to the Librarian and Archivist of Canada, Dr. Daniel J. Caron, for the opportunity afforded him by the Library and Archives Canada to pursue this work. Special thanks are due to my colleagues in the Strategic Research Branch, Dr. Richard Brown, Mr. Ihtesham Rashid, Dr. Zeïneb Gharbi and Mrs. Susan Franklin for their ongoing support and encouragement. The analysis, views and opinions expressed in this paper are those of the author and do not necessarily reflect the official position or policies of the Library and Archives Canada or the Government of Canada. The author also acknowledges the helpful and probing comments made by the editor David Wood and the anonymous reviewers.

References

1. Smith, A. Library of Parliament. The Roles and Responsibilities of Central Agencies. URL http://www2.parl.gc.ca/Content/LOP/ResearchPublications/prb0901-e.pdf.
2. Dix, A. and Talis. CSV Meta Description, March 2011. URL http://tiree.snipit.org/talis/tables/.

3. Australian Government. Australia To Open Office Of Information From November 2010 | Gov Monitor, a. URL http://www.thegovmonitor.com/civil_society_and_democratic_renewal/governance/australia-to-open-office-of-information-from-november-2010-33051.html.
4. Australian Government. Freedom of Information Act 1982, b. URL http://www.comlaw.gov.au/Details/C2010C00387. C2010C00387.
5. Australian Government. Freedom of Information Amendment (Reform) Act 2010, c. URL http://www.comlaw.gov.au/Details/C2010A00051. C2010A00051.
6. Australian Government. Australian Information Commissioner Act 2010, d. URL http://www.comlaw.gov.au/Details/C2010A00052. C2010A00052.
7. Australian Government. Government Response to the Report of the Government 2.0 Taskforce, e. URL http://www.finance.gov.au/publications/govresponse20report/index.html.
8. Australian Government. Project 7: Whole of Government Information Publication Scheme, f. URL http://gov2.net.au/projects/project-7/.
9. Australian Government. Freedom of Information (FOI) Reform, November 2010. URL http://www.dpmc.gov.au/foi/foi_reform.cfm.
10. Berners-Lee, T. Linked Data - Design Issues. URL http://www.w3.org/DesignIssues/LinkedData.
11. Brito, J. and United States. *Hearings on 'Transparency Through Technology: Evaluating Federal Open-Government Initiatives'. 112th Congress, 1st session, Friday, March 11, 2011*. Subcommittee on Technology, Information Policy, Intergovernmental Relations and Procurement Reform, [Washington, D.C. :, 2011. URL http://oversight.house.gov/images/stories/Letters/Brito_Testimony-Bio_3-11-11.pdf.
12. Brown, R. Macroappraisal in the Twenty-First Century: Towards a New Documentary Framework for Public Memory. In *The future of memory: the digital archival heritage*, Santiago de Compostela, Spain, November 2010, forthcoming. Arquivo de Galicia.
13. Canada. Open Data Pilot Project, March 2011a. URL http://www.data.gc.ca/default.asp?lang=En&n=F9B7A1E3-1.
14. Canada. Government of Canada Open Data Portal - Backgrounder, March 2011b. URL http://www.data.gc.ca/default.asp?lang=En&n=CA05CAF7-1.
15. Canada. Speech from the Throne, June 2011c. URL http://www.speech.gc.ca/local_grfx/docs/sft-ddt-2011_e.pdf.
16. Canada and Lambert, A.T. Final report, Royal Commission on Financial Management & Accountability (Lambert report). Technical report, Canada, Ottawa, 1979.
17. Canada. Task Force on Government Information and D'Iberville Fortier. *To know and be known: the report of the Task Force on Government Information*, volume 1. Queen's Printer, 1969.
18. Heting Chu. *Information representation and retrieval in the digital age*. ASIST monograph series. Published for the American Society for Information Science and Technology by Information Today, Medford, N.J., 2nd ed edition, 2010. ISBN 9781573873932 (hc).
19. Caron, D.J., Library and Archives Canada. The Recordkeeping Initiative: Findings of Assessment Projects and the Way Forward. URL http://www.lac-bac.gc.ca/government/news-events/007001-6301-e.html.
20. Caron, D.J., Library and Archives Canada. Shaping our Continuing Memory Collectively: A Representative Documentary Heritage, March 2010. URL http://www.lac-bac.gc.ca/obj/013/f2/013-449-e.pdf.
21. Caron, D.J. and Library and Archives Canada. Memory Institutions in the 21st Century: The Need for Convergence and Collaboration. In *The War of Independence Reconsidered: Librarians and Archivists – Past, Present and Future.*, Banff, Alberta, May 2010. Archives Society of Alberta (ASA).
22. Reynolds, D. and Epimorphics. An organization ontology, May 2010. URL http://www.epimorphics.com/public/vocabulary/org.html.

23. Devey, M., Côté, M.-C., Bain, L. and McAvoy, L. Celebrating 10 Years of Government of Canada Metadata Standards. In *International Conference on Dublin Core and Meta-data Applications, DC-2010–Pittsburgh Proceedings*, 2010. URL http://dcpapers.dublincore.org/ojs/pubs/article/download/1046/994.

24. Dunleavy, P. and Margetts, H. The second wave of digital era governance. In *American Political Science Association Conference*, Washington DC, USA., September 2010. American Political Science Association Conference. URL http://eprints.lse.ac.uk/27684/.

25. Erickson, J. DOIs, URIs and Cool Resolution, a. URL http://bitwacker.wordpress.com/2010/02/04/dois-uris-and-cool-resolution/.

26. Erickson, J. The DOI, DataCite and Linked Data: Made for each other!, b. URL http://bitwacker.wordpress.com/2010/01/19/the-doi-datacite-and-linked-data-made-for-each-other/.

27. Fekete, J. and Plaisant, C. TreeML Specification, a. URL http://cs.marlboro.edu/courses/fall2006/tutorials/information_visualization/TreeML.

28. Fekete, J. and Plaisant, C. DTD describing a tree structure for visualization, b. URL http://www.nomencurator.org/infoVis2003/download/treeml.dtd.

29. Golub, K. and Tudhope, D. Delivering a Terminology Registry. Poster at LIDA conference, Dubrovnik and Mljet, Croatia, 2-7 June 2008, 2008. URL http://www.ukoln.ac.uk/projects/trss/dissemination/Lida08-golub.pdf.

30. Heer, J., Card, S.K. and Landay, J.A. Prefuse: a toolkit for interactive information visualization. In *Proceedings of the SIGCHI conference on Human factors in computing systems*, pages 421–430, 2005.

31. Hudon, M. and Hjartarson, F. Governments meet people: Developing metathesauri in the framework of "government online" initiatives. In *Advancing knowledge: Expanding horizons for information science: Proceedings of the 30th Annual Conference of the Canadian Association for Information Science, 30 May-1 June 2002, Toronto, Canada*, pages 46–60, 2002.

32. ISO 15489-1:2001. Information and documentation – Records management –Part 1 :General. Technical report, International Organization for Standardization (ISO), 2001.

33. ISO/IEC 42010:2007. Systems and software engineering - recommended practice for architectural description of software-intensive systems. Technical report, International Organization for Standardization (ISO), 2007.

34. Library and Archives Canada. Disposition. URL http://www.lac-bac.gc.ca/government/disposition/index-e.html.

35. Library and Archives Canada. Appraisal Methodology: Macro-Appraisal and Functional Analysis, Part A: Concepts and Theory, October 2001. URL http://www.lac-bac.gc.ca/government/disposition/007007-1035-e.html.

36. Library and Archives Canada. How to Register a Controlled Vocabulary, March 2006. URL http://www.collectionscanada.gc.ca/government/controlled-vocabularies/007004-3000-e.html.

37. Library and Archives Canada. Government of Canada Core Subject Thesaurus in SKOS/RDF, May 2011. URL http://en.thesaurus.gc.ca/default.asp?lang=En&n=EAEAD1E6-1.

38. Library of Congress. FDsys Helps GPO Provide Access to Federal Digital Publications, March 2011. URL http://www.digitalpreservation.gov/news/2011/20110301_news_zwaard_briefing.html.

39. Matte, F. What we learned from Gomery: Managing the scope of document discovery, 2008. URL http://www.lac-bac.ca/obj/023023/f2/023023-3404d-e.pdf.

40. Miles, A. and Pérez-Agüera, J. SKOS: Simple Knowledge Organisation for the Web. *Cataloging & Classification Quarterly*, 43(3):69–83, 2007. doi: 10.1300/J104v43n03_04.

41. Obama, B. Remarks by the President in State of Union Address, January 2011. URL http://www.whitehouse.gov/the-press-office/2011/01/25/remarks-president-state-union-address.

42. Organisation for Economic Co-operation and Development. *Modernising government: the way forward*. OECD Publishing, May 2005. ISBN 9789264010499.

43. Desrochers, P., Smith, S., and Library and Archives Canada. Recordkeeping Directive 101: Everything you wanted to know, but were too afraid to ask. ARMA Conference, 2008. URL http://www.slideshare.net/pdesrochers/recordkeeping-directive-101-everything-you-wanted-to-know-but-were-tooafraid-to-ask.

44. Brown, R. and Caron, D.J.. The Documentary Moment in the Digital Age: Establishing New Value Propositions for Public Memory. *Archivaria*, 71:1–20, 2011.

45. Brown, R., Caron, D.J., and Library and Archives Canada. Creating Documentation Standards for Government Programs, Services and Results: A Developmental Framework and Guide for Business Managers and Information Resource Specialists, March 2008. URL http://www.lac-bac.gc.ca/obj/007001/f2/007001-5000.1-e.pdf.

46. Rusbridge, C. What are the advantages of DOIs as dataset identifiers in citations? URL http://friendfeed.com/chrisrusbridge/74f80839/what-are-advantages-of-dois-as-dataset.

47. Sydney Morning Herald, AAP. I'll end secrecy: Rudd - Federal Election 2007 News - Federal Election 2007. http://www.smh.com.au/news/federal-election-2007-news/ill-end-secrecy-rudd/2007/11/21/1195321837158.html. URL http://www.smh.com.au/news/federal-election-2007-news/ill-end-secrecy-rudd/2007/11/21/1195321837158.html.

48. Baker, T. and Keizer, J.. Linked Data for Fighting Global Hunger: Experiences in setting standards for Agricultural Information Management. In David Wood, editor, *Linking enterprise data*, pages 177–201. Springer, New York NY Heidelberg, 2010. ISBN 9781441976642.

49. Treasury Board of Canada Secretariat. Directive on Recordkeeping, a. URL http://www.tbs-sct.gc.ca/pol/doc-eng.aspx?section=text&id=16552.

50. Treasury Board of Canada Secretariat. Canada's Performance Report 2008-09: The Government of Canada's Contribution, b. URL http://www.tbs-sct.gc.ca/reports-rapports/cp-rc/2008-2009/cp-rc06-eng.asp.

51. Treasury Board of Canada Secretariat. Policy Framework for Information and Technology, July 2007a. URL http://www.tbs-sct.gc.ca/pol/doc-eng.aspx?id=12452&section=text.

52. Treasury Board of Canada Secretariat. The Management, Resources, and Results Structure Policy: Instructions to Departments for Developing a Management, Resources, and Result Structure, July 2007b. URL http://www.lac-bac.gc.ca/webarchives/20071123053135/http://www.tbs-sct.gc.ca/pubs_pol/dcgpubs/mrrsp-psgrr/id-cm/id-cm_e.asp.

53. Treasury Board of Canada Secretariat. Policy on Access to Information, April 2008. URL http://www.tbs-sct.gc.ca/pol/doc-eng.aspx?id=12453&section=text.

54. Treasury Board of Canada Secretariat. Implementation Report No. 112 -Info Source 2009 Requirements, March 2009. URL http://www.tbs-sct.gc.ca/atip-aiprp/impl-rep/2009/112-imp-mise02-eng.asp.

55. Treasury Board of Canada Secretariat. Canada's Performance 2009-2010: The Government of Canada's Contribution, November 2010a. URL http://www.tbs-sct.gc.ca/reports-rapports/cp-rc/2009-2010/cp-rctb-eng.asp.

56. Treasury Board of Canada Secretariat. Standard on metadata, June 2010b. URL http://www.tbs-sct.gc.ca/pol/doc-eng.aspx?id=18909&section=text.

57. Treasury Board of Canada Secretariat. Policy on Management, Resources and Results Structures, February 2010c. URL http://www.tbs-sct.gc.ca/pol/doc-eng.aspx?id=18218&section=text.

58. W3C. SKOS/FAQs, Janu 2010a. URL http://www.w3.org/2001/sw/wiki/SKOS/FAQs.

59. W3C. W3C Library Linked Data Incubator Group, June 2010b. URL http://www.w3.org/2005/Incubator/lld/.

60. W3C. Library Linked Data Incubator Group Charter, June 2010c. URL http://www.w3.org/2005/Incubator/lld/.

61. Weber, M. *The theory of social and economic organization.* Simon and Schuster, July 1997. ISBN 9780684836409.
62. Woodstox. ValidateXML. http://woodstox.codehaus.org/ValidateXML. URL `http://woodstox.codehaus.org/ValidateXML`.
63. Zeng, M.L. and Qin, Jian. *Metadata.* Neal-Schuman Publishers, New York, 2008. ISBN 9781555706357 (pbk. : alk. paper). URL `http://www.loc.gov/catdir/toc/ecip0816/2008015176.html`.

Chapter 9
Linking Australian Government Data for Sustainability Science - A Case Study

Qing Liu, Quan Bai, Li Ding, Huong Pho, Yun Chen, Corné Kloppers, Deborah
L. McGuinness, David Lemon, Paulo de Souza, Peter Fitch, and Peter Fox

Abstract

Sustainability science has been viewed as a new discipline which focuses on the
complex interactions between nature and society. It demands intensive integration of
data from different sources within different domains. Governments collect and generate huge amounts of scientific data and thus are in a unique position to support sustainability research. However, there are many challenges in discovering and re-using
government data. In this chapter, first, we survey the sustainability related datasets
published by the Australian government. We believe this is the critical first step to
identifying the opportunities and issues and advancing the Australian Government
2.0 agenda. Second, we investigate the role of Linked Data in integrating a selection
of Australian government datasets to generate sustainability science hypotheses and
support the data analysis. We discuss the challenges based on our survey experience
and present some recommendations for data publishing and analysis.

9.1 Introduction

Sustainability science [16, 7] has been viewed as a new discipline attracting attention from academia and industry. Focusing on the complex interactions between
nature and society, sustainability science investigates problem-driven frameworks
to create, manage and apply relevant knowledge in support of decision-making for
sustainable development [7].

The United Nations defined five priorities through its 'WEHAB' framework for
sustainable development: Water, Energy, Health, Agriculture and Biodiversity [20].
This vision not only unveils the interdisciplinary nature of sustainability research,

Correspondance author: Qing Liu, Tasmanian ICT Centre, CSIRO, GPO BOX 1538, Hobart, TAS
7001, Australia, e-mail: Q.Liu@csiro.au. See the List of Contributors for full contact details.

but also demands intensive integration of data in the listed disciplines from all possible sources. In order to answer sustainability science questions, researchers usually need to find datasets from different sources and mash-up the datasets to find correlations among the data from different disciplines. Although sustainability scientists may own several datasets, they frequently need to obtain additional datasets from other sources.

Government entities have historically and continue to collect and maintain large amounts of data required for use in their decision making processes. In the past twenty years, the development of e-government infrastructure gradually opened such governmental data to the public on the Web, usually via query-based visual human computer interfaces. Beginning in 2009, the emerging world-wide open government data activities further opened up direct raw data access to reduce the cost of developing visual data access applications and thereby enhanced the transparency of government operations. In 2010, following the US and UK, the Australian Government committed to an open government based on a culture of engagement, built on better access to and use of government held information, and sustained by the innovative use of technology.

The Australian government has published a large number of government datasets on its official data registry portal - Data.gov.au. Upon investigation of this site, we found a substantial number of datasets that can be used in support of sustainability science despite the fact that many were not originally created for that purpose.

There are still many challenges in reusing Australian government data for sustainability science research. First, governmental datasets are maintained by a number of independent agencies. Without understanding the responsibilities of each government agency and how different agencies operate, it is often hard for users to find relevant and useful data quickly. Second, all these datasets are published in a wide range of different formats. To analyze the relationships among the datasets, significant efforts are required to either transform the various data formats into a common representation or to create mappings between the representations in order to facilitate data integration. Finally, there are many semantic ambiguities contained in the published the data. To integrate the datasets together, it requires users to have a clear understanding of how the concepts could be mapped together and then make sense of them. Given the complexity involved in sustainability science, significant efforts are required to make the datasets published by the Australian government discoverable and re-usable for sustainable development.

Linked Data [3], an important part of the Semantic Web[21], presents an opportunity to build a world-scale data space in which data from different providers can be easily aggregated, and fragmented information from multiple sources can be integrated, to achieve a more comprehensive view. We believe that sustainability science may be an excellent area in which Linked Data technology could play a critical role in connecting the above five disciplines of 'WEHAB' framework. In this chapter, we investigate the role of Linked Data in integrating a selection of Australian government datasets to generate sustainability science hypotheses and support the related analysis. This work shows our preliminary work on proving the viability of Linked

Government Data in sustainability science research, and we deliver the following key contributions:

- A survey of Australian open government data sources and how they are related to different disciplines of 'WEHAB' framework;
- A case study exhibiting the practical value of linking Australian open government data in advancing sustainability research;
- Recommendations for data publishing and data analysis for sustainability science based on our experience and lesson learned.

The rest of the chapter is organized as follows: Section 9.2 introduces some background concepts and related work. In Section 9.3, we survey the open sustainability related datasets published by the Australian government agencies; Section 9.4 presents the case study by introducing the Linked data-based infrastructure and the datasets selected; a Linked data-based analysis is also discussed to analyze the relationships among the datasets integrated; Section 9.5 presents some challenges and recommendations for publishing and linking Australian government datasets based on our experience and lesson learnt from our case study; This is followed by *Conclusion*.

9.2 Background and Related Work

In this section, first we introduce the background of sustainability science. Then the Semantic Web and Open Government Data are discussed.

9.2.1 Sustainability Science

Sustainability science has its origins in the concept of sustainability development. According to the World Commission on Environment and Development (WCED), convened by the United Nations in 1983 (also known as the Brundtland Commission), sustainable development is development that meets the needs of the present without compromising the ability of future generations to meet their own needs [19]. Sustainability science provides an essential framework for sustainability.

Today sustainability is viewed as a critical issue by all nations around the world. The opportunity to develop the emerging discipline of sustainability science has never been greater.

Six fundamental questions of sustainability science have been proposed by Kates *et al.* [12]. Of these six, in this work we are trying to study the question: "How can today's operational systems for monitoring and reporting on environmental and social conditions be integrated or extended to provide more useful guidance for efforts to navigate a transition toward sustainability?"

Since sustainability science tries to understand the integrated ï£¡wholeï£¡ of environmental, social and economic systems, it is essential to connect academia, industry and government from scientific, social and economic disciplines. There are two main obstacles that impede the progress of answering the above question [14]:

- The complexity of the problems: This is because the sustainability crisis is caused by a multitude of factors. It is a challenge to have an integrated view of the overall problems;
- The specialization of the scholarship that seeks to address them: While a complex problem may cover multiple disciplines, most existing studies have been conducted from a highly restricted perspective within an individual discipline using partial observations and limited problem solving techniques.

In short, knowledge structuring of issues has been identified as an essential first step in the effort to acquire a comprehensive view of sustainability issues which are both complex and interconnected.

Since the key information for sustainability are generated by multi-disciplines and multi-organizations, a major part of knowledge structuring will entail building up the tools that provide an "overview" of what is known. Sustainability science can construct and coordinate a framework within which the vast amount of data can be easily accessed [13]. This requires a massive global cooperative effort. A systematic approach for bringing the data together, both structurally and semantically, is essential to provide an integrated analysis across disciplines and across organizations.

Government pervades some of the critical aspects of information collection and generation to improve its policies, regulation and service delivery. Information held by government agencies represents the local and public knowledge and expertise. It is a national resource that provides essential information to study sustainability science.

Government data provides a fantastic opportunity to bring the vast amount of data together and to have a comprehensive view of sustainability issues. In return, the proposed solutions based on better understanding of the complex problems will help government to make better decisions related to supporting long term sustainability.

However, the data published by the government could be viewed as a two-edged sword: we want it, but when we get it, how could we make it meaningful? Data discoverability, data description and data analysis are the three main obstacles to the reusability of government published data.

9.2.2 Semantic Web and Open Government Data

Semantic Web [2] offers a web-based infrastructure for preserving semantic structure of data and supporting advanced logical inference. The W3C's semantic web standards, including RDF, RDFS, OWL, and RIF, provide a common ground for machines to share and integrate data.

Linked Data presents an opportunity to build a global data space in which data from different providers can be aggregated, and fragmented information from multiple sources can be integrated, to achieve a more comprehensive view. However, the current applications that consume the data are not designed to enable exploiting Linked Data capability to its full potential.

Targeting transparency, enabled by the advance of Internet technology and the World Wide Web, and driven by governmental policies and regulation directives, infrastructures for opening government data has been developed and evolved as part of the e-government practices since 1990s [11]. While downloadable files has been widely used by individual government agencies in publishing government data, interoperability infrastructure has also been extensively investigated in 2000s [10], e.g. web service based data publishing (e.g. [15]) and semantic web based data publishing (e.g. [9]). While semantic technologies, e.g. taxonomy[6], glossary [17], and thesaurus [5], are already being used to enhance understanding of government data, ontologies are used in providing a large-scale solution for integrating distributed open government data.

Recently, a number of countries around the world started dedicated websites to catalog and publish open government data on the Web, e.g. Data.gov was released in 2009 following US President Obama's "Memorandum on Transparency and Open Government" [22], Data.gov.uk was released in 2010 following UK Prime Minister 's "Letter to Government departments on opening up data" [4], and Data.gov.au was released in 2010 following Australian Government's "Declaration of Open Government" [1]. Although not all government data (e.g. criminal investigation data, personal identity data) are suitable for unrestricted public accessing (e.g. a number of US government data are protected by FOIA (Freedom of Information Act)[1]), most data related to sustainability science are non-sensitive and open to general public.

Our work differs from existing semantic web based approaches to that we emphasize Linked Data principle, where published datasets may be used in the way not expected by the curator and datasets are incrementally linked in a collaborative environment. Moreover, we focus on Australian open government data, which is different from the well-known Data.gov and Data.gov.uk that have already adopted Linked Data in data publishing. Therefore, this work enlightens the path for deploying Linked Data at Data.gov.au and the follow up use in sustainability science context.

9.3 Survey of Australian Government Data for Sustainability Science

In this section, we survey some of the Australian government agencies that publish datasets which may contribute to the 'WEHAB' framework for sustainable develop-

---

[1] http://www.foia.gov/

ment: water, energy, health, agriculture and biodiversity. We believe this is a critical first step to identify the issues and opportunities of using government datasets for sustainability research. In what follows, we first review some government agencies that publish sustainability related datasets, and then summarize how these datasets can be used in contributing to the above five disciplines.

9.3.1 National Data Service

9.3.1.1 Data.gov.au

Data.gov.au[2] (DGA) is the official n open data portal that "provides an easy way to find, access and reuse public datasets from the Australian Government and state and territory governments". Since the goal of this site is to promote community engagement to reuse raw Australian government data, the data published on this site are under open licences. The site is created in response to n Government's "Declaration of Open Government" and the Government 2.0 Taskforce [18]. Currently, it is maintained by the Department of Finance and Deregulation.

The site provides both a list of downloadable datasets and a collection of links to other peer Australian dataset catalogues or sources. Approximately 230 datasets are currently listed on this site and they are grouped into 27 categories, such as environment, geography, finance, health, and geography. Public users can browse the list of datasets by jurisdiction or category. The datasets are curated and published by 68 federal/state/territory government agencies.

Each dataset is associated with the metadata which includes the dataset information (annotation, date published, data updated, category, keyword and license), agency information (agency and jurisdiction) and data coverage (temporal coverage, spatial coverage and granularity). The dataset may be in one or more of the following file formats: xml (eXtensible Markup Language), csv (Comma-Separated Value Lists), txt (Raw Text files), xls (Excel Spreadsheet), kml/kmz (Keyhole Markup Language), ESRI Shapefiles (Geodata overlays) and others.

We detect sustainability related datasets using the following heuristics. First, we leverage the category metadata to locate relevant datasets, e.g. Environment and Health. Second, we use well known domain phrases in 'WEHAB' framework to match dataset titles, descriptions and keywords, e.g. land, water, marine, and forest. Last but not the least, a manual verification was used to keep the matching in high quality. These methods helped us to find a small number of relevant datasets[3], e.g. land use, vegetation coverage, forest, world heritage, marine protected area, Integrated Marine and Coastal Rationalization, Murray-Darling Basin Boundary - Water Act 200.

The agencies that contribute to the 'WEHAB' related datasets include:

---

[2] http://data.gov.au

[3] These methods is primarily done by hand to collect examples. Our future work will design automatic tools for exhaustively listing relevant datasets.

- Commonwealth of Australia: Department of sustainability, environment, water, population and communities, GeoScience Australia, Department of agriculture, fisheries and forestry;
- Victoria State: Sustainability Victoria, Department of Justice, Department of planning and community development, Department of sustainability and environment;
- New South Wales State: Department of environment, climate change and water, Rural fire service
- Australian Capital Territory: Territory and Municipal Services
- Queensland State: Department of environment and resource management
- South Australia: Department for environment and Heritage

9.3.1.2 Australian Bureau of Statistics

The Australian Bureau of Statistics[4] (ABS) is a national agency devoted to undertake surveys to collect estimates from Australian organizations and community to produce high quality and objective statistical data to meet its mission to "assist and encourage informed decision making, research and discussion within governments and the community, by leading a high quality, objective and responsive national statistical service."[5]

The ABS cover a wide range of interest with some key deliverable in population and housing, surveys on research and development in business, higher education, general government and non-profit sectors. These surveys allows the ABS to compile and publish comprehensive statistical data products.

As of today, ABS publishes 6423 datasets[6] covering 5 different general topics, including Economy, People, Environment & Energy, Industry and Regional.

9.3.1.3 Australian National Data Service

The Australian National Data Service[7] (ANDS) aims to (a) partner with researchers and research organizations to help them meet their data management ambitions; and (b) transform the disparate collections of shareable research data around Australia into a commons of discoverable research resources. It provides a mesh of searchable web pages describing n research data collections. ANDS does not hold the actual data, but points to the location where the data can be accessed.

---

[4] http://www.abs.gov.au

[5]   http://www.abs.gov.au/websitedbs/d3310114.nsf/
51c9a3d36edfd0dfca256acb00118404/325a67193dc1ae1bca256b21001c4078!
OpenDocument

[6]   http://www.abs.gov.au/ausstats/abs@.nsf/filternavwebpage?
readform

[7] http://ands.org.au/

The data providers register their data in the ANDS collection registry. Currently there are about 1425 datasets provided by the Australian universities, Australian Institute of Marine Science, n Institute of Marine Science, the Commonwealth Scientific and Industrial Research Organization (CSIRO) *etc*. The metadata describes subjects, spatial coverage, distributor, point of contact and the url link to the datasets. The data format are varied which depends on the data providers.

Many datasets could contribute to the 'WEHAB' framework through ANDS portal. As an example, Murray-Darling Basin Sustainable Yields Future Climate Data published by CSIRO is used to assess the range of possible climate conditions around the year 2030. The data could be accessed from the CSIRO file system.

9.3.1.4 GeoScience Australia

Geoscience Australia[8] (GSA) is an agency within the Resources, Energy and Tourism portfolio. It provides geoscientific information and knowledge which enables government and community to make informed decisions. It focuses on the issues such as the global attractiveness of Australia's offshore and onshore exploration, improved resource management and environmental protection. It plays a key role in developing a sustainable energy supply for Australia's future.

The data could be accessed from databases or downloaded as file such as ArcView Shapefile, ArcInfo Export or MapInfo mid/mif. Each dataset has metadata to describe the scale, release date, spatial coverage and abstract. Extended metadata describes the temporal coverage, dataset states and data quality *etc*. which meets the GA metadata standards.

The datasets available from Geoscience Australia include Earth Monitoring, Earth Observation and Satellite Imagery, Energy, Greenhouse Gas Storage, Groundwater, Hazards, Marine and Coastal, Minerals *etc*. For example, New South Wales coastal Waterways Geomorphic Habitat Mapping datasets maps the geomorphic habitat environments (facies) for 131 New South Wales coastal waterways.

9.3.1.5 Australian Social Science Data Archive

n Social Science Data Archive[9] (ASSDA) provides a national service for the collection and preservation of computer readable data relating to social, political and economic affairs and to make these data available for further analysis.

Specifically, it includes ageing, demography, economics, education, employment, environment, conservation and land use, health, social welfare etc*etc*. The data could be downloaded in multiple formats: stata, NSDstat, DIF, DBase, text, delimited, SAS, and CSV. Metadata describes document, study, data and variables are published as well.

---

[8] http://www.ga.gov.au

[9] http://www.assda.edu.au/index.html

9.3.2 Agencies with Dedicated Data Hosting Services

Apart from the well-organized dataset registry and dataset repositories listed above, many other Australian government agencies publishes their curated government data via their own data catalog. In this suvery, we focus on the federal government agencies. There are many state/territory agencies who also provide sustainability related data.

9.3.2.1 Australian Bureau of Agricultural and Resource Economics and Sciences

The Australian Bureau of Agricultural and Resource Economics and Sciences (ABARES) is a research organization within the n Government Department of Agriculture, Fisheries and Forestry. ABARES produce tools, models, data and metadata to help agricultural, fisheries and forestry industries and government make decisions. ABARES maintains a data catalog[10] listing agriculture related datasets.

The data products published by ABARES cover areas such as agriculture, food, forest, fisheries, energy, minerals, productivity, water and electricity. Pdf and Excel are the two main formats used to publish data.

9.3.2.2 Bureau of Meteorology

The Bureau of Meteorology[11] (BOM) is Australia's national weather, climate and water agency. It deals with the harsh realities of natural environment, including drought, floods, fires, storms, tsunami and tropical cyclones.

Climate summarizes the average, range and variability of weather elements, e.g. rain, wind, temperature, fog, thunder, and sunshine, observed over many years at a location or across an area. In order to understand the climate better, the Bureau collects a wide range of data from the atmosphere, oceans and land surface. For example, rainfall datasets record mean monthly and mean annual rainfall values across Australia in the form of two-dimensional array data. The mean data are based on the standard 30-year period 1961-1990. Water information is also managed to monitor, assess and forecast its availability, condition and use.

The data published are in various format: pdf, image, xml, text file and maps etc*etc*. The metadata describes the spatial and temporal coverage, dataset status, access, data quality, abstract, and contact information.

---

[10] http://www.abares.gov.au/data

[11] http://www.bom.gov.au

9.3.2.3 Australian Institute of Health and Welfare

The Australian Institute of Health and Welfare[12] (AIHW) is a major national agency set up by the Australian Government to provide reliable, regular and relevant information and statistics on Australia's health and welfare. The data portal of this agency is hosted at http://www.aihw.gov.au/data/.

The data and resources collected by AIHW include cancer data, chronic disease indicators, incidence of mortality, disability data, alcohol and other drugs, hospital-related data, mental health data *etc*. Data could be retrieved through database query, through tables published in html or downloaded in xls format.

9.3.2.4 Integrated Marine Observing System

The Integrated Marine Observing System[13] (IMOS) is supported by Australian government to meet the needs of marine climate research. The system provides data in the open oceans around out to a few thousand kilometers as well as the coastal oceans.

IMOS focuses on providing continuous data streams of ocean processes. The datasets cover the monitoring of seasonal, broadscale structure of the global ocean down to 2,000 meters, the monitoring of physical, chemical and biological parameters from both commercial vessels and research vessels, data stream from the full fleet of coastal and deep ocean gliders.

The data are accessible through the electronic Marine Information Infrastructure with netCDF, HDF or GeoTIFF as data format. Applying ISO 19115 standard, the metadata describes data identification, temporal and spatial coverage, reference system, data quality, and contact information.

9.3.3 Other Agencies

There are still many agencies that does not even have a dedicated page for listing dataset. Instead, their data are typically embedded in their programs and publications. In what follows, we name a just few to show the potentials but not list them exhaustively.

---

[12] http://www.aihw.gov.au

[13] http://imos.org.au

9.3.3.1 Department of Sustainability, Environment, Water, Population and Communities

The department of Sustainability, Environment, Water, Population and Communities[14] (DSEWPC) is responsible for implementing the Australian Government's policies to protect our environment and heritage, and to promote a sustainable way of life.

The data could be accessed from the three major information systems under DSEWPC: environmental resources information network, national vegetation information system and discover information geographically. They provide data in the area of environment quality, land, water, biodiversity and heritage. Most data published on DSEWPC are accessible only via visual interaction interface, and it is not obvious to access raw data from its website.

One example of biodiversity related dataset is "Overview of Feral and Managed Honeybees in Australia"[15]. This dataset contains several data table, one of which states the approximate average numbers of hives of honeybees maintained by beekeepers in each Australian state during the 1980s. The data is not easy to reuse as it only provide multi-year average data and the data is formatted in HTML table.

An example of water related datasets is Australian Wetlands Database which provides online access to information on Ramsar wetlands.

9.3.3.2 Murray-Darling Basin Authority

The Murray-Darling Basin Authority[16] (MDBA) administrates the basin which is Australia's most important agricultural area producing over one-third of Australiaï£¡s food supply. It is also home to more than 2 million residents.

The information on water in storage in the Murray-Darling Basin is published in the weekly report. More details could be could be accessed through state water information.

9.3.4 Summary

Table 9.1 summarizes the sources, data format used to publish data and how each data source contributes to the 'WEHAB' framework. Two major observations are:

- **Observation 1**: Different government agencies may contribute the datasets to the same 'WEHAB' discipline from different perspectives. It is not easy for

---

[14] http://www.environment.gov.au

[15] http://www.environment.gov.au/biodiversity/invasive/publications/bees/distribution.html

[16] http://www.mdba.gov.au/

Source	Water	Energy	Health	Agriculture	Biodiversity	Format
DGA	*	*	*	*	*	xml, csv, txt, xls, kml/kmz, Shapefile
ABS	*	*	*	*		csv, srd, xls, html
ANDS	*		*	*	*	varied
GSA	*	*		*	*	shapefile, ArcInfo export, map-info mid/mif, db query
DSEWPC	*	*		*	*	pdf, html
BoM	*	*	*			pdf, gif, xml, txt, html, map
MDBA	*				*	pdf, html
IMOS	*				*	netCDF, HDF, GeoTIFF, csv
ABARES	*	*		*	*	pdf, xls
AIHW			*			xls, html
ASSDA			*			stata, NSDstat, dif, db, txt, delim-ited, sas, csv

Table 9.1 Data Source and 'WEHAB' Discipline

users to identify the useful datasets quickly without understanding the responsibilities of each government agency and how the agency operates.

- **Observation 2**: Different data formats are used to publish datasets by different
  government agencies. To link the datasets together, extra efforts are required to
  convert the datasets into a common format if it is possible.

There are many other issues identified during this survey process. We will discuss
the details in Section 9.5.

9.4 Linking Australia Government Data for Sustainability Science - A Case Study

In this section, we present a case study, as a proof of concept, to show that finding,
linking and using open government data is viable and useful to support highly interdisciplinary sustainability science research. This case study implements a prototype
system with three highlights: (i) Linked Data production and consumption is viable.
We also show a viable infrastructure that can convert Australian open government
data into Linked Data and produce user-friendly user interface for accessing and
mashing up such data. (ii) Relevant raw data exists. We show that there exists some
downloadable and relevant open government data in many Australian government
agencies' website, and they can be easily linked by their temporal-spatial features.
(iii) Linked Open Government Data is useful. We show the collected Linked Data
can be used to help sustainability researchers to create interesting hypotheses towards unexpected discoveries and deeper data analysis. In what follows, we elabo-
rate these three highlights with implementation details.

9.4.1 Linked Data-based Data Management System

We develop a prototype data management system to facilitate users to access and analyze published open government data from different sources. Figure 9.1 illustrate the system's architecture. In *Data Collection* process, the system collects datasets from several Australian government agencies listed in previous section. As there is no standard data publication format in Australia, the collected raw datasets are encoded using various formats such as xls, csv, txt, csv and pdf. In *Data Conversion* process, the system reuse RPI's data conversion tools [17] to convert the collected raw data into Linked Data and store the converted data into an RDF triple store.

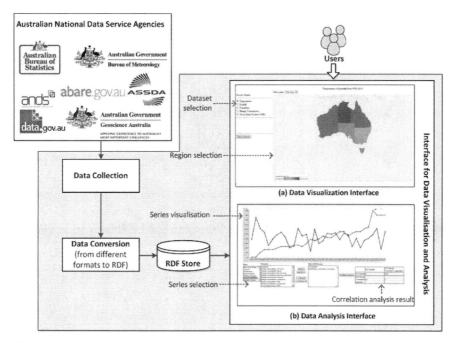

Fig. 9.1 System Infrastructure

We also build a general-purpose interactive user interface to support users visually explore and analyse the Linked Data.

Our prototype supports online visual temporal-spatial analysis. As shown in Fig. 1(a), users can visually select one dataset (e.g. Energy Consumption Data), then a statistical measure in the dataset (e.g. Energy Consumption in agriculture) ,and then a time range (e.g. 1979-1980) to display the corresponding dataset query results on a Google Map. The darkness of the color of each state is determined by the corresponding statistical value obtained from the query.

---

[17] the tools are listed at http://logd.tw.rpi.edu/tools_technologies

By clicking the "Data Analysis" button in the visualization (see Fig. 1(a)), users can enter the data analysis interface which is shown in Fig. 1(b). In this interface, users can select and visualize multiple datasets using line-chart. In addition, users can also analyze the correlations among selected datasets by clicking the "Correlation Analysis" button. After the button is clicked, the correlation table of the selected data will be shown in the right-bottom panel of the interface.

9.4.2 Sustainability Related Datasets Collection and Conversion

The case study starts with dataset discovery, where we manually find a selection of relevant datasets from the Australian open government data sources. In particular, we focus on temporal-spatial statistical raw datasets, i.e. datasets that contains temporal dimension (in which year(s) the data item was recorded), spatial dimension(which state the data item is about), and statistical dimension (each of which corresponds to a numerical value and a specific measure, such as temperature and consumed electricity power in GWh). To simplify data linking and correlation analysis, "Year" and "State" are selected as the levels of granularity for temporal feature and spatial feature respectively[18]. We also limit the selected datasets to tabular data which can be easily represented by CSV, so as to avoid complex structrual alignment. Once collected the datasets, we used tools from the TWC LOGD Portal [8] to convert the selected raw dataset into Linked Open Government Data.

The conversion process was executed following typical LOGD production workflow in the TWC LOGD Portal. We first download the original datasets from the Web to create a local snapshot. For the datasets that are not originally stored in CSV format, we manually convert those files into CSV files using tools such as Microsoft Excel. Most of the resulting CSV files are formatted as data table, where each row contains statistical numbers for all Australian states during a certain year (e.g., table 9.2). In order to facilitate SPARQL based data integration, we adopt "cell-based conversion", i.e. creat an instance of statistical item for each cell (except the first column) as shown in the following example. In the example, the temporal, spatial and statistical dimensions are captured by three triples respectively.

```
@prefix void: <http://rdfs.org/ns/void#> .
@prefix energy_09_c09: <http://logd.tw.rpi.edu/source/abare-gov-au/dataset/
    energy_09_c09/version/2011-Jan-21/> .
@prefix energy_09_c09_vocab: <http://logd.tw.rpi.edu/source/abare-gov-au/
    dataset/energy_09_c09/vocab/> .
@prefix e1: <http://logd.tw.rpi.edu/source/abare-gov-au/dataset/
    energy_09_c09/vocab/enhancement/1/> .
@prefix rdf: <http://www.w3.org/1999/02/22-rdf-syntax-ns#> .
@prefix ov: <http://open.vocab.org/terms/> .
@prefix dbpedia: <http://dbpedia.org/resource/> .
@prefix xsd: <http://www.w3.org/2001/XMLSchema#> .
```

---

[18] we also observed datasets using multi-year temporal period as temporal granularity, but we can always copy such average to individual years to better align datasets. Similarly, we can aggregate quarterly data into yearly statistics.

```
energy_09_c09:total_energy_consumption_3_7
    void:inDataset <http://logd.tw.rpi.edu/source/abare-gov-au/dataset/
      energy_09_c09/version/2011-Jan-21> ;
    rdf:type energy_09_c09_vocab:total_energy_consumption ;
    e1:year "74-75" ;
    e1:state dbpedia:Tasmania ;
    rdf:value "71.3"^^xsd:decimal ;
    ov:csvRow "3"^^xsd:integer ;
    ov:csvCol "7"^^xsd:integer .
```

Specifically, five datasets from different Australian government agencies are selected for the analysis. Two datasets in environment domain, and the rest are in
society domain, coving energy, economics and demographics. With such a diverse
collection of datasets, we expect to see interesting correlations among them including unexpected hypotheses.

Energy:
We select a set of energy consumption data (Tables c - c8, Australian energy
consumption, by fuel energy units [19]) from n Bureau of Agricultural and Resource
Economics and Sciences (ABARES)[20], which contains the statistics of energy
consumptions in different industries of the seven Australian states and territories
(not including ACT). The statistics is based on financial years[21] and covers
the period from "1960-61" to "2007-08". The data is published in Excel format.
We need manually convert the data from excel to CSV first and then convert to RDF.

	NSW	VIC	QLD	SA	WA	TAS	NT
89-90	1230.4	1099.8	691.8	301.9	473.0	96.6	52.5
90-91	1228.6	1090.9	702.0	287.4	488.4	97.6	55.0
91-92	1219.4	1108.7	715.0	296.9	496.4	89.3	56.9
92-93	1249.1	1104.7	758.5	300.1	522.0	90.1	57.2
93-94	1276.7	1102.5	793.2	304.8	554.1	92.0	58.5
94-95	1314.6	1152.2	847.3	304.4	592.7	92.4	61.8
95-96	1351.2	1184.9	882.7	296.6	630.2	93.0	67.0
96-97	1380.6	1202.7	914.1	299.7	649.6	94.8	69.7
97-98	1382.0	1286.3	968.5	311.9	662.6	95.8	70.4
98-99	1413.8	1318.3	983.8	327.2	672.8	95.7	73.2
99-00	1426.3	1346.3	1009.7	328.0	688.5	95.8	76.4
00-01	1455.6	1341.5	1025.7	330.3	712.5	94.4	74.0
01-02	1451.1	1376.3	1063.6	329.2	727.4	98.1	74.3
02-03	1477.7	1385.4	1107.2	337.7	771.6	102.6	74.5
03-04	1507.0	1414.4	1189.6	335.8	786.8	110.6	78.2
04-05	1532.0	1429.9	1231.9	341.4	791.7	116.0	82.5
05-06	1504.0	1477.0	1314.9	323.6	807.0	120.0	93.7
06-07	1529.0	1463.4	1309.0	317.2	916.0	125.9	109.3

Table 9.2 Total Energy Consumption (unit: PJ, petajoule)

---

[19]   http://www.abare.gov.au/publications_html/energy/energy_09/C_
09.xls

[20] catalog page: http://www.abare.gov.au/publications_html/data/data/
data.html

[21] In Australia the financial year runs from July 1 to June 30 of the following year.

Population:

"n Demographic Statistics, Jun 2010" from Bureau of Statistics (ABS)[22] is included in this case study. This dataset contains the quarterly estimation of the resident populations (ERP) of Australia and the states and territories based on the results of the 2006 Census of Population and Housing held on 8th August 2006. Since most of other data in this case study are yearly based, we only extracted the data of June in each year from the original data-set. The data is published in Excel format. We manually extract the required data from the file and put into the CSV. Then the data is converted into RDF.

	NSW	VIC	QLD	SA	WA	TAS	NT
89-90	5834021	4378592	2899283	1432056	1613049	462188	163728
90-91	5898731	4420373	2960951	1446299	1636067	466802	165493
91-92	5962569	4455002	3029950	1456512	1658045	469826	168086
92-93	6004880	4472387	3109788	1460674	1677669	471659	170734
93-94	6060190	4487570	3187113	1466138	1703009	472939	173375
94-95	6126981	4517387	3265109	1469429	1733787	473673	177552
95-96	6204728	4560155	3338690	1474253	1765256	474443	181843
96-97	6276961	4597201	3394671	1481357	1794992	473605	186912
97-98	6339071	4637820	3447725	1489552	1822668	471967	189880
98-99	6411370	4686402	3501421	1497819	1849733	471430	192735
99-00	6486213	4741339	3561537	1505038	1874459	471409	195561
00-01	6575217	4804726	3628946	1511728	1901159	471795	197768
01-02	6628951	4863084	3714798	1521127	1926111	472766	199411
02-03	6672577	4923485	3809214	1531278	1953070	477646	200046
03-04	6707189	4981467	3900910	1540434	1982637	482770	202063
04-05	6756457	5048602	3994858	1552514	2017088	486327	206373
05-06	6816087	5126540	4090908	1567888	2059381	489951	210627
06-07	6904942	5221310	4195981	1585794	2112967	493204	214804

Table 9.3 Population (unit: person)

Economics:

We select "Table 1. Gross State Product, Chain volume measures and current prices" in ABS's "5220.0 Australian National Accounts: State Accounts"[23] as the economic indicator in this case study. This data-set contains state and territory estimates of gross domestic product and its components, in current price and chain volume terms, for the years "1989-90" to "2009-10". Same process as for the Population dataset is applied to the economic data.

Environment:

Two sets of environmental data, i.e., rainfall and temperature data, are included in this case study. Both of them are obtained from a data portal called Australian Cli-

22 www.abs.gov.au/AUSSTATS/abs@.nsf/DetailsPage/3101.0Jun%202010?OpenDocument
23 www.abs.gov.au/AUSSTATS/abs@.nsf/DetailsPage/5220.02009-10?
OpenDocument

	NSW	VIC	QLD	SA	WA	TAS	NT
89-90	142075	111636	63530	30327	39707	8699	4313
90-91	147061	113133	65925	30793	40949	8559	4683
91-92	150452	112515	68568	31170	42437	8788	4521
92-93	155534	118500	73946	32405	44748	9281	4631
93-94	162413	124029	78044	34084	48352	9554	4651
94-95	172293	129912	84278	35495	51869	10224	4957
95-96	184189	137867	89241	37562	56055	10875	5413
96-97	196418	144387	93729	38669	57971	11043	5622
97-98	206884	152026	99850	41002	62468	11630	5916
98-99	219890	160536	105540	41972	64131	12057	6303
99-00	233777	171978	110971	44311	69501	12384	7434
00-01	246657	182431	119715	47973	76508	12628	8675
01-02	261522	193883	131858	51620	82477	13691	8732
02-03	276785	205388	139883	54212	87644	14607	9124
03-04	295653	220941	154506	57866	92731	16186	9698
04-05	313270	232194	170888	60162	102968	17206	10877
05-06	329899	243728	191400	64002	121560	18415	12250
06-07	353113	259789	211150	69073	141847	20460	13783

Table 9.4 Gross State Product (unit: $Millions)

mate Variability & Change (ACVC)[24], which is provided by Australian Bureau of Meteorology (BoM).

ACVC provides an open interface to visualize and download time series data related with climate change. However, users can only download single time series, e.g., average rainfall in January in Victoria from 1950-2010, from ACVC. To include the downloaded time series for analysis in this case study, we downloaded individual time series one by one, and then combine them to a unified time range, i.e., financial year. For example, for rainfall data of each state, first we downloaded average rainfall of the twelve months (twelve time series); then, extract rainfall values which belong to a same financial year (July to June) from the twelve time series and sum them together to get the average rainfall value for that (financial) year; finally the yearly average rainfall values were combined together to form a new time series. The raw dataset is published in CSV format.

9.4.3 Linked Data-based Analysis

With linked data management system and collected data, we now show how our prototype helps the advance of sustainability science. In principle, linking data from different resources enables many cross-domain analysis towards correlation discovery over human and nature systems.

In this case study, we conduct several correlation analysis using the collected dataset as evidences to justify the practical value of linked open government data for sustainability science.

---

[24] http://www.bom.gov.au/cgi-bin/climate/change/timeseries.cgi

	Mean Temperature (unit: °C)							Rainfall (unit: mm)						
	NSW	VIC	QLD	SA	WA	TAS	NT	NSW	VIC	QLD	SA	WA	TAS	NT
50-51	17.34	14.54	22.2	19.48	22.0	10.51	24.31	687.07	698.36	799.48	337.34	220.99	1304.62	621.18
51-52	17.19	13.59	22.88	19.0	22.14	9.57	25.0	477.42	804.75	408.08	216.78	193.18	1636.27	225.3
52-53	16.96	13.73	22.69	18.85	22.13	10.03	24.67	543.15	688.38	622.87	264.32	213.23	1399.75	514.64
53-54	16.97	13.44	22.68	18.61	22.03	9.88	24.8	446.28	702.25	691.98	280.47	204.57	1634.9	357.81
54-55	17.47	13.92	22.79	19.27	22.3	10.08	25.0	707.09	728.81	893.51	380.06	291.54	1184.33	549.75
55-56	16.58	13.86	22.5	18.93	22.01	10.38	25.1	901.17	947.26	883.25	321.9	241.59	1913.97	544.05
56-57	16.51	13.06	22.49	18.89	22.29	9.43	25.09	406.8	642.27	700.77	286.34	171.54	1523.06	574.43
57-58	17.63	13.66	23.53	19.26	22.82	9.72	25.58	420.49	550.54	579.5	259.72	154.91	1423.48	376.65
58-59	17.16	13.9	23.04	19.06	22.6	10.13	25.46	604.53	688.91	570.47	310.73	213.03	1365.18	463.66
59-60	17.29	13.97	22.94	19.31	22.1	10.16	25.43	492.2	716.64	541.61	412.99	192.32	1475.44	475.59
60-61	16.85	14.07	22.53	19.27	22.37	10.56	25.25	521.33	687.48	434.48	307.97	147.33	1158.87	324.21
61-62	17.23	14.46	23.02	19.48	22.76	10.73	25.1	633.42	617.7	610.1	269.6	147.36	1320.66	413.34
62-63	17.12	13.82	23.17	19.47	22.33	9.68	25.43	726.46	684.63	699.6	413.24	212.02	1190.37	444.61
63-64	17.05	13.98	23.01	19.31	22.57	9.93	25.36	503.59	601.04	508.89	264.76	112.31	1435.95	323.15
64-65	16.87	13.33	23.26	19.21	22.58	9.51	25.47	327.15	671.85	491.19	275.92	161.95	1679.66	419.44
65-66	17.55	14.01	23.08	19.85	22.45	10.17	25.27	419.26	609.23	442.73	352.78	215.89	1093.2	458.17
66-67	17.12	13.96	22.95	18.76	21.67	10.23	24.09	549.64	603.42	585.32	377.47	233.93	1053.67	646.61
67-68	17.58	14.48	23.1	19.75	22.21	9.98	25.19	459.4	562.9	647.65	446.77	249.66	1501.77	611.79
68-69	17.12	13.68	23.33	18.82	21.77	9.99	24.65	537.15	698.46	372.97	320.84	237.71	1702.39	512.24
69-70	16.89	13.64	23.39	19.17	22.69	10.24	25.45	502.5	706.25	485.8	213.49	125.48	1373.17	366.7
70-71	16.84	14.12	22.75	19.2	22.33	10.49	24.96	616.16	755.88	740.57	316.41	195.59	1811.44	445.95
71-72	16.6	13.59	22.99	18.84	22.26	10.24	25.23	511.42	627.79	670.38	230.17	182.69	1312.37	545.73
72-73	18.09	14.45	23.84	20.21	22.98	10.55	26.1	525.9	693.55	611.79	370.0	261.39	1520.3	517.72
73-74	17.6	14.68	23.01	19.41	21.96	10.96	24.48	927.62	904.74	1217.71	531.59	508.97	1326.29	1035.33
74-75	16.63	13.62	22.64	18.95	22.11	9.93	24.34	520.7	691.8	638.91	411.01	259.85	1772.05	718.42
75-76	17.28	14.54	22.82	19.02	21.97	10.77	24.07	748.12	711.79	900.48	389.73	361.05	1545.14	888.6
76-77	16.83	13.63	22.57	18.88	22.44	9.99	24.3	612.2	694.51	813.17	239.55	174.53	1470.33	672.14
77-78	17.71	14.24	23.08	19.86	22.92	10.17	24.92	489.62	570.76	478.03	363.21	183.3	1197.05	544.8
78-79	17.15	14.15	22.62	19.19	22.31	10.36	24.55	562.77	705.53	823.98	337.25	309.35	1328.5	620.83
79-80	17.84	14.12	23.78	19.83	22.99	10.45	26.07	391.06	604.83	485.76	403.65	251.13	1416.15	511.69
80-81	18.36	14.95	23.48	20.22	22.74	11.14	25.66	449.73	667.98	716.19	335.92	250.89	1473.26	563.65
81-82	17.46	14.42	23.41	19.71	22.18	10.65	25.63	463.62	610.41	554.27	425.36	203.8	1367.09	669.25
82-83	18.02	14.34	23.42	19.88	22.77	10.21	24.79	450.06	461.32	571.14	348.34	143.31	1149.53	497.69
83-84	16.82	13.73	23.13	19.37	22.6	10.35	25.02	699.82	683.88	643.83	419.37	268.53	1178.53	650.54
84-85	17.16	14.01	23.24	19.41	22.56	10.18	25.1	483.71	609.68	562.33	302.03	174.86	1544.05	506.7
85-86	17.32	13.81	23.55	19.55	22.79	10.26	25.99	464.16	652.78	514.4	312.74	150.34	1391.81	385.4
86-87	17.75	13.44	23.69	18.92	22.0	10.03	25.31	577.28	765.17	583.29	323.5	285.34	1428.42	563.62
87-88	17.54	14.59	23.77	19.82	22.89	11.02	25.83	627.41	621.17	496.19	301.17	198.51	1077.98	430.7
88-89	17.91	14.63	23.91	19.72	22.56	10.99	25.62	754.07	760.64	755.05	381.51	350.14	1529.06	584.85
89-90	17.32	14.17	23.2	19.46	22.44	10.72	25.43	604.14	639.67	702.28	245.42	198.63	1238.43	376.53
90-91	18.18	14.55	23.45	20.37	23.16	10.32	25.9	470.43	656.61	698.55	308.59	173.83	1295.35	590.67
91-92	17.4	13.97	23.67	19.92	22.86	10.24	26.1	467.48	649.6	454.81	355.35	214.87	1450.92	352.97
92-93	17.14	13.84	23.55	19.25	22.21	10.47	25.41	600.54	818.79	480.86	375.02	308.15	1430.6	603.27
93-94	17.36	13.97	23.55	19.66	22.36	10.46	25.27	545.19	779.12	543.88	286.56	246.93	1459.52	512.83
94-95	17.24	13.99	23.47	19.49	22.5	10.28	25.0	463.77	585.27	502.65	447.66	181.85	1318.35	549.06
95-96	17.35	13.45	23.92	19.89	23.06	9.76	25.91	540.86	670.12	596.65	347.44	167.72	1445.05	446.67
96-97	17.47	14.05	23.2	19.94	22.73	10.18	25.29	550.67	587.82	679.18	482.71	255.3	1421.54	585.51
97-98	18.14	14.04	24.14	19.88	23.18	10.44	25.97	473.03	520.42	684.7	333.64	243.17	1172.9	504.34
98-99	17.65	14.28	23.9	20.1	22.61	10.74	25.81	641.01	625.35	815.73	579.6	220.68	1348.06	661.3
99-00	17.3	14.54	23.1	19.8	21.63	10.97	24.54	684.27	624.88	778.66	648.3	285.55	1149.53	867.96
00-01	18.07	14.79	23.37	20.47	22.35	11.04	24.64	554.96	633.5	714.77	448.1	270.56	1307.84	1001.91
01-02	17.58	13.97	23.69	19.36	22.35	10.61	24.97	409.64	612.62	495.21	369.92	243.77	1347.66	580.55
02-03	18.41	14.64	24.01	20.19	23.13	11.04	25.45	349.18	462.76	444.14	329.61	190.63	1423.21	523.68
03-04	17.91	13.96	24.14	20.26	22.61	10.17	25.59	461.83	594.84	577.05	466.25	235.14	1548.31	757.02
04-05	17.99	14.27	23.87	20.24	23.38	10.53	25.92	504.18	621.77	501.07	258.51	148.99	1127.54	372.17
05-06	18.09	14.39	24.25	20.05	22.06	10.69	25.42	461.98	571.48	640.04	501.35	234.31	1487.0	812.27
06-07	18.49	14.97	23.72	20.66	23.18	10.94	25.48	448.15	478.63	578.49	388.1	193.89	1061.66	605.75
07-08	17.85	14.91	23.23		23.11	11.06	25.63	522.02	489.29	652.4	338.65	128.28	1146.48	476.95
08-09	17.95	14.36	23.55	20.08	22.71	10.51	25.45	543.67	497.7	791.52	380.7	206.98	1287.66	624.49
09-10	18.46	15.3	23.71	20.65	23.54	11.36	25.66	551.6	685.62	734.43	276.57	277.24	1468.95	707.59

Table 9.5 Mean Temperature and Rainfall in Australian States

Statistical datasets covering states' population, energy consumption and gross state product (GSP) are listed in Table 9.2, Table 9.3 and Table 9.4, respectively (Note: we only include data in a common period, i.e., 89-90 to 06-07, in the tables.). Intuitively, it is natural to see more populate will lead to higher energy consumption and higher GSP. In sustainability science, it would be great to observe non-increasing trend of the energy consumption per capita (total energy consumption divided by population).

	NSW	NT	QLD	SA	TAS	VIC	WA
NSW		0.961	0.981	0.948	0.898	**0.991**	0.981
NT	0.961		0.982	0.878	0.94	0.965	0.972
QLD	0.981	0.982		0.912	0.934	0.985	0.983
SA	0.948	0.878	0.912		**0.841**	0.954	0.893
TAS	0.898	0.94	0.934	**0.841**		0.915	0.899
VIC	**0.991**	0.965	0.985	0.954	0.915		0.972
WA	0.981	0.972	0.983	0.893	0.899	0.972	

Table 9.6 Correlations of Total Energy Consumption in Different Australian States

	NSW	NT	QLD	SA	TAS	VIC	WA
NSW		0.373	**0.699**	0.572	0.014	0.618	0.259
NT	0.373		0.605	0.687	-0.024	0.072	0.673
QLD	**0.699**	0.605		0.599	0.053	0.338	0.335
SA	0.572	0.687	0.599		0.106	0.486	0.51
TAS	0.014	-0.024	0.053	0.106		0.483	**-0.144**
VIC	0.618	0.072	0.338	0.486	0.483		-0.095
WA	0.259	0.673	0.335	0.51	**-0.144**	-0.095	

Table 9.7 Correlations of Total Rainfall among Different Australian States

	NSW	NT	VIC	QLD	SA	WA	TAS
NSW		0.424	0.74	0.671	**0.85**	0.582	0.574
NT	0.424		**0.096**	0.676	0.533	0.708	0.099
VIC	0.74	**0.096**		0.272	0.723	0.33	0.853
QLD	0.671	0.676	0.272		0.626	0.534	0.326
SA	**0.85**	0.533	0.723	0.626		0.673	0.576
WA	0.582	0.708	0.33	0.534	0.573		0.236
WA	0.574	0.099	0.853	0.326	0.576	0.236	

Table 9.8 Correlations of Mean Temperature among Different n States

Apart from the linear correlations between any pairs of the three measures, we further analyse how the states are correlated over individual measure. A statistical analysis on the datasets shows that all state has strong linear correlations on the "energy consumption" measure (see Table 9.6). From this table, we observe that correlation among different states' energy consumption is between 0.841 (TAS & SA) to 0.991 (VIC & NSW).

Correlations among state environment data are much lower than that of the society data (see Table 9.5). As shown in Table 9.7 and 9.8, the correlation in environment data is mainly based on the geo-locations of the states.

Through analysis, we also find that there are some potential patterns between environment data and society data. For example, the three series in Figure 9.2 are the normalized value of personal residential energy consumption increase rate, the normalized value of mean temperature and the normalized value of GSP per capita increase rate of Tasmania. Through correlation analysis (see Table 9.9), we found that GSP has a very big impact on personal residential energy consumption with a

	TAS Mean Temp.	TAS GSP Incr. Rate (Per Capi.)	Personal Resi. Ener. Cons. Incr. Rate
TAS Mean Temp.		0.179	0.185
TAS GSP Incr. Rate (Per Capi.)	0.179		0.688
Personal Resi. Ener. Cons. Incr. Rate	0.185	0.688	

Table 9.9 Correlations among the Personal Residential Energy Consumption Increase Rate, the Mean Temperature and the Gross State Product Increase Rate (Per Capita) of Tasmania.

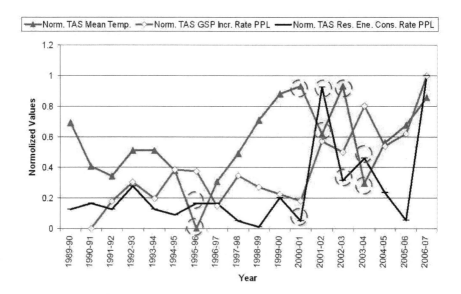

Fig. 9.2 Normalized Residential Energy Consumption Increase Rate Per Capita, Normalized GSP Increase Rate Per Capita, and Normalized Mean Temperature in Tasmania

correlation of 0.688, and temperature does not have strong correlation with personal energy consumption (only with a correlation of 0.185). However, in Figure 9.2, it can be found that the peak values of residential consumption are always combined with temperature valley values (dash circles in the figure). The reason behind this fact could be that heating is a major residential energy consumption unit in Tasmania.

9.5 Discussion

In this section, first we describe the challenges identified based on our survey experiences. This is followed by recommendations for government data publishing and analysis.

9.5.1 Challenges

Two observations are presented in Section 9.3. Here we summarize the major challenges related to linking Australian government data for sustainability science as follows:

Data Discoverability: there are several reasons leading to the difficulties in locating useful data quickly:

- Some sources only support very simple search functions such as simple keyword search. The search results may include not only the datasets but also the policies, project and/or research papers, which are are often viewed as a different kind of data, and one that might not be included in data search query answers.
- Based on the *Observation 1*, it is not easy to locate the right datasets for users without understanding the government agencies' responsibilities and data structures. Every agency may have its own specializations and data is usually published using an agency-centric view;
- Different agencies use different data categorizations thus causing difficulties for users who are trying to find the data quickly;

Data Description: there are two aspects of data description that present difficulties for identifying and linking data:

- Semantic ambiguity: an example we found most often is the concept of a year. Some agencies use financial year to describe data but others use a calendar year. This presents difficulties when trying to analyze the relationship between the two datasets due to their different temporal coverage. Extra efforts are required to transfer data into forms with the same temporal coverage;
- Various data formats: as described in *Observation 2*, this presents difficulties for linking and understanding the data;
- Granularity: datasets are published with different granularity and different spatial coverage and/or different temporal coverage. Extra efforts are required to transform the data to an agreed granularity for data linking and analysis if possible.

Data Analysis: the ultimate goal of linking data for sustainability science is to analyze the interactions among different disciplines. Even when we solve the data discoverability and data description problems and all the data are stored using a common RDF format, questions still remain concerning how best to analyze the Linked Data. Problems reaming that could not be solved using SPARQL queries.

9.5.2 Recommendations

Given the complexity of sustainability science, there are a lot of challenges to develop a seamless integration of Linked Data from multiple disciplines. The challenges come from not only the technology side but also the governance side. The public sector information, published by the n government, is liberated as a key national asset. To enlighten the path for deploying Linked Data at Data.gov.au, we present the following recommendations:

- **Recommendation 1**: There are many commonalities among the data published by the different government agencies from not only but also the other countries. To avoid duplication of effort, coordinated efforts are required to identify the common vocabularies for various domains for the purpose of re-use and linkage.
- **Recommendation 2**: To enable the existing data discoverable, guidance on converting data from the existing data model (*e.g.* relational data model, CSV *etc.*) to the RDF model for general, non-application-specific usage is needed for publishing data as Linked Data.
- **Recommendation 3**: To enhance data discoverability, collaborative efforts from different agencies and coordinated governance are required to deliver a better data access service. The service should not only be comprehensive, but also well documented and include examples;
- **Recommendation 4**: To enhance data re-usability, better data analysis services are required to realize the full value of public sector information;

9.6 Conclusion

In this chapter, we investigate a Linked Data approach for supporting sustainability researchers in their efforts to create and investigate sustainability science hypotheses.

Such hypotheses generation and evaluation requires intensive integration of data from different sources from a wide range of domains. A survey of sustainability related datasets published by the Australian government agencies has been conducted based on the WEHAB framework. A case study was presented to examine the practical value of linking Australian open government data in advancing sustainability research. Based on our experiences and the lesson learned, we summarize the challenges of re-using data published by the government agencies and present our recommendations for future government data deployment.

As a possible future study, we will investigate automatic tools to discover all the relevant datasets and enhance the Linked Data-based analysis functions.

Acknowledgements The Tasmanian ICT Centre is jointly funded by the Australian Government through the Intelligent Island Program and CSIRO. The Intelligent Island Program is administered by the Tasmanian Department of Economic Development, Tourism and the Arts. This research is supported by the Water for a Healthy Country Flagship and the Wealth from Oceans National Research Flagship of CSIRO.

The authors would like to thank the anonymous reviewers and the editor for thoroughly reading the article and providing thoughtful comments. Also thanks Peter Marendy for the proofreading.

References

1. Australian Government. Declaration of open government. http://www.finance.gov.au/e-government/strategy-and-governance/gov2/declaration-of-open-government.html, January 2010.
2. Berners-Lee, T., Hendler, J. and Lassila, O. The semantic web. *Scientific american*, 284(5):28–37, 2001.
3. Bizer, C., Heath, T. and Berners-Lee, T. Linked data - the story so far. *International Journal on Semantic Web and Information Systems*, 5:1–22, 2009.
4. Cameron, D. Letter to government departments on opening up data. http://www.number10.gov.uk/news/statements-and-articles/2010/05/letter-to-government-departments-on-opening-up-data-51204, 2010.
5. Chen, Chao-chen, Yeh, Jian-hua, and Sie, Shun-hong. Government ontology and thesaurus construction: A taiwanese experience. In Fox, E., Neuhold, E., Premsmit, P. and Wuwongse, V. editors, *Digital Libraries: Implementing Strategies and Sharing Experiences*, volume 3815 of *Lecture Notes in Computer Science*, pages 263–272. Springer Berlin / Heidelberg, 2005. 10.1007/11599517_30.
6. Cheng, Chin Pang, Lau, G.T., Law, K.H., Pan, J. and Jones, A. Improving access to and understanding of regulations through taxonomies. *Government Information Quarterly*, 26(2):238 – 245, 2009. Building the Next-Generation Digital Government Infrastructures.
7. Clark, W.C. and Dickson, N.M. Sustainability science: The emerging research program. In *Proceedings of the National Academy of Sciences of the United States of America*, volume 100, pages 8059–8061, 2003.
8. Li, Ding, Lebo, T., Erickson, J.S., DiFranzo, D., Williams, G.T., Li, Xian, Michaelis, J., Graves, A., Zheng, Jin Guang, Shangguan, Z., Flores, J., McGuinness, D.L. and Hendler, J. TWC LOGD: A Portal for Linked Open Government Data Ecosystems. *Journal of Web Semantics (special issue on semantic web challenge 2010*, 2011.
9. Glassey, O. Developing a one-stop government data model. *Government Information Quarterly*, 21(2):156 – 169, 2004.
10. Guijarro, L. Interoperability frameworks and enterprise architectures in e-government initiatives in europe and the united states. *Government Information Quarterly*, 24(1):89 – 101, 2007.
11. Jaeger, P.T. and Bertot, J.C. Transparency and technological change: Ensuring equal and sustained public access to government information. *Government Information Quarterly*, 27(4):371 – 376, 2010. Special Issue: Open/Transparent Government.
12. Kates, R.W., Clark, W.C., Corell, R., Hall, J.M., Jaeger, C.C., Lowe, I., McCarthy, J.J., Schellnhuber, H.J., Bolin, B. Dickson, N.M., Faucheux, S., Gallopin, G.C., Gruebler, A., Huntley, B., JŁger, J., Jodha, N.S., Kasperson, R.E., Mabogunje, A., Matson, P., Mooney, H., Moore, B. III, O'Riordan, T. and Svedin, U. Sustainability science. *Science*, 292:641–642, 2001.

13. Kauffman, J. Advancing sustainability science: report on the international conference on sustainability science. *Sustainability Science*, 4:233–242, 2009.

14. Komiyama, H. and Takeuchi, K. Sustainability science: building a new discipline. *Sustainability Science*, 1:1–6, 2006.

15. Medjahed, B., Rezgui, A., Bouguettaya, A. and Ouzzani, M. Infrastructure for e-government web services. *IEEE Internet Computing*, 7:58–65, January 2003.

16. National Research Council. *Our Common Journey: A Transition Toward Sustainability*. Natl. Acad. Press, Washington, DC, 1999.

17. Stirling, D.A. Epa glossaries: The struggle to define environmental terms. *Government Information Quarterly*, 24(2):414 – 428, 2007.

18. The Australian Government. The government 2.0 taskforce report, 2009.

19. United Nations. Report of the world commission on environment and development. *General Assembly Resolution*, 42/187, 1987.

20. United Nations World Summit on Sustainable Development (2002) WEHAB Framework Papers. http://www.johannesburgsummit.org/html/documents/we hab_papers.html.

21. W3C Semantic Web Activity. http://www.w3.org/2001/sw/.

22. White House. Memorandum on transparency and open government. http://www.whitehouse.gov/the_press_office/TransparencyandOpenGovernment, January 2009.

Chapter 10
The Web is My Back-end: Creating Mashups with Linked Open Government Data

Dominic DiFranzo, Alvaro Graves, John S. Erickson, Li Ding, James Michaelis, Timothy Lebo, Evan Patton, Gregory Todd Williams, Xian Li, Jin Guang Zheng, Johanna Flores, Deborah L. McGuinness, and Jim Hendler

Abstract Governments around the world have been releasing raw data to their citizens at an increased pace. The mixing and linking of these datasets by a community of users enhances their value and makes new insights possible. The use of *mashups* — digital works in which data from one or more sources is combined and presented in innovative ways — is a great way to expose this value. Mashups enable end users to explore data that has a real tangible meaning in their lives. Although there are many approaches to publishing and using data to create mashups, we believe Linked Data and Semantic Web technologies solve many of the true challenges in open government data and can lower the cost and complexity of developing these applications. In this chapter we discuss why Linked Data is a better model and how it can be used to build useful mashups.

10.1 Introduction

The deluge of raw data that has recently become available due to government transparency initiatives around the world presents developers with new opportunities to create web-based *mashups*, or light-weight compositions of data and services displayed in compelling ways. Mashups based on linked open govenment data are an important new form of application that enable users in a variety of contexts to discover patterns and correlations that previously may not have been apparent.

Government datasets have been published using a variety of approaches ranging from web services [5] with RESTful APIs [14] (Application Programming Interfaces) to downloadable "dump" files. As a result of these initiatives, users and developers are now able to access and derive benefits from data representing a rich variety of domains including financial markets, health, government, and environment. At the time of this writing the Programmable Web portal[1] lists over 3,000 APIs that are available for accessing data on the Web, proof of the growing interest amongst producers in getting their data online and developers in consuming this data.

Correspondance author: Dominic DiFranzo, Tetherless World Constellation, Rensselaer Polytechnic Institute, 110 8th St., Troy, NY 12180, USA, e-mail: difrad@rpi.edu. See the List of Contributors for full contact details.

[1] http://www.programmableweb.com/apis/directory

Many examples exist of compelling mashups that have been based on open government datasets. In one case, two EPA-published datasets containing data about ground ozone readings and information about collection sites were combined to visualize the levels of ground ozone in different parts of the US[2]. In another case, foreign aid supplied by the US was compared with that of the UK government. In this second example, not only were datasets from different governments used, but it was also necessary to translate currency from British pounds to US dollars in order to create a comprehensible visualization[3].

A key benefit of creating mashups using the methods described here is that they enable users to make certain observations that are not evident from individual datasets alone. Different organizations may collect data representing aspects of a phenomenon, making it difficult to observe it as a whole. For example, a phenomenon like heavy snow will be relevant to different organizations: The National Oceanic and Atmospheric Administration (NOAA) might report data related to the weather, while data from the Department of Agriculture (USDA) may focus on the effect of the snow on crops; the Department of Education (ED) could utilize this information to determine the conditions under which schools should close. Each organization will include data related to this event in one or more of their datasets, but it is not until we mash them up together that we can have a complete picture of the phenomenon.

10.2 Motivation

Government datasets published under open data principles contain a wealth of information that can impact the decisions and actions of stakeholders ranging from individuals to organizations. For example, the US Centers for Medicare and Medicaid Services releases data documenting the quality and services of every hospital and nursing home in the United States that accepts Medicare and Medicaid. If presented in the right context, this data could enable citizens to compare the hospitals in their area and enhance their medical decision-making process. Presented in a different context, organizations could use this data to compare and contrast the quality of medical care around the US and investigate what outside factors might be involved. In yet another context, community leaders could use this data to target medical care delivery problems in their area and leverage it to develop solutions. All of this can be accomplished with a single dataset, presented in the appropriate context for the user.

Much more is possible when datasets are interlinked based on their related fields and entities. For example, the US Department of Labor publishes unemployment rates for every county in the US. By linking unemployment data with hospital metrics, a possible correlation between the unemployment rate and the quality of hospitals in a given area can be investigated. Raw data by itself can be difficult to parse and understand; a table of data devoid of context is unlikely to be meaningful to an end user. As seen in the example above, a single dataset might be useful by itself, empowering individuals, organizations and communities in many different ways. By linking datasets, a user can obtain a better insight on the context related to the data by looking to other datasets. Mashups based on Linked Data enable stakeholders at many levels to experiment, to discover connections, and to pose questions and rapidly test hypotheses about how and why things happen. The mashup culture of prototyping, linking, experimenting and visualizing helps to bring out the full potential of open government data.

An important advantage of mashups in the government space is the agility and low cost with which they can be developed compared with alternative approaches, including the creation of standalone applications by contract developers. Previously, a visualization project could take weeks or even months for a software contractor to implement and cost on the order of thousands of dollars.

---

[2] http://www.data.gov/semantic/Castnet/html/exhibit

[3] http://data-gov.tw.rpi.edu/demo/linked/aidviz-1554-10030.html

This meant that organizations and small communities with limited resources could not easily use government data to address their specific questions or to guide their decision-making processes. Mashups may be built in hours or days using free tools and services readily available on the Web, including tools like Google Visualizations [7] and Protovis [4]. Rapid learning curves enable communities, organizations and even individuals to create their own mashups using open government data without having to hire outside developers or domain experts. Web-accessible visualization tools and APIs enable developers to focus on the important work of linking and mashing the actual data. Communities and organizations now have the ability to not only build and use mashups for their own goals, but also to test and experiment with different ideas and hypotheses without the risk of wasting time and money. Stakeholders can now engage in an iterative, rapid prototyping process to learn and discover more about the specific datasets they care about, and to build better visualizations to communicate their message and achieve their goals.

10.3 Linked Data

The Linked Data premise is that data should "work" in the same way the Web of Documents currently works; we argue that developers will be more productive building mashups based on the emerging Web of Data based on Linked Data principles.

A key advantage of the Linked Data approach is that it is decentralized, enabling providers to be spread out and their datasets referenced from across the Web. Unlike traditional APIs which provide a single source for data access and querying, datasets published using Linked Data principles may be hosted, queried and referenced across many sources. This works much like the current Web, in which documents are hosted and accessed by systems distributed across the world.

Linked Data is inherently modular; no coordination or planning is required to link concepts and ideas from different datasets together. Any Linked Data can be mashed up or combined with any other Linked Data. The beauty of this approach is that the "real" mashup takes place within the data graph itself, not in the application code as it must with web API-based development. And because links between the datasets are actually in the data itself, they are accessible and reusable to other developers and users. This is analogous to the current Web of Documents: anyone can put up a web page and link from it to any other web page on the Web, and consumers do not need to coordinate or seek permission from the owners of any of the web pages they link to.

These factors combine to make Linked Data a more scalable approach for the construction of open government data mashups. It is easy to extend Linked Data that has already been published; this remains true even as the definitions and structure of the data change over time. Following Linked Data principles, anyone can publish semantic data and link to any other semantic dataset. Unlike proprietary APIs, the core technologies that make up Linked Data — HTTP URIs (Universal Resource Identifiers), RDF (the basic data description language for the Semantic Web) and SPARQL (a query language for RDF) — are open standards and are W3C (World Wide Web Consortium) recommendations. This allows developers who combine web application skills with knowledge of RDF and SPARQL to reuse their knowledge as they encounter new datasets. Applications built using standard Semantic Web technologies can more easily use new semantic datasets that they weren't originally built for. By using SPARQL in tandem with Linked Data, developers have much more freedom with the types of queries and questions their mashups can ask from the datasets. Developers are not restricted by a simple interface to access and query the data anymore, but rather have access to a complete, robust query language to accomplish their goals.

The Linked Data approach facilitates reuse by exposing the dataset data model to developers and users. This transparency enables developers and users to see exactly how the datasets are structured and can help the community understand, improve and reuse these models. This reuse is what allows standards to get started and grow, which in turn allows for greater reuse and linking of data. This reuse is an extremely important point as it also helps to lower the cost of building applications and mashups. For example, by using Linked Data the BBC has been able cover and include a wider area of topics and information in the many areas they care about, all the while being able to contribute back to these datasets and systems to help build a better web of data. This allowed them to have a better, more complete and consistent information portal while saving in costs of managing and building the dataset and services that were already available for reuse. [9]

Linked data mashup developers can use the same visualization APIs, web services, programming environments, frameworks, and platforms in the same way as for web API-based mashups. Indeed, LOGD mashups often use web services to send SPARQL queries using standard REST methods, and get SPARQL results back in any of the formats web developers are familiar with (JSON, XML, RSS, etc). The transition to Linked Data does not require web developers to substantially change their patterns for building applications and visualizations, and it enables them to take advantage of and contribute to the Web of Data.

10.3.1 Alternatives to Linked Data

In this section we discuss other approaches to creating data-driven mashups and contrast them with the benefits of Linked Data.

10.3.1.1 Raw Files

One of the simplest methods for publishing data on the Web is publishing raw data in downloadable "dump files." In this approach developers can download these files and use them to create mashups, but this approach may lead to several problems:

- **Lack of context:** The first problem for mashup developers using dump files is understanding what the data is about. To reduce this problem, some organizations assign relevant names to their files as well as "README" files in the same directory with metadata and a description of the files. One of the problems with this is that the description is not in the data, making up for the developer to understand the inherent relations between the different values in the dataset. For example, it is difficult for developers to understand when a field accepts a range of values (instead of a any numerical value): Expressing this restrictions in the data itself (as it is done using Linked Data) makes it easier for developers to understand and simplifies applications and mashups.
- **Difficulty of reuse:** Another related problem raw files create is that for every new developer trying to reuse the data, she will have to start understanding the data from scratch. Depending on the complexity of the data, this cost (in terms of time and effort of the developer) may be too big, discouraging people from using this data.
- **Raw data cannot be uniquely identified** Another problem that appears is the lack of unique identifiers for the entities that data describes. For example, if records from different datasets are identified by the number "1324" it is not clear that they describe the same entity. Another example is when two or more datasets describe information about "New York," do they mean New York *City* or New York *State*?
- **Difficuty searching other datasets:** When using raw files as a main publishing mechanism, searching for other datasets that describe the same entities can be very time consuming; typically this will require the developer to manually look for these new datasets using search engines and other mechanisms. Linked Data allow to specify explicitly where and how (by URI dereferencing) to find more relevant information about a certain entity.

10.3.1.2 Relational Databases

Another alternative is to use Relational Databases (RDBs). The main benefit is the maturity, scalability and robustness of this technology. However, in a dynamic environment, RDBs present different issues:

- **Must know the schema** *a priori*: One of the biggest problems with RDBs is that developers need to know the schema — tables, indexes and other objects — up front in order to make a successful (and efficient) query. Part of the knowledge related to the data is expressed in this schema and hence developers must be aware of both instead of being concerned only about the data. Linked Data relies on RDF, a schema-less data model; with RDF the structure of the data is in the data itself and not determined by a schema.
- **Lack of Flexibility:** In general, with RDBs small changes in the data may require a change in the schema including the addition of new tables, primary and foreign keys, changing column types and so forth. Linked Data's inherent graph structure enables stakeholders to mix data from different sources more easily.
- **Difficult to Share:** Another problem arises when users share and reuse datasets stored in RDBs: Different RDB engines uses slightly different versions of SQL making it difficult to import the data from one engine to another.
- **Reuse and Security:** Most RDBs are not designed to be used in the open Web; applications must access the database using some security scheme, typically user/password on the organization's internal network). It is therefore difficult for developers outside the organization to use the data stored in the RDB. On the other hand, Linked Data is focused in sharing the data on the Web; most endpoints available are open for any developer. Also, it is possible to download dumps of the datasets so others can use it in their own endpoints.

10.3.1.3 APIs (Application Programming Interface)

Current mashup development practices make heavy use of traditional web services and APIs. RESTful [14] APIs in recent years have been more widely used as a means to expose structured data to developers, enabling applications to retrieve data from web services and other applications through standard HTTP requests. For example, using the Twitter search API, a developer can use a HTTP GET request on `http://search.twitter.com/search.json?q=#semweb` to retrieve a JSON file full of tweets containing the hash `#semweb` in them.

The RESTful API approach is attractive because it enables developers to easily query data using almost any platform or programming environment. In the open government data space we have seen many of these APIs emerge to help developers build applications. These APIs come from both the private sector (e.g. Sunlight Foundation, MapLight.org, FollowTheMoney.org) and public sector (e.g. Recovery.gov, TradeStats Express, Business.gov Web Service API). RESTful APIs, while incredibly useful for accessing data, pose several challenges in terms of their development and application:

- **Data APIs only answer the queries they were built to answer.** An important aspect of Web users is that their nature can be described as a "long tail", which means there is never a truly "average" user [2]. Data providers should assume that a large percentage of users will want to ask questions of their data, make connections and discover things that the providers might not have anticipated. Mashup developers may seek answers from the data that are not supported by an API or available through a very complex composition of their services.
- **Data APIs by themselves are not standards.** Each API has been designed around the particular service its creator wishes to provide. Knowing how to query using one API does not imply knowledge of how to use another. REST is a standard architecture that many of these APIs are based on, but the specific implementation and interface design of individual APIs can vary greatly. This means each time one encounters a new API, one must re-learn how to handle queries, what types

of queries are supported, what format they come in, etc. The need to learn every new API makes it difficult to add and mash new APIs together.

- **Data APIs are opaque.** Many APIs make it difficult to see, reuse or improve the underlying data or data model. Time and energy has been expended modeling and structuring data to create a usable API, but the resulting data model invariably gets hidden from developers and users. A better approach would make such data models systematically available for other systems and datasets to reuse and to be improved by the community. Moreover, data is "trapped" inside these APIs, creating "data silos" which only return the results of the queries that the given API supports, in the formats that it allows. Because of this, the linking and mashing of data in a mashup must happen in the application code of the mashup rather than natively within the graph. This means that linking must be hard-coded in the mashup and can't be easily reused by other developers and users, forcing developers to start each new mashup from scratch. Developers spend time and resources determining how to interconnect the results from their chosen APIs, but it is difficult for others to reuse this work.

Beyond the specific constraints imposed by APIs, there are other challenges developers must face when creating mashups, the biggest of which is *data quality*. It is critically important that developers use "good" data that is well-defined and understood. Developers must establish the history of the data, its origins, how was it collected, and especially what processing has been performed on it so that it can be presented correctly. A cursory review of the many raw government dataset catalogs worldwide reveals that data quality varies greatly, with no established standards. Moving forward, Linked Data practitioners must find ways to help improve this situation across the board to help developers and users understand and use these datasets correctly.

10.3.2 Challenges when using Linked Data

Although using Linked Data can alleviate many of the challenges in mashup development, there are still many risks that need to be addressed and understood. In this section we address a few of the considerations that need to be taken in using Linked Data in mashups.

- **Changes in the Data:** The data selected for use in mashups or applications could change, move, or update in ways developers cannot predict. Development can be very difficult as one cannot predict all the ways in which the data can change. This can be addressed to some extent by dataset creators and providers using standard vocabularies and communicating better with the community about planned changes to datasets, how they plan to archive old data, and what mechanisms they plan to use to migrate to new data and schemas.
- **Data Quality:** The publication of a dataset as Linked Data does not automatically mean it is of high enough quality to be easily used in applications. In practice, linked datasets can still be very inconsistent, metadata and provenance information can be missing or incomplete and the schema and data model could be poorly documented or poorly designed. The data itself could also be missing values or be poorly mapped to other datasets. Data publishers need to find ways to evaluate Linked Data better, and develop mechanisms to help communities engage in the organizations and maintenance of Linked Datasets.
- **Reliance on Outside Services:** Building mashups and applications with Linked Data can mean that you often rely on services that you don't directly control. This means you are at the mercy of the uptime and maintenance of other organizations. If a SPARQL endpoint for the dataset you use goes down, there is nothing you can immediately do to "fix" it, which means that your application or mashup is also down, or at best incomplete.

As we can see, there is still a disparity between some of the promises and functionality of Linked Data, and how it is currently used and released in practice. Many of these issues are not due to actual limitations in Linked Data itself, but in how it is commonly used and released. Data providers and consumers need to come together to help mature link data practice.

10.4 Workflow for Developing Linked Data Mashups

The objective of Linked Data-based mashups is to replace APIs and other transitional backends for mashups and applications with Linked Data accessed through SPARQL queries. With this approach the power of semantics and semantic technologies can be leveraged while still utilizing familiar visualization tools and programming environments.

10.4.1 Converting, Understanding and Enhancing Linked Data

The TWC mashup workflow consists of several steps[4]. First, raw data must be converted into RDF, the fundamental data model for the Semantic Web. There are many tools and converters that may be employed for this; at TWC we have built our own tool, `csv2rdf4lod` [10], that converts tabular data such as raw CSV (comma-separated values) files into RDF. The `csv2rdf4lod` tool, including its source code and documentation, has been released as an open source project[5] to enable other developers and data publishers to follow TWC's model for their own data conversions.

The next step is in many ways the hardest and most time-consuming when building mashups from any data: gaining a deeper working understanding of the datasets that will be the basis of the mashup. There are no step-by-step procedures or automated processes for this; it requires developers to do research and to manually inspect the data. Many interesting datasets have been released by a number of government agencies and organizations, but they all vary in the metadata and data dictionaries released with their datasets as well as the actual structure of their data. There are few standards in this regard and it can be very difficult to understand the context, definitions and history of the data we want to work with. Even when dataset metadata is available it may be difficult to work with the data absent the proper domain knowledge for the dataset. For example, we might be interested in a dataset containing "readings of ground ozone around the United States over time," but if we do not know that ground ozone is considered an air pollutant, then we will not see a potentially valuable use of this data. Understanding the data involves researching the organizations that have released the data, the processes they've used in collecting and publishing data, and gaining some of the domain knowledge that the data represents.

Once we understand the data better, our goal is to enhance the converted RDF and to introduce links to other datasets. We also annotate the dataset with the metadata and provenance information we've found through our research to help other developers and data consumers more easily use the data without having to start from scratch. These enhancements enable the dataset to become more reusable and saves the time and resources of others in using open government data. At TWC we re-apply the `csv2rdf4lod` converter again to enhance our datasets with ranges and descriptions of the different properties found in the data.

Equipped with an understanding of the context and broader domain knowledge of the data, we can target other datasets that may be good candidates to link to and mash. We also look for common properties between datasets to use as "bridges" to link them together. For example, if two datasets both have geographic information (e.g., describing facts about different US states), we are able to link these values (in the form of URIs denoting each state) to get a more complete picture of what is happening, based on data about different states drawn from multiple datasets.

Different strategies may be used to link resources from multiple datasets. First, if we have a deep understanding of the datasets involved and what their values mean we can directly claim that

---

[4] For a more comprehensive discussion of the TWC LOGD conversion process, please see Timothy Lebo, et.al., *Producing and Using Linked Open Government Data in the TWC LOGD Portal* (this volume)

[5] https://github.com/timrdf/csv2rdf4lod-automation/

two URIs should be linked. A common example of this is asserting that two URIs represent exactly the same entity; (for example, New York State). Hence we can say that

```
ex1:resourceA owl:sameAs ex2:resourceB .
```

where `owl:sameAs` is the predicate to express identity of instances in OWL [11]. It is possible to express semantically different relations, for example using predicates from SKOS [13] (`skos:broader`, `skos:narrower`) or Dublin Core [15] (`dc:relation`). Another possibility is to use literals to discover potential links between URIs. For example, consider two datasets that both provide information about US states. One uses `New York` as a state name while the other uses `NY`. We could then establish that both entities refer to the same concept and use `owl:sameAs` to link them. Sometimes links are less obvious and depend on domain knowledge of individual datasets and the level of abstraction desired; for example, the URI for the "President of the United States" and the current president may be identical, but only during a determined period of time.

A string literal like `NY` may be "promoted" into a URI that is unique across the whole web. For example, consider a dataset providing average rainfall data for all states in the US for the year 2009. The string `NY` occurring in this dataset can be promoted into a URI like `http://example.com/average_rainfall_2009/NewYork`. Other references to the state of New York in other datasets may then be linked via this new URI. Consider then a second dataset listing the populations of all the states in the US for the year 2009 and which refers to the state of New York as `http://other-example.com/population-2009/New_York`. These two URIs may be explicitly linked together using `owl:sameAs` as mentioned above. Once linked in this way, these datasets may be queried together to obtain results for average rainfall and population in 2009 for the state of New York. Another benefit of linking datasets by introducing explicit URIs is that other developers may reuse these links and add their own to datasets they are interested in. Currently this can be a time-consuming process; there are tools that can help make this process easier, but there still must be a human in the loop.

10.5 Case Studies

We now present detailed case studies illustrating how mashups may be used with linked open government data. First, we show how diverse datasets were used to create an iPad/iPhone application that enables users to review the visitors to the White House and who they visited. Next, we present a mashup that displays information related to crime, transport and education in the UK. Lastly, we show how US and UK government data may be used to compare the levels of foreign aid provided by these governments to other countries.

10.5.1 Whitehouse Visitor Log Demo

Our first case study examines a mashup developed by TWC based on visitor records from the White House[6]. The *Whitehouse Visitor Log* Demo enables users to search for visitors to the White House and the people they met. For the subset of White House employees with Wikipedia pages the mashup displays information including their title, an image, a short biography and their homepage. A user for example can search for "POTUS" (President of the United States) to reveal the top 25 people who have visited him, displayed using a table, bar chart and pie chart, in addition to information about him retrieved from Wikipedia. This additional, linked information provides the

---

[6] `http://logd.tw.rpi.edu/demo/white-house-visit/search`

user with additional context about this person and perhaps some additional insight into why specific people might be visiting him.[7]

Our first step in creating the mashup was to obtain, study and convert the raw data. The data for the White House Visitor Search came from the White House Visitor Logs dataset [8], published as a CSV file that included information on the first and last name of everyone who has visited the White House, when they made their visit and the staff member they visited. In working with this dataset we made the assumption that an individual's name uniquely identified them in the dataset and that there would be no overlap, meaning there wouldn't be two people with the same name. In general this will not be true, but given the dataset and accompanying documents and metadata it was a reasonable assumption to make. We used the `csv2rdf4lod` conversion tool to convert this raw data into RDF.

Based on our RDF version of the visitor logs dataset, we explored ways to link this data with other outside datasets. We knew for example that many of the White House employees had pages written about them on Wikipedia and would therefore also have records in DBpedia [3], a semantic data version of the information found at Wikipedia. DBpedia provided us with a great target to link into and allowed us to query for more information about the people in our original dataset. To demonstrate this we manually found 30 White House employees who could be linked to DBpedia; using this information we were able to enhance the White House Visitor dataset with links to DBpedia.

With these linked data "hooks" in place we could then query the White House Visitor dataset, obtain the DBpedia links for the correct results, use these URIs to query the SPARQL endpoint for DBpedia[9] and get additional results like the employee's picture, title and homepage from Wikipedia.

In addition to our web mashup, we wanted to explore creating a mashup based this data for mobile platforms. Publishing a Semantic Web application in the mobile space required a different focus on the presentation of the data, especially due to restricted display space and the fact that the existing suite of visualization tools used in the web based version were written in Adobe Flash, making them —at the time of this writing— unusable on iOS. Since we expected this work would be presented at locations where wireless access was prohibited, caching mechanisms were necessary in order to store data on the device in the event that a network connection was unavailable.

The mobile version of the application provides a simple wrapper around three libraries: one that provides an RDF data model, another that provides methods for performing SPARQL queries and iterating over the results of SPARQL select statements, and a third that generates pie graphs of retrieved data. SPARQL results are serialized out to a cache directory in additional to any supplementary data retrieved from external sources.

As with the web mashup, the mobile app takes advantage of linked data by performing queries against sites like DBpedia that may provide additional annotations about an individual, including their current office and title. Also, by using the Freebase Globally Unique ID (GUID) retrieved from DBpedia the mobile app can perform image lookups. DBpedia also includes links to the New York Times linked data, and the mobile application can search through the New York Times API [10] to find recent articles discussing the individuals in question. Figure 10.1 provides a screenshot of the mobile White House Visitor Log applications.

Since a single lookup can potentially produce up to five queries that must be executed, the mobile app includes options for adjusting the `LIMIT` clause in the SPARQL query, providing better responsiveness to the user when the query is limited to a smaller set of results. The user is also given control over what linked data sources will be used to build a profile of the individual. By

---

[7] One obvious extension of this would be to display available information about the visitor, including their party affiliation and employer.

[8] `http://www.whitehouse.gov/briefing-room/disclosures/visitor-records`

[9] `http://dbpedia.org/sparql`

[10] `http://data.nytimes.com`

default, DBpedia, Freebase, and the New York Times are all enabled. Turning off these options can increase application performance by reducing the number of external queries at the cost of limiting the comprehensiveness of the results, given that the Data.gov datasets are extremely targeted.

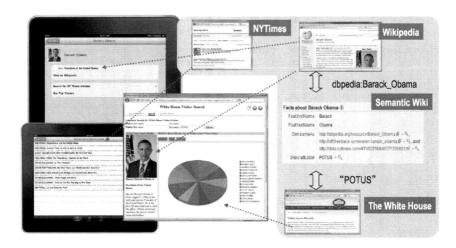

Fig. 10.1 Screenshot of the mobile version of TWC's White House Visitors Demo. This mashup enables users to explore which White House employees have been visited and by whom. By linking URIs of different people to those in DBpedia, Freebase and other external datasets, it is possible to obtain more detail information about these people.

10.5.2 See UK

"See UK"[11] is an application that displays information related the United Kingdom taken from multiple datasets from *data.gov.uk*. The user can select what information to be displayed from different datasets available related to crimes, public transportation, and public education.

Users can visualize crimes by different classifications like burglary, robbery, and others. By switching to public transportation, See UK can display where each train or bus station is in any area. Finally, the application can show different information related to schools, students enrollment, absences, among others. All of these datasets and visualizations together allow users to see different geo-related correlations. For example a parent could see the crime statistics for the bus stop their children may use to get to school. Policy makers and community leaders can see if there are any correlations between school absences and youth related crime, allowing them to find areas that need better attention.

The mashup allows users to select an area by indicating its postcode or by clicking on it in a map; Depending on the level of zoom, this area can be a ward, a county or a region (including several counties). Once the user selected an area, displays a pie chart displaying the values using by colors (green when crime is low, red when is high). The outer layers of the pie reflect the values for the adjacent areas to the one selected.

---

[11] http://apps.seme4.com/see-uk/

The data is described using RDF and it was collected from different datasets internally. See UK uses 4Store as a triple store and as SPARQL endpoint for the backend while the front-end is implemented using PHP and JQuery. A screenshot of SeeUK can be seen in Figure 10.2.

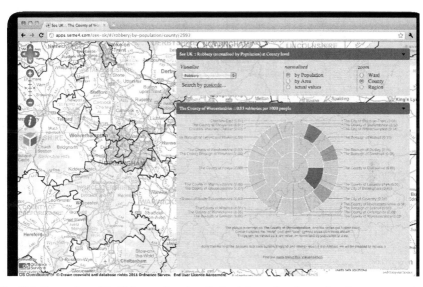

Fig. 10.2 Screenshot of SeeUK, a mashup that display information about education, transportation and crimes in the United Kingdom. Users can specify an area in the map and a pie chart will display the value for that area and its neighbors.

10.5.3 Comparing USAID (US) and DFID (UK) Global Foreign Aid

In this TWC-created mashup, foreign aid figures provided by the United States Agency for International Development (USAID)[1] and United Kingdom's Department for International Development (DFID)[2] from 2007 are jointly presented via the interface.

Here, each aid-receiving country is shaded based upon total USAID and DFID aid received. Upon clicking a particular country, three pie charts are presented:

1. A comparison of total USAID and DFID spending.
2. A breakdown of USAID spending by category.
3. A breakdown of DFID spending by category.

Additionally, contextual information for each country is pulled in from two sources:

---

[1] http://www.data.gov/raw/1554/

[2] http://data.gov.uk/dataset/dfid-statistics-on-international-development

1. **The New York Times Article Database**[3]: This provides news stories involving foreign aid efforts.
2. **The CIA World Factbook**[4]: This provides demographic data, such as literacy rate and life expectancy.

The first step in designing this mashup involved processing raw data from USAID and DFID — published in Microsoft Excel spreadsheets – into RDF using the `csv2rdf4lod` tool described earlier. Following this, three issues had to be resolved to effectively mash up data from these two agencies with the contextual information described above:

1. **Country Names**: Slight variations on labels assigned to countries could be observed between USAID, DFID data (e.g., "Congo (Kinshasa)" versus "Congo (Dem Rep)") and CIA World Factbook data.
2. **Currency**: USAID and DFID figures were represented in the raw data using US Dollars and Pound Sterling, respeciviely.
3. **Fiscal Year**: Additionally, USAID and DFID figures were represented with different fiscal years (April 6th to April 5th in the UK, versus October 1st to September 30th in the US).

To resolve the country name mapping issue, an RDF-based vocabulary was defined which assigned a unique ID to each aid receiving country. Attached to these IDs would be sets of country labels, corresponding to potential variations across datasets. This approach established label equivalence among datasets, and helped facilitate SPARQL-based retrieval of content from multiple data sources.

The currency issue was resolved by performing a conversion calculation at the application level. The currency conversion step was accomplished by representing DFID figures in US Dollars, using an RDF-based record of currency exchange figures from January 2006 to January 2008. These figures were derived from a CSV file downloaded from the online currency conversion service oanda.com.

Finally, the fiscal year issue was resolved by normalizing DFID figures to the US fiscal year. This was accomplished an application-based calculation which averaged DFID figures reported for the UK 2006 and UK 2007 fiscal years.

Designing this demo helped illustrate some current challenges faced by developers in mashing up international data.

First, an appropriate agency-to-agency mapping had to be determined. Both USAID and DFID are tasked with managing foreign aid contributions. However, it could be argued that other agencies in both the US (e.g., the Department of Agriculture) and UK would need to be considered to establish a better comparison. Without a standardized inter-agency comparison for developers to reference, such mappings will remain a matter of debate.

Second, the USAID and DFID data required prior processing before any form of mashup could be made. Specifically, the data had to be normalized to a common currency and fiscal year. As with the first issue, the specific processing steps may not be agreed upon by all developers. Nonetheless, such processing must be carried out in some form to enable mashups of international data to be produced.

10.6 Teaching the Art of Mashup: Workshops and Hack-a-thons

The Tetherless World Constellation has hosted a number of events, usually presented as *workshops* or *hackathons*, for teams from government and non-governmental organizations (NGOs). In these hands-on events we've demonstrated the potential of Semantic Web technology and Linked Data

---

[3] http://developer.nytimes.com/docs/article_search_api

[4] https://www.cia.gov/library/publications/the-world-factbook

best practices and have shown how to create visualizations and mashups relevant to the particular audience.

10.6.1 Motivation and Audience

The focus of TWC-run workshops and hackathons is to show others the true advantages of using Linked Data when creating mashups and to motivate attendees to do it themselves. Each mashup development step is covered in depth and participants are encouraged to practice the methods in "real time" using their own data. Attendees at TWC workshops and hackathons typically are stakeholders from a variety of backgrounds; it is not unusual to find web developers and hackers intermingled with data analysts, managers and government contractors.

10.6.2 Event organization

Workshops and hackathons conducted by members of the TWC team usually consist of an audience from the stakeholder organization, one or more tutors and one or more "featured" speakers. A hackathon agenda will typically include the following steps:

1. **Presentation:** Speakers and tutors are introduced and the objective for the meeting is presented.
2. **Introduction to Semantic Web:** The speaker presents a brief overview of the Semantic Web, covering its goals, its potential and the current technology available. This also includes a brief high-level description of Linked Data and how it is applied to Open Government Data.
3. **Group presentation:** Attendees form groups, introduce themselves and decide what they want to accomplish with their demo. Each group presents their goal to the other groups.
4. **Group work:** The Groups code their demos, basing their work on the tutorials and demos discussed during the presentation and the introductory Semantic Web and Linked Data material. Depending on the number of tutors and groups, tutors might work with one group directly or they might roam between groups, providing guidance and answering questions.
5. **Final presentation:** At the end of the hackathon — at the end of a day, or the next day if it lasts for 24 hours — groups present their progress, ideally showing a finished demo. The group explains what techniques and tools they used and the challenges and difficulties they encountered.

10.6.3 Tools and resources

Nearly all of the tools used in TWC workshops are documented in the TWC Linking Open Government Data (LOGD) Portal (http://logd.tw.rpi.edu) as well as its Wiki-based predecessor (http://data-gov.tw.rpi.edu). Through these sites users learn how to use semantic technologies by working through a number of tutorials dealing with many aspects of mashup creation (http://logd.tw.rpi.edu/tutorials) or by worked examples in our "Demos" section (http://logd.tw.rpi.edu/demos), where users can review the actual source code. Another important resource is the LOGD dataset catalog (http://logd.tw.rpi.edu/datasets) which lists all the datasets converted to-date by the TWC team. Each dataset may contain different versions and enhancements, so each converted dataset on TWC LOGD also has a description page with more details.

In addition to the TWC LOGD dataset catalog, an important tool we use to create mashups during hackathons is the LOGD SPARQL Proxy (http://logd.tw.rpi.edu/sparql) which provides an endpoint for several of the more popular datasets. The proxy enables developers to query the data and obtain the results in different formats (XML, JSON, etc.) according to their needs. When data needs to be converted that is not available from the TWC LOGD catalog, the TWC-developed cdr2rdf4lod converter may be used to convert tabular data to RDF [10].

In most of our hackathons the TWC team has promoted a lightweight, rapid approach to development. For example, we find that using client-side JavaScript as a programming model leads to less complexity in terms of configuration and installation than using server-side languages. Since most of the development done during these events is based in HTML and JavaScript, the list of requirements for creating demos is simple: a modern browser, a text editor and an Internet connection. Moreover, there are multiple external tools and services written in JavaScript that can be easily integrated into mashups. We have found that Google Visualizations [7] is particularly well suited for this due to its simplicity and short learning curve. We have also explored other visualization tools, such as Yahoo! Pipes [6], Simile Exhibit [8] and others.

Finally, we use Drupal [12] as a Content Management System (CMS) for publishing data, demos and tutorials. Drupal provides a robust and well-tested infrastructure that can be extended by adding external modules developed by the Drupal community. In particular, our team has customized the TWC Drupal6 instance, enabling it to publish RDFa [1] related to datasets, demos, people and others from our SPARQL endpoint embedded in XHTML pages.

10.6.4 Lessons Learned

Based on our experience leading or participating in a large number of workshops and hackathons we have found that there are certain factors that will improve the experience for participants, instructors and tutors:

- **Group composition:** It is not always the case that groups will consist of technology-savvy participants. This makes it difficult for the group to work together to create a new demo, for example due a lack of experience in web development. Organizers should mix up the composition of groups to ensure that each has members from different backgrounds.
- **Preparation of materials:** If the background and concerns of the audience are known ahead of time, organizers should prepare a set of tutorials and demos specifically designed with these interests in mind. For example, if the majority of attendees work on environmental issues, tutorials and demos should be created or adapted using datasets from that particular domain. An example of a demo created specifically for one of these events can be seen at http://logd.tw.rpi.edu/mashathon2010/example/2. In this case the TWC team demonstrated mashups that mixed data describing the cigarette taxes with data specifying the number of books in each state.
- **Publication of results:** Attendees should be encouraged to "take home" a final working product they can review with their colleagues after the hackathon. We recommend that demos created during the event remain publicly available so attendees can revisit them after the event. For example, the results from a hackathon done in August 2010 can be visited at http://logd.tw.rpi.edu/mashathon2010.

10.7 Conclusions

In this chapter we have considered the role played by mashups in unleashing the full potential of open government data. We have examined the pros and cons of other popular approaches for developing mashups based on raw data, relational databases and RESTful APIs and have argued that the Semantic Web technologies provides distinct technical advantages due to the inherent benefits of Linked Data. We have outlined a step-by-step procedure for creating mashups based on the linked open government data published through the TWC LOGD Portal. Finally, we have presented a model plan for hosting a government data hackathon event including the organization of the event, the tools that should be used, and specific recommendations based in our experience that will enable attendees to better understand the principles of mashups and explore real use cases as they create compelling mashups based on linked open government data.

References

1. Adida, B. and Birbeck, M. RDFa primer 1.0: Embedding rdf in XHTML. *W3C working draft*, 12, 2007.
2. Anderson, C. The long tail. *Wired*, 12(10), October 2004.
3. Auer, S., Bizer, C., Kobilarov, G., Lehmann, J., Cyganiak, R. and Ives, Z. DBpedia: A nucleus for a web of open data. *The Semantic Web*, 4825:722–735, 2007.
4. Bostock, M. and Heer, J. Protovis: A graphical toolkit for visualization. *IEEE Transactions on Visualization and Computer Graphics*, pages 1121–1128, 2009.
5. Curbera, F., Duftler, M., Khalaf, R., Nagy, W., Mukhi, N. and Weerawarana, S. Unraveling the Web services web: an introduction to SOAP, WSDL, and UDDI. *Internet Computing, IEEE*, 6(2):86–93, 2002.
6. Fagan, J.C. Mashing up Multiple Web Feeds Using Yahoo! Pipes. *Computers in Libraries*, 27(10):8, 2007.
7. Google Inc. Google Visualization API `http://code.google.com/apis/visualization/documentation/gallery.html`.
8. Huynh, D.F., Karger, D.R. and Miller, R.C. Exhibit: lightweight structured data publishing. In *Proceedings of the 16th international conference on World Wide Web*, pages 737–746. ACM, 2007.
9. Kobilarov, G., Scott, T., Raimond, Y., Oliver, S., Sizemore, C., Smethurst, M., Bizer, C. and Lee, R. Media meets semantic web — how the bbc uses dbpedia and linked data to make connections. In *Proceedings of the 6th European Semantic Web Conference on The Semantic Web: Research and Applications*, ESWC 2009 Heraklion, pages 723–737, Berlin, Heidelberg, 2009. Springer-Verlag.
10. Lebo, T. and Williams, G.T. Converting governmental datasets into linked data. In *Proceedings of the 6th International Conference on Semantic Systems*, pages 1–3. ACM, 2010.
11. McGuinness, D.L., Van Harmelen, F. et al. OWL web ontology language overview. *W3C recommendation*, 10:2004–03, 2004.
12. Mercer, D. *Drupal: Creating Blogs, Forums, Portals, and Community Websites*. Packt Publishing, 2006.
13. Miles, A. and Bechhofer, S. SKOS simple knowledge organization system reference. 2008.
14. Richardson, L. and Ruby, S. *RESTful web services*. O'Reilly Media, 2007.
15. Weibel, S., Kunze, J., Lagoze, C. and Wolf, M. Dublin Core metadata for resource discovery. *Internet Engineering Task Force RFC*, 2413, 1998.

Acronyms

Readers are referred to the glossary for definitions.

ABARES Australian Bureau of Agricultural and Resource Economics and Sciences
ABS Australian Bureau of Statistics
ACT Australian Capital Territory
ACVC Australian Climate Variability & Change
AEMET Agencia Estatal de Meteorologica (Spanish Meteorological Office)
AIHW Australian Institute of Health and Welfare
ANDS Australian National Data Service
API Application Programmer Interface
BOM (Australian) Bureau of Meteorology
CSH Canadian Subject Headings
CSIRO (Australian) Commonwealth Scientific and Industrial Research Organization
CST Government of Canada Core Subject Thesaurus
CSV Comma-Separated Value data format
D2RQ Database to RDF Queueing
DAG Directed Acyclic Graph
DC Dublin Core Element Set
DCMI Dublin Core Metadata Initiative
DDC Dewey Decimal Classification
DFID Department for International Development of the United Kingdom
DNS Domain Name System
DOAP Description of a Project vocabulary
DOI Digital Object Identifier
DSEWPC Australian Department of Sustainability, Environment, Water, Population and Communities
DTD Document Type Definition
EAD Encoded Archival Description
e-Gov Electronic Government
ETL Extract, Transform and Load
EPA U.S. Envronmental Protection Agency
FDsys Federal Digital System
FAR U.S. Federal Acquisition Regulations
FLOSS Free/Libre/Open Source Software
FOAF Friend of a Friend ontology
FOIA Freedom of Information Act of the United States
GC Government of Canada

GIS   Geographic Information Systems
GML   Geographic Markup Language
GORs   Government Office Regions of England
GPO   U.S. Government Printing Office
GSA   General Services Administration (U.S.), Geoscience Australia (Australia)
GSP   Gross State Product
GRDDL   Gleaning Resource Descriptions from Dialects of Languages
HTML   Hypertext Markup Language
HTTP   Hypertext Transfer Protocol
ICT   Information and Communications Technology
IETF   Internet Engineering Task Force
IGN   National Geographic Institute of Spain
IMOS   Integrated Marine Observing System of Australia
INE   National Statistic Institute of Spain
ISO   International Standards Organization
IT   Information Technology
KOS   Knowledge Organization System
LCC   Library of Congress Classification
LCSH   Library of Congress Subject Headings
LED   Linking Enterprise Data
LOD   Linked Open Data
LOGD   Linking Open Government Data portal at TWC
MARC   MAchine-Readable Cataloging system
MIME   Multipurpose Internet Mail Extensions
MODS   Metadata Object Description Schema
MRRS   Management, Resources and Results Structure
N3   Notation 3
OGD   Open Government Data
OWL   Web Ontology Language
PAA   Program Activity Architecture
POTUS   President of the United States
PSI   Public Sector Information
R2RML   Relational to RDF Markup Language
RDB   Relational Database
RDF   Resource Description Framework
RDFa   Resource Description Framework Attributes
RDFS   Resource Description Framework Schema
RDF/XML   Resource Description Framework eXtensible Markup Language serialization format
RMMS   Government of Canada Records Management Metadata Standard
RVM   Répertoire de vedettes-matière
REST   Representational State Transfer
RFC   Request for Comments
RPI   Rensselaer Polytechnic Institute
SCOVO   Statistical Core Vocabulary
SKOS   Simple Knowledge Organisation System
SOA   Service Oriented Architecture
SOAP   Simple Object Access Protocol
SPARQL   SPARQL Protocol and RDF Query Language
SQL   Structured Query Language
SSN   Semantic Sensor Network Ontology
TSV   Tab-Separated Value data format
TWC   Tetherless World Constellation at RPI
URI   Uniform Resource Indicator
URL   Uniform Resource Locator

USDA   United States Department of Agriculture
USAID   United States Agency for International Development
UUID   Universally Unique Identifier
VoID   Vocabulary of Interlinked Datasets
W3C   World Wide Web Consortium
WCED   World Commission on Environment and Development
WEHAB   Water, Energy, Health, Agriculture and Biodiversity framework of the United Nations
XHTML   Extensible Hypertext Markup Language
XML   Extensible Markup Language
XSD   XML Schema
XSLT   Extensible Stylesheet Language Transformations

Glossary

Readers are encouraged to also see the acronym list.

Abox One of two types of statements in an ontology (the other being Tbox). Abox statements represent facts (or "assertions", hence the "A"), e.g. John is a Person (where Person is a defined class).

Application Programmer Interface An abstraction implemented in software that defines how others should make use of a software package such as a library or other reusable program.

Backward chaining A method of reasoning that begins with a conclusion being sought and works backward to determine if any data supports that conclusion. Backward chaining is the reverse of forward chaining.

Big O notation A definition of the worst case performance of a mathematical function, often a computer algorithm.

Canadian Subject Headings An English language thesaurus on Canada and Canadian topics for use in bibliographic records, maintained by Library and Archives Canada. Compare to RVM and LCSH.

Closed world The presumption that what is not known to be true must be false. The assumption underlying relational databases, most forms of logical programming, OWL DL and OWL Lite.

Controlled vocabularies Carefully selected sets of terms that are used to describe units of information; used to create thesauri, taxonomies and ontologies.

Database to RDF Queueing A mechanism to query information in traditional management systems such as relational databases via the SPARQL query language. D2RQ may refer to the language definition or the Open Source Software project.

Data warehouse A storage and retrieval system for enterprise information designed to centralize information from other stores to facilitate cross-system querying and reporting.

DBPedia An RDF representation of the metadata held in Wikipedia and made available for SPARQL query on the World Wide Web.

Dewey Decimal Classification A commonly used proprietary system of library classification, currently maintained by The Online Computer Library Center (OCLC).

Directed Acyclic Graph A directed graph (like RDF) with the additional restriction that no loops or cycles are permitted. A cycle is a path from a given node that would allow one to find their way back to the starting node.

Directed graph A graph in which the links between nodes are directional (they only go from one node to another). RDF represents things (nouns) and the relationships between them (verbs) in a directed graph. In RDF, the links are differentiated by being assigned URIs.

Document Type Definition A type of schema for defining a markup language, such as in XML or HTML (or their predecessor SGML).

Domain Name System The Internet's mechanism for mapping between a human-readable host name (e.g. www.example.com) and an Internet Protocol (IP) Address (e.g. 203.20.51.10).

Dublin Core Element Set A vocabulary of fifteen properties for use in resource descriptions, such as may be found in a library card catalog (author, publisher, etc). The most commonly used vocabulary for Semantic Web applications.

Dublin Core Metadata Initiative An open international organization engaged in the development of interoperable metadata standards, including the Dublin Core Element Set.

Encoded Archival Description A standard for encoding archival finding aids using Extensible Markup Language (see XML), maintained by a partnership of the U.S. Library of Congress and the Society of American Archivists.

Enterprise For the purposes of this book, any human organization that uses computer systems to store, retrieve and analyze information.

Federal Digital System An electronic information management system to authenticate, preserve, version, and provide permanent public access to U.S. federal government information operated by the U.S. GPO (see GPO).

Forward chaining A method of reasoning that begins with statements of all the relevant facts and infers new facts based on a set of rules. Equivalent to the logical operation *modus ponens*. The reverse of forward chaining is backward chaining.

Free/Libre/Open Source Software A generic and internationalized term for software released under an Open Source license.

Friend of a Friend A Semantic Web vocabulary describing people and their relationships for use in resource descriptions.

Government of Canada Records Management Metadata Standard A metadata element set for records management systems used in the Government of Canada.

Government of Canada Core Subject Thesaurus A bilingual (French and English) thesaurus of terms used in information resources of the Government of Canada.

Graph A collection of objects (represented by "nodes") any of which may be connected by links between them. See directed graph.

Hypertext Markup Language The predominant markup language for hypertext pages on the Web. HTML defines the structure of Web pages. A family of W3C standards.

Hypertext Transfer Protocol The standard transmission protocol used on the World Wide Web to transfer hypertext requests and information between Web servers and Web clients (such as browsers). An IETF standard.

International Standards Organization A network of the national standards institutes of 162 countries that cooperate to define international standards. Defines many standards including in the context of this book formats for dates and currency.

Internet Engineering Task Force An open international community concerned with the evolution of Internet architecture and the operation of the Internet. Defines standards such as HTTP and DNS.

Jena An Open Source Software implementation of a Semantic Web development framework. Supports the storage, retrieval and analysis of RDF information. See http://openjena.org and compare to Mulgara and Sesame.

Knowledge Organization System A tool or system that provides an organized interpretation of knowledge structures.

Library of Congress Classification A system of library classification developed and maintained by the U.S. Library of Congress.

Library of Congress Subject Headings A thesaurus of subject headings for use in bibliographic records, maintained by the U.S. Library of Congress.

Linked data A pattern for hyperlinking machine-readable data sets to each other using Semantic Web techniques, especially via the use of RDF and URIs. Enables distributed SPARQL queries of the data sets and a "browsing" or "discovery" approach to finding information (as compared to a search strategy).

Linked Open Data An open community project to interlink data on the Semantic Web using URIs and RDF.

Linking Government Data The use of tools and techniques of the Semantic Web to connect, expose and use data from government systems.

MAchine-Readable Cataloging system A family of formats for the representation of bibliographic information in libraries (ISO 2709, ANSI/NISO Z39.2).

Management, Resources and Results Structure Government of Canada policy linking the management of government resources and program results to their organizational structures. It provides a representation of how a department is managed through a) strategic outcomes; b) program activity architecture (PAA); and c) governance structure. See also PAA.

Metadata Information used to administer, describe, preserve, present, use or link other information held in resources, especially knowledge resources, be they physical or virtual.

Metadata Object Description Schema A bibliographic description system intended to be a compromise between MARC and DC metadata. Implemented in XML Schema (see DC, MARC, XSD).

Mulgara An Open Source Software implementation of an RDF database. Supports the storage, retrieval and analysis of RDF information. See http://mulgara.org and compare to Jena and Sesame.

Multipurpose Internet Mail Extensions A means of representing binary content in textual messages, such as in electronic mail and HTTP. An IETF standard.

Notation 3 An RDF syntax intended to be readable by humans. See also Turtle.

Ontology A formal representation of relationships between items in a directed graph structure. See taxonomy.

Open world The presumption that what is not known to be true may yet be true if additional information is later obtained. The assumption underlying RDF and OWL Full.

Pattern A general reusable approach to solving a commonly occurring type of problem.

Program Activity Architecture A component of a MRRS. It provides a hierarchical linkage for all departmental programs and activities to a departmentÕs strategic outcomes. It documents how Government of Canada departments allocates and manages its resources to achieve their intended results. See also MRRS.

Protocol A set of instructions for transferring data from one computer to another over a network. A protocol standard defines both message formats and the rules for sending and receiving those messages.

Public Sector Information Information created by a government in the course of governing.

Quad store A colloquial phrase for an RDF database that stores RDF triples plus an additional element of information, often used to collect statements into groups.

RDF database A type of database designed specifically to store and retrieve RDF information.

Répertoire de vedettes-matière A partially bilingual (English and French) thesaurus of terms in French hosted and developed by Université Laval. It is complemented by the Canadian Subject Headings (CSH) developed by Library and Archives Canada.

Representational State Transfer An architectural style for information systems used to greater or lessor degree on the Web and explains some of the Web's key features, such as extreme scalability and robustness to change.

Request for Comments A document submitted to the IETF. Internet standards started as RFCs and are often referenced by their RFC numbers.

Resource Description Framework RDF: An international standard for data interchange on the Web. A W3C standard.

Resource Description Framework Attributes An RDF syntax encoded in HTML documents. A W3C standard.

Resource Description Framework Schema The simplest RDF vocabulary description language that provides much less descriptive capability than SKOS or OWL. A W3C standard.

Resource Description Framework eXtensible Markup Language serialization format An RDF syntax encoded in XML. A W3C standard.

Schema A data model that represents the relationships between a set of concepts. Some types of schemas include relational database schemas (which define how data is stored and retrieved), taxonomies and ontologies.

Semantic technologies The broad set of technologies that relate to the extraction, representation, storage, retrieval and analysis of machine-readable information. The Semantic Web standards are a subset of semantic technologies and techniques.

Semantic Web An evolution or part of the World Wide Web that consists of machine-readable data in RDF and an ability to query that information in standard ways (e.g. via SPARQL).

Semantic Web standards Standards of the World Wide Web Consortium (W3C) relating to the Semantic Web, including RDF, RDFa, SKOS and OWL.

Service Oriented Architecture A set of architectural design guidelines used to expose services, often as Web Services.

Sesame An Open Source Software implementation of a Semantic Web development framework. Supports the storage, retrieval and analysis of RDF information. See http://www.openrdf.org and compare to Jena and Mulgara.

Simple Knowledge Organisation System A vocabulary description language for RDF designed for representing traditional knowledge organization systems such as enterprise taxonomies in RDF. A W3C standard.

Simple Object Access Protocol A protocol over HTTP for exchanging structured information in XML to and from Web Services.

SPARQL Protocol and RDF Query Language A query language standard for RDF data on the Semantic Web; analogous to the Structured Query Language (SQL) for relational databases. A W3C standard.

Structured Query Language A query language standard for relational databases.

Taxonomy A formal representation of relationships between items in a hierarchical structure. See ontology.

Tbox One of two types of statements in an ontology (the other being Abox). Tbox statements describe a knowledge system in terms of controlled vocabularies (or "terminology", hence the "T"), e.g. A Person is a Mammal.

Term For the purposes of this book, an entry in a controlled vocabulary, schema, taxonomy or ontology.

Triple An RDF statement, consisting of two things (a "subject" and an "object") and a relationship between them (a verb, or "predicate"). This subject-predicate-object triple forms the smallest possible RDF graph (although most RDF graphs consist of many statements).

Triple store A colloquial phrase for an RDF database that stores RDF triples.

Tuple An ordered list of elements. RDF statements are 3-tuples; an ordered list of three elements.

Turtle An RDF serialization format, designed to be easier to read than others such as RDF/XML. A subset of N3.

Uniform Resource Indicator A global identifier for the Web standardized by joint action of the W3C and IETF. A URI may or may not be resolvable on the Web (see URL).

Uniform Resource Locator A global identifier for Web resources standardized by joint action of the W3C and IETF. A URL is resolvable on the Web and is commonly called a "Web address".

Universally Unique Identifier A large hexadecimal number that may be calculated by anyone without significant central coordination and used to uniquely identify a resource. A standard of the Open Software Foundation.

U.S. Government Printing Office An agency of the U.S. Congress tasked with printing and making available documents of the U.S. Government.

Web 2.0 A colloquial description of the part of the World Wide Web that implements social networking, blogs, user comments and ratings and related human-centered activities.

Web 3.0 A colloquial description of the part of the World Wide Web that implements machine-readable data and the ability to perform distributed queries and analysis on that data. Considered synonymous with the phrases "Semantic Web" and "The Web of Data".

Web Ontology Language A family of knowledge representation and vocabulary description languages for authoring ontologies, based on RDF and standardized by the W3C. Standardized variants include OWL Full, OWL DL (for "description logic") and OWL Lite.

World Wide Web Consortium An international community that develops standards for the World Wide Web. Defines standards such as HTML, XML and RDF.

eXtensible Hypertext Markup Language A family of versions of HTML based on XML and standardized by the W3C.

eXtensible Markup Language A specification for creating structured textual computer documents. Many thousands of XML formats exist, including XHTML. A family of standards from the W3C.

XML Schema Limitations on the content of an XML document that defines what structural elements are allowed.

eXtensible Stylesheet Language Transformations Declarative programs to transform one XML document into another XML document.

Index